KU-320-978

Restaurant Babylon

www.transworldbooks.co.uk

By the same author

The Taming of Eagles
My Canapé Hell
Shagpile
The Wendy House
Hotel Babylon
Tuscany for Beginners
Air Babylon
The Stork Club
Fashion Babylon
Beach Babylon
Pop Babylon
Wedding Babylon
Hospital Babylon

Restaurant Babylon

IMOGEN EDWARDS-JONES
& Anonymous

BANTAM PRESS

LONDON · TORONTO · SYDNEY · AUCKLAND · JOHANNESBURG

TRANSWORLD PUBLISHERS
61–63 Uxbridge Road, London W5 5SA
A Random House Group Company
www.transworldbooks.co.uk

First published in Great Britain
in 2013 by Bantam Press
an imprint of Transworld Publishers

Copyright © Imogen Edwards-Jones 2013

Imogen Edwards-Jones has asserted her right under the Copyright,
Designs and Patents Act 1988 to be identified as the author of this work.

This book is a fictional account based on the experiences and recollections of the
author's sources. In some cases, names and sequences or the detail of events have
been changed to protect the privacy of others. The author has
stated to the publishers that, except in such respects not affecting the
substantial accuracy of the work, the contents of this book are true.

A CIP catalogue record for this book
is available from the British Library.

ISBNs 9780593069905 (hb)
9780593069912 (tpb)

This book is sold subject to the condition that it shall not,
by way of trade or otherwise, be lent, resold, hired out,
or otherwise circulated without the publisher's prior
consent in any form of binding or cover other than that
in which it is published and without a similar condition,
including this condition, being imposed on the
subsequent purchaser.

Addresses for Random House Group Ltd companies outside the UK
can be found at: www.randomhouse.co.uk
The Random House Group Ltd Reg. No. 954009

The Random House Group Limited supports the Forest Stewardship Council® (FSC®),
the leading international forest-certification organisation. Our books carrying the
FSC label are printed on FSC®-certified paper. FSC is the only forest-certification scheme
supported by the leading environmental organisations, including Greenpeace. Our paper
procurement policy can be found at www.randomhouse.co.uk/environment

Typeset in 11.5/16pt Sabon by Falcon Oast Graphic Art Ltd.
Printed and bound in Great Britain by
CPI Group (UK) Ltd, Croydon, CR0 4YY

2 4 6 8 10 9 7 5 3 1

MIX
Paper from
responsible sources
FSC
www.fsc.org
FSC® C016897

For Rafe

Acknowledgements

With very grateful thanks to the wonderful Eugenie Furniss, and the handsome Doug Young and all at Transworld for their fabulousness.

And to all those people whose time and patience I called upon during the hours and days I spent interviewing them in restaurants, bars, private clubs and at kitchen tables. I am extremely grateful, as I could not have done this without your humour, kindness and cooperation. I would especially like to thank my dear, wonderful friend Henry. What a ham!

Prologue

All of the following is true. Only the names and some circumstances have been changed to protect the guilty. All the
anecdotes, the stories, the characters, the situations, the highs,
the lows, the scams, the drugs, the misery, the love, the death
and the insanity are exactly as was told to me by Anonymous
– a collection of some of the finest chefs, maître d's, sommeliers, owners and insiders working in the restaurant industry
today. However, for legal reasons the stories now take place in
a fictitious restaurant with a fictitious owner. Narrated by
Anonymous, thousands of hours of experience and knowledge
have been compressed into twenty-four. Everything else is as it
should be. The chefs shout, the owners smile, and the rich just
carry on eating. It's just another twenty-four hours in one of
London's finest dining establishments.

6–7 a.m.

I must change that ring tone. There're only so many times you can listen to sodding *Mission Impossible* without wanting to stick it in a chicken and rotisserie the hell out of it for the next six hours. Christ, my head hurts. A man of my age should not be drinking jägerbombs in some nameless Soho dive with a steel door and sweat sliding off the walls at four in the morning. It's pathetic. I've been in the restaurant business long enough to know it's either vodka or a fine red wine, and bed before the birds; anything else will make you wish you hadn't been born. And right now I'd like to return to the cosy confines of a snug womb, never to surface again.

Where the hell's my phone? I sit up. My brain joins me a few seconds later. My small, smoke-choked flat comes into focus. It's still dark outside but the orange glow of the nearby street-light illuminates the sad, single room in all its filthy glory. I inhale and then yawn. The air smells of fags, alcohol and guilt. I was only supposed to be staying here for a few months. It was a quick pit stop before my divorce came through, but it's been over six months now. Most of which has been spent sleeping in this crappy armchair. I've got a bed. Quite a nice one, actually. I managed to save it from the fire sale that was the breakdown of my marriage and it's got White Company linen and plenty of pillows. But I just don't seem to get into it much. By the time I get home, I'm usually too many sheets to the wind to get further than the armchair, and there I remain until morning. Or until some sod wakes me up.

Finally I spot my phone, next to the skid-marked mirror, the rolled-up twenty-pound note, and the pile of Camel full-strength fighting for butt space in the ashtray. Oh shit, I think, looking at the flashing screen. It's Adam.

'What?' I say, my lips cracking. My mouth is drier than a Mormon wedding. 'This had better be good.'

'It's shit, mate,' shouts Adam, his thick Aussie accent echoing cavernously around whichever hellhole he is currently frequenting. 'It's totally shit! Some fucking sturdy bird's had a shag in the dunny and I'm up to my cock in water.'

I frown. Talking of water, I really fancy a glass. I slowly pull myself out of the chair and, stumbling towards the kitchen sink, I trip over a pair of black high heels.

'It's unbelievable how much damage a big, fat arse can do!' continues Adam. 'One of the basins is totally fucked. It's hanging off the wall, the pipe's bust and there's water all the way through to the gents. Mate, it's a disaster! I've called Pavel six times already this morning but I think he must have pissed off back to Poland, which is a bit rich because he hasn't told me, or you, or anyone, and now we are in the shit. Quite literally.'

'There's shit as well?'

'Well, no, not literally.'

'Oh.' I look back down at the shoes.

'Is Gina with you?' he asks. 'From the club? The one you offered a job to?'

'Oh, her,' I reply finally, as the whole sorry evening comes slowly ebbing back.

Quite what Adam and I thought we were doing last night I do not know. Nico, the deputy manager of Le Bar, which I own and Adam runs, was going back to Italy after eighteen months of mixing mojitos and martinis, and we were giving him a bit of a send-off. Normally I tend just to show my face at these sorts of events and then bugger off, as it is not a great look to get plastered with your own troops. The last thing they need to witness is their boss getting totally legless, feeling up the waiting staff, and helping himself to the bar. It makes it a little difficult to give them a bollocking the next morning when you, yourself, are in disgrace. Also, an all-night club crawl is not really necessary for a forty-something bloke with two failed marriages behind him. It stinks of desperation.

But, obviously, I did not heed my own advice and shall certainly regret it today. And I've got one of those days. I really don't need this hangover and I certainly don't need to be woken up at this unearthly hour.

I am such an idiot. I can't believe I allowed myself to be

persuaded to 'go on'. The last time Adam and I hit Soho we ended up in the very same dive we went to last night and I thumped him. Adam was being all lippy and pissed and had attracted the attention of some heavy blokes at the bar. Suited and booted, straight from work in his best Gucci, we'd had a catch-up dinner, discussing staff problems (particularly Damon, who has a whiff of the dodgy about him), and the whole thing got out of control, as it tends to do with Adam. We moved on to my divorce from Sketchley (as Adam insists on calling my ex) and on to his obsession with Pippa, or more accurately Pippa the head chef at my brasserie La Table's tits. Anyway, it was around three and we were on the vodka tonics and these big lads covered in tats started lining up by the bar, crunching their knuckles, baring their tiny Tic Tac teeth and looking our way. Adam, full of booze, blow and bravado, whipped off his Gucci jacket and turned to me.

'Come on, mate,' he slurred. 'Let's get 'em.'

Given the choice between being pummelled into a small doughball by the butch blokes at the bar or knocking Adam out, I chose the latter. I swung round and hit him so hard on the cheek that he keeled over immediately. The blokes at the bar looked stunned, and quite possibly a little disappointed that I had curtailed their fun. Adam, on the other hand, was so sodding grateful the next day, because he'd managed to get out of the bar, jaw intact, that he bought me a magnum of Laurent Perrier Rosé which must have set him back at least £90 as a thank-you. The small bruise below his right eye, he concluded, was a lot better than what might have been.

So, given the previous welcome we'd received in the dive bar, I am amazed we went back. We must have been drunk. *Obviously* we were drunk.

Alcohol is a big problem in this business. It is a major part of it. I mean, you don't go into the restaurant industry if you haven't a hint of the epicurean about you. It is not the sort of profession that attracts people who don't like a good time, who aren't a little bit greedy, or keen on their booze. I've worked with seven head chefs over the past fifteen years and I have taken four of them to open AA meetings. One of them was so out of control we had to hold an intervention in the kitchen with all the staff around and, eventually, we managed to persuade him he had a problem. The fact that he used to come to work drunk and was constantly swigging from a bottle of Jack Daniel's (why is it always Jack Daniel's?) he kept under the pass was apparently 'nothing to worry about'. Anyway, I haven't spoken to him in a while. I think he's sobered up now and is running his own place in some seaside town near Norwich.

'Norfolk,' as Adam once said, 'where chefs go to die.'

But chef burn-out is common. The hours, the lack of light, the stress of the kitchen – after a while they all get this vampiric waxy white look that makes them appear like they've recently been exhumed. The shelf life of a chef is often quite short. The trick is to catch them when they're young and on the way up, when they're brilliant and creative and full of energy and ideas, when they are happy to do the hours and not have a family life. Then you ditch them when they peak and plateau and have nothing left to say. The smart ones get out then; they get a nice fat hotel somewhere, with their own kitchen garden and some overpriced rooms out the back. And then there are the others who just fall by the wayside.

I have this exact problem at my other place at the moment. I've had Le Restaurant for five years now and my head chef, Andrew James, is rather quickly and surely tumbling off the rails. He's always been one of those shouty little shits who gets right in your face before he calls you a cunt. But when you've got a Michelin star in your pocket, you tend to get away with that sort of kitchen 'banter'. However, in the last couple of months he's been missing days, shouting more, whacking the commis around, dishing out the slaps and committing the most cardinal of chef sins: he's been inconsistent in his cooking. So, after much talking and cajoling, I have managed to persuade him to walk, and I have also managed to lure his more charming and talented ex-number two, Oscar Richards, back from where he's been training with Michel Bras in southern France. Quite how I achieved such a Ban Ki-moon feat I shall never know. But Oscar arrives in a couple of hours to initiate the handover; meanwhile I have exploding toilets in Le Bar and, seemingly, a new colleague in my bed to contend with.

'So did you get to first base?' quizzes Adam with a smutty chuckle.

'A gentleman doesn't share details,' I declare, slightly embarrassed by the fact that I'd clearly fallen asleep in my chair before I could even take my socks off.

'Oh,' he replies. 'Is she still there?'

'No,' I lie, peeking my head around the door to see a nest of blonde hair on one of my numerous pillows. 'She left.'

'So I'll call Pimlico Plumbers, seeing as Pavel has pissed off into the ether?'

'Isn't there anyone else?'

'I know they're expensive—'

'Just do it. I'm on my way.'

Any excuse not to deal with the bedroom blonde. You'd have thought that two divorces and two children I barely have monthly access to would have made me a little more circumspect about pulling random women in subterranean nightclubs, but I've always found a pretty girl hard to resist. I remember a friend of my dad's once telling me that when he ran a restaurant in the seventies he didn't sleep alone for five years. They had some rooms over the top and they were constantly in use, even between courses. Customers would take a break between the boeuf bourguignon and the apple pie for a swift one upstairs.

'They're quick those Brummies,' he used to say. 'The pudding never got cold.'

Outside, and the streets of London hang heavy with a chilly, dank fog. It is the last week of November and there is that distinct cinnamon whiff of Christmas in the air. The restaurant business loves Christmas. It adores it almost as much as a gift-paper-shredding three-year-old, high on sugared almonds. and it makes us feel just as ill. All year long we wait for it; gagging for it because in many an establishment up to 90 per cent of our annual profit can be made in the last four weeks of the year. It is a licence to print money. But it is also the most exhausting, ball-aching twenty-eight days of your life. If you can survive Christmas in a kicking West End joint, you can get through almost anything.

I have three places in the West End – Le Restaurant, Le Bar and La Table – and, at all three of these venues, we're preparing to welcome the festive season in with the largest bear hug and the sleightest of hand, as we pat you on the back and dip your pocket at the same time. You give: we take. But hopefully you'll be so gently anaesthetized by fine wines and bonhomie, you won't feel a thing until your credit card statement at the end of January.

My bachelor pad, such as it is, is above La Table – the newest addition to my nascent empire. A forty-seater brasserie serving premium quality soups, salads and steaks with all-day lattes of every intolerant special need, we are mainly after the yummy mummy market as there is a private school handily not far from the site. We are turning over a useful £28,000 a week but the rent is a steep £4,000, so I have a chat booked in with Pippa and her tits today as we've got to have a little re-think about our margins. I need to get our GP (gross profit) up or we're in trouble.

A ten-minute walk up the road on Jackson Street, just near Conduit Street where Mayfair teeters towards Soho, I have a bar and a restaurant at either end of the road. Le Restaurant, my pride and joy, my pain and the mistress of both my divorces, was the first place I opened. A sixty-cover restaurant, it took ten years of graft to get there and another two years to get a Michelin star, which we have managed to retain for the last three. Although quite how we made the grade last year is anyone's guess, what with Andrew's inconsistency and Sketchley's feather-spitting front-of-house attitude towards any pretty girl who walked into the room. And bearing in mind we were well-reviewed by A. A. Gill in the *Sunday Times*, Giles Coren in the Saturday edition of *The Times* and Fay Maschler in the *Evening Standard*, we had plenty of them, holding the porky hands of fat-walleted businessmen as they swung through the revolving door.

Not bad for a bloke from Kidderminster with two O-levels (Pottery and Geography) and a BTEC from Stratford College. Back then I wasn't really focused on the job, it was just something to do, with my limited options and qualifications. I remember using my Escoffier, *Le Guide Culinaire*, to roll my joints on. Pages from *Hering's Dictionary of Classical and Modern Cookery* and Saulnier's *Le Répertoire de la Cuisine* were used for roaches between lessons. But, you know, I was seventeen years old and my parents had more or less washed their nice middle-class hands of me: what else was a lad to do except get drunk at lunchtime and waste the afternoons freeze-drying his books in the new-fangled machine they'd just taken delivery of at the college?

And then, after learning some rudimentary knife skills and how to spatchcock a partridge, I was released into the wonderful world of West Midlands cuisine, where the women were blondes, the carpets were shag pile, and the cars were almost always Jags. Not that this culinary cabal was remotely interested in receiving me.

The first place I worked, a symphony of pale pink napery and mock Tudor beams, I was bullied, beaten and locked in the chest freezer for three hours in my first week. The second week I was bundled into the walk-in fridge and forced to stay there shivering and shaking next to thirty-one prawn cocktails for the next five hours, half of my whole ten-hour shift. When I was finally released, with blue lips and a cock the size of a button mushroom, no one uttered a word.

The worst night came a couple of months later. It was a fine-dining fortieth-birthday-party extravaganza. Some bloke, big in car dealerships, had taken over the place and I was ordered to do eighty-five Parma Ham and Melon. I made the mistake of leaving half a blue label on one of the melons and the restaurant manager – Frank was his name – came marching back into the kitchen and shouted: 'What fucking cunt chef fucking cunting did this?'

I made the foolish mistake of owning up. I said I was terribly sorry. I think I even grovelled.

Then the head chef said, 'Yes, you will be fucking sorry.' And he head-butted me, knocking me out cold. I hit the deck and was dragged out by my feet, and put back into the walk-in fridge for the rest of service. I was the lowest of the low.

Correction. *Paul* was the lowest of the low. He was the *plongeur* and he had, as was common in those days, learning difficulties. The poor bloke was subject to much more bullying and baiting than I was. I remember he was once bet £10 to eat his own shit sandwich, which he was only too willing to do, between two slices of bread. It was appalling. Eventually, he was pushed so hard that he snapped and punched the head chef during the middle of service. I have to say it was hard not to slap him on the back and congratulate the worm for turning at last. He was fired, of course, on the spot, but he did return to reap a delicious revenge.

The night following Paul's dismissal we had a banquet for some one hundred and fifty people. It was, naturally, coq au vin (it was a salubrious establishment) all prepared in flats (a stainless steel dish that contained ten portions of coq). The starters were back and the mains were away, when suddenly Frank comes steaming back into the kitchen shouting, 'What the *fuck* is going on? What have you done to the coq au vin, chef?'

'Nothing,' I replied.

'It tastes of fucking Domestos!' he yelled back, his old champagne breath getting right up my nose.

Transpires that Paul was a lot smarter than anyone ever gave him credit for and, as he'd collected his wages that day, he'd slipped a bottle of Domestos into the coq. The shit really hit the fan that night. One hundred and fifty mains were returned and another one hundred and fifty fillet steaks were cooked very medium rare (due to time constraints) and served with a selection of ropey old battoned carrots we happened to have in the fridge.

But now I've got a bar, a brasserie, and a destination restaurant with a £3 million turnover and one star. Although the star is not mine, and nor does it belong to the restaurant, and when Andrew pisses off, which he will do next week, we'll be crawling with Michelin inspectors checking to see if they'll give it back. But still, it's a long way from Kidderminster. It's a long way from Frank and it's a long way from the shit chef with a hard head and a penchant for dumping commis in the freezer.

That's what I like about the restaurant business, it is all about reinvention: Gordon, Heston, Marcus, Marco, the list goes on – we're all boys from the provinces making it in the big smoke. There's a touch of Dick Whittington syndrome in chef world; get it right and the streets of London really are paved with gold. Get it wrong and you end up in Norfolk!

I can hear Adam's Aussie twang from here as I turn the corner into Jackson Street. Le Bar was an old Edwardian town house that I spent rather too much money (half a million quid) gutting and transforming into the sort of place to attract the high-spending cocktail crowd. We get the art trade from Bond Street, we get fashionistas and the hairdressers from Bruton Street and we are close enough to Hanover Square to get the Condé Nast girls as they leave Totty Towers on their way home. They favour a cocktail called a Skinny Bitch – vodka, lime and soda – which has about as many calories at the three Haribo they've eaten all day.

As you walk into Le Bar there's a long glossy black bar to the right, with plenty of fat black leather perching stools nestled along its length. We have some low leather armchairs and small round cocktail tables with low-lit lamps on the left for couples and gangs of four. Towards the back, next to the indoor palms and taller standard lamps, there are larger soft sofas and more comfortable armchairs for the serious drinkers, as well as a couple of crimson-velvet booths with banquette seating which always go first. We serve a few small plates from the tiny basement kitchen, mainly chips, fish goujons and plates of honey-coated chipolatas, along with olives, nuts and Chinese cracker things that I find utterly unpalatable, but which seem to go down well with the Totty Towers crowd. The place works. We are turning over £70,000 a week. The lighting is low and the music is loud enough not to make conversation essential.

'Thank Christ!' declares Adam as I walk through the door. In his early thirties, slim and fit, with plenty of thick dark hair and pale eyes, Adam's the sort of bloke girls write their phone number on. He's funny, charming and knows how to work a room. He's also got the stamina of an ox. He quite often stays up the whole night and kicks on through to the next day. The only way you'd know is his insistence on a Bloody Mary for breakfast.

'Check this out,' he says, nodding over his shoulder.

I follow him through the swing doors and into the toilets at the back. The black and white checked floor is covered in about two inches of water, although the white tiled walls appear to be surviving; the light bulbs around the mirrors are working but in the middle of the row of three basins, one hangs limply from the wall, swinging on its own plumbing.

Adam shakes his head. 'Can you believe it? It's totally rooted.'

'It looks bad,' I acknowledge.

'I mean how fucking fat was she?'

'How d'you know it was a big girl?'

'Damon said he saw her go in with some chubby chaser.' He nods. 'Arse the size of Texas.'

'What's the water damage like?' I can feel it beginning to seep into my leather-soled Church's shoes.

'It'll be fine,' says Adam. 'The plumber's on his way and I'll get the cleaners to mop up. We'll be fine by lunch – before then, probably.'

'Great,' I cough, patting down my jacket pocket for my cigarettes. 'A couple of bulbs there also need replacing in the mirrors and how are the toilets?' I poke my head into the cubicle.

Running any place like this is all about the details. Are the glasses clean? Is the bar shining? Why isn't that curtain hanging properly? Why is that mirror dirty? What's happened to that lampshade? When were the lavs last cleaned? Where's the loo paper? Walk into any place with any restaurateur and they just can't help themselves. Once glance of their gimlet eye and they'll be able to spot a crooked painting, a smeared fork and an un-plumped cushion at sixty paces. We're worse than any thin-lipped dowager duchess with OCD. My pet-hate? Trainers. Anyone who turns up in a pair of trainers gets sent home on the spot. I came in here last week and caught two of my staff wearing them behind the bar. I sent them both up to Oxford Street with £50 each to buy new shoes and personally shoved their best Nikes in the bin. I don't give a shit. There are standards.

My phone goes. 'Oh, that's the dealer,' I say, checking the number. 'He's waiting for me down the road.'

Adam shoots me a wink and taps the side of his nose. 'Make mine two,' he grins.

7–8 a.m.

Five minutes later and I'm slowly sinking deep into the front seat of Reza's over-heated Mercedes. It must be about thirty degrees in here and half the seat springs are broken. The number of customer backsides must have given it repetitive strain injury. There is very little air in the car and what there is is laced with leather, flatulence and Magic Tree. I start to lick ten-pound notes off from a roll in my pocket, while he takes small paper packets out of a larger plastic bag.

'This is top quality stuff,' he sniffs, scratching his luxuriantly black sideburns. His fingernails are manicured and his left pinky is squeezed into a large flashy signet ring. 'It was all harvested at dawn. Iranian,' he adds. 'The quality is so much better.'

'I've gone right off the Spanish stuff,' I agree, counting out another tenner. 'It's all adulterated. I am not paying fifty pounds for ten grams of floral waste.'

'It's cut with crap,' he laughs, 'but look at thi up a small packet. 'Red gold.'

Reza's been my saffron dealer for three year affable chap with his own delivery business to half the restaurants in the capital. He also deals caviar, which I do purchase occasionally, but now that the sturgeon's been slaughtered into near extinction by the Russians up their end of the Caspian Sea, it seems a tad unethical to take it from the Iranians, just because they've got a few left. I know you can get farmed eggs these days from obscure places like Uruguay, and I think even the French are having a go. But I'm a fan of those old big blue caviar tins and even those old yellow-lidded pots that the Russian sailors used to sell door-to-door fresh off the docks. Also, so much of it's been tampered and played with now it's often not worth the expense.

Saffron, on the other hand, we seem to get through by the packet load. It is also not cheap, around £6,000 a kilo, but when you consider it takes five hundred thousand crocus flowers to produce one kilo, you can see why. The stigmas must be hand picked between dawn and ten in the morning – after that they lose their colour and scent. They are then dried and are ready for use. Iranian saffron is darker than its European cousin, an autumnal red, and the aroma is denser.

'Wow,' I say, inhaling the sweet spicy scent. 'It smells fantastic. One hundred pounds for two?'

'Perfect.' He yawns. 'Are you sure you don't fancy some caviar?'

'No thanks, mate.'

'Isn't Oscar starting this week?'

'How do you know that?'

'I hear all the gossip.' He grins, broadly flashing a gang of golden molars that are clearly doubling as his pension plan.

'Starts today, in fact.'

'He's a nice man,' he says, taking my fistful of tenners and counting them. 'I remember him from before.'

'Mmm,' I agree, looking over the maroon velvet tissue box on the dashboard and into the cobbled mews beyond.

There, sitting on the back doorstep of the restaurant, rolling up an unsuspicious-looking fag, is one of my commis chefs, Sean. I like Sean. He's a young lad, full of Irish charm and in the early stages of Celtic tattoos. He's got a couple of symbols on each forearm, the plug earring, the bolt through the eyebrow, and he occasionally comes in with various shaved areas on his head. He looks exhausted.

'Thanks, Reza,' I say, getting out of the car and pocketing the saffron. 'I'll give you a call soon.' Closing the door behind me, I make my way towards Sean as he lights up. 'You all right, mate?' I say, raising my voice as I come down the alley. He looks over; his eyes are rimmed red and his face is ashen. 'Been here long?' He stares up at me and I am pretty sure he is trying to focus. 'You OK?'

'Oh, Boss!' He nods. 'Fine, mate, fine. I went out last night and I had some sleep but, you know, I thought I'd come in early.'

Bollocks, I think, looking at him. I know a dirty stop-out when I see one and Sean's come straight from a club. 'Good,' I lie. 'Just so long as you're OK. You've got a long shift to get through.'

'Tip-top, Boss.' He sniffs, exhaling his fag smoke in circular puffs.

'You coming in?' I ask, opening the back door.

'One sec,' he says, taking another large lug on his roll-up before flicking it across the cobbles.

I've met the likes of Sean many times before; they're all keen and interested in cooking, they've been to college, got the skills and come to London to become the next Gordon Ramsay, with their face on the telly, their home in a magazine, and a wife endlessly photographed endlessly shopping. But they get a bit distracted by the nightlife and the club scene on the way. I had one commis chef who started here eight months ago who used to pop an E up his arse at the beginning of service. He reliably informed Andrew that it made for an easy ride, putting it up the arse, and it meant he didn't get too high too quickly. Being a relatively straight bloke from Bradford, Andrew took a dim view of this 'entre nous' and Chris, I think his name was, was out on his Eed-up backside before you could say 'come down'.

Talk to anyone in the business and they'll tell you there's plenty of drugs on the scene. Mainly coke and on both sides of the pass. The chefs are doing it to stay awake; the commis chefs are doing it out of exhaustion, misery and boredom; the maître d's are chopping out because they're hungover from the night before; the waiters are sharpening up before a shift – and out front there are punters, girlfriends, wives, partners (both business and sexual) all hungry for a line along with their wine. It's rife. It's London. It's everywhere. We're forever getting the *Evening Standard* hacks coming in to swab our toilets during London Fashion Week. It's tiresome. They just can't help themselves; it's quite sad really that they can't come up with another idea.

But coke is mainly rife in those hip places where the food is secondary to the fun: brasseries, chains, places where they flip burgers, flatten chickens and fry courgettes into chips. There, the turnover and the atmosphere are as high as the crowd and so are the chefs backstage.

It is less usual, although obviously not unheard of, in a Michelin-starred kitchen. Although who can forget the sad death of David Dempsey, head chef at Restaurant Gordon Ramsay, who fell from a block of flats after a night out on cocaine? But when you've got stars and staff and a soufflé that goes up or down in three and half minutes, you tend to be too much of a control freak to be under the influence of anything. Although I did hear recently that one of the hottest chefs in town at the moment has succumbed to the blow and you can begin to taste it in his cooking. It's not quite so precise, not quite so perfect as before. But the pressure to be good and stay at the top of your game is usually reason enough to 'just say no' and focus. Just ask Gordon and Marco. I was told they were both 'far too square' to take drugs – unlike myself, who has always been a little bit partial.

In the old days, I remember spending many an early morning quite literally sniffing my away around Covent Garden market, apologizing for my terrible 'cocktail cold' while feeling up the cavolo nero. We'd have loads of nights out on the pop and chop – champagne and cocaine – and lock-ins were a regular thing in the first West End restaurant I worked in, learning to turn potatoes and pick bloody frisée lettuce for fifteen hours a day.

But things have changed, as indeed has Covent Garden. Andrew or I might still pop down there for a few essentials but we are much more likely now to use our own suppliers. We used to use Secretts, Greg Wallace's place just outside Godalming. They have great asparagus, but they've got a bit pricey for us, so we've moved on to Rushtons The Chef's Greengrocers who, although they have a place in New Covent Garden, deliver to our door.

We spend about £20,000 a year on veg but over £400,000 a year on meat, plus fish and wine. These are big contracts and you'd have thought that suppliers would be keen to keep them. But we had this bastard bloke who was always late with his order and consistently overweighed his produce, gently charging us a little extra every time, so we've recently moved to H. G. Walter in West Kensington, who supply The River Café. The legendary Caff, of course, gets first dibs at everything. The nicest grouse, the best partridge, the springiest lamb. But they've been with them for years and are the sort of restaurant that uses a whole prime £20 chicken to make even their most basic stocks; so you can't really begrudge them their top spot in the queue.

We're looking into our fish supplier at the moment. Last week the turbot came packed in a whole load of ice that, strangely, seemed to be included in the price. And when you're paying nearly £25 a kilo for one of the ugliest fish around and they include the ice, you know you can't trust the sod. So I am thinking of moving to this new bloke who apparently buys directly off the boats in Essex. Ben's Fish, I think he's called. You speak to him in the morning, he'll tell you what he thinks they are bringing in and it arrives shiny and spanking fresh (ice not included) at around four that afternoon. He does a few places in the Islington area at the moment, Moro, St John and Trullo, and I'm debating whether to join them. Boat to plate in less than eight hours is a good USP. Most of the fish we get at the moment is at least twenty-four hours old.

With ingredients, it's all about freshness and provenance. The organic argument is a little bit supermarket. In the trade, husbandry and where you're sourcing your supply is far more important. Either your restaurant is completely organic or it's not. There's simply no point in shoving the word 'organic' in front of a dish or an ingredient and hoping it's going to impress the henna brigade – it just makes the place look amateur. Whether your beef has been butchered and hung properly and where it came from are far more important. And contrary to what the layman might think, if any of us comes across a great supplier or a source of good meat, we are much more likely to share the contact than hoard it. Great suppliers are rare and they need to be nurtured and encouraged, otherwise they go out of business. The more restaurants use the good ones, the more likely they are to survive.

Equally, there's nothing like a few charlatans to really put you off your coddled eggs. There's always a crooked supplier, and plenty of crooked chefs, to keep you on your toes. The oldest trick in the book is for the chef to over order and to sell on out the back. In one of the places where I used to work, the head chef was on a percentage from the fish guy. The fish would be delivered, and a third of it would disappear and be sold on. Then the delivery guy and the chef would split the proceeds fifty-fifty. He was only caught because another delivery bloke wanted in on the scam and when they refused, he shopped them both.

As an owner you have to be on it all the time, checking the invoices and watching the stock, otherwise you'll wake up one day to a terrible surprise. I remember my first boss in London told me how he went to dinner once at his head chef's flat only to find his tables, his chairs, his cutlery, his salt and pepper pots all making an appearance. His chef had lifted the lot from the restaurant. He even ended up tucking into his own meat.

'I can tell you what we ate,' he told me. 'Pork and fucking prunes. I have never been able to eat it since.' Eventually he fired the bloke when he worked out that he'd paid for seventy-five turkeys one Christmas and had only served twenty-five lunches.

Theft is as rife as drugs in this business, but there are levels. Some theft is acceptable, expected even, like light-fingered bar staff walking off with the odd bottle of house white, customers pocketing the pepper or walking out with a wine bucket under their jumper, pretending to be pregnant. And some, such as my last barman, selling my wine out the back of Le Bar, or the waitress who stole £5,000 from my office, is patently not. But you live, you learn – and you watch everyone like a bloody hawk. And if something doesn't tally up, or look right, then it invariably isn't.

Much like Sean. I swear he is looking greyer and sweatier by the minute. Most of the chefs are in now. I have just seen Barney getting changed into his whites in the corridor and slipping on his black crocs. Half my staff favour Birkenstocks and the others don black Crocs. I suppose they are comfortable and waterproof but, personally, I can't stand the things.

'All right, Barney?' I ask as he walks towards me, buttoning up the front of his white double-breasted jacket.

'Just checking the prep list,' he smiles, walking towards the noticeboard. 'I want to be ahead of the game before Oscar gets here.'

'Sure,' I nod. 'Did you work with him before?'

'Bit before my time,' he says, running his finger down the list. 'I think I'll crack on with the *mirepoix*.'

The *mirepoix* consists of finely chopped carrots, onions and celery, which are fried gently in either butter or olive oil until they are reduced and translucent. It's made daily, or every other day, and is the mainstay for many dishes. It takes about two hours of hard graft and it is not a job one would normally volunteer for, unless, of course, one is trying to impress a boss, or indeed a shiny new incoming head chef. Meanwhile Sean's pulled the puntarelle straw and is slowly but surely cutting the spiky leaves off at the root. It's a nightmare job where each leaf is sliced off and then split in two before being soaked and curled in cold water to take away some of the bitter taste. Personally, I'd take the *mirepoix* over that any day.

In the far corner Alfonso is preparing the cuttlefish and, in the back kitchen, I can see Giovanna kneading the sourdough before its final proving. It will be baked and sliced fresh and warm for the breadbasket at lunchtime. She's been the pastry chef here ever since we opened and she is always the first in at around seven. In her late forties, with grey Thatcher hair contained in a small cap, she must have some of the coldest hands in the business, which is a crucial asset when it comes to putting together a millefeuille. Over at the other end of her bench she has a pile of blood oranges she's got to juice, sieve and make into a deliciously delicate ruby-coloured jelly before noon today. She's got her work cut out.

All this – staff, ingredients and prep time – has to be factored into the cost of a dish. So when I hear people telling me what a rip-off restaurants are these days, it does get me more than a little wound up. In fact, the quickest way to be ripped-off is not to book Heston's fourteen-course tasting menu at The Fat Duck at £195 per head, but to go out for a pizza. The cost of a pizza is negligible; it's less than a quid to make and you can bash out dozens of them in the time it takes for you to debone a duck. You can then charge up to £15 for the pleasure of your margarita. Now that's what I call a mark-up.

If you go somewhere posh, where they charge £30 for a main including VAT, it would have cost the restaurant around £7.50 to get it on the plate, and on top of that you have to think about rent, napery and staff costs. We are all aiming for a GP of about 70 per cent; if we hit that then we are happy. We normally times the food cost by three, or four if we think we can get away with it. Having said that, what you lose on the swings you make up with on the side dishes.

Restaurants love a side dish, almost as much as they love a vegetarian option or indeed a bowl of soup. Side dishes are posh pizza. We sell them at £4 or £5 a pop and they cost pennies to make. Buttered spinach? 20 pence to make, £5 on the plate. Chips? 15 pence to make, £4.50 on the plate. A nice beetroot salad? 30 pence to make, £7 on the plate. Macaroni cheese? 50 pence to make (cheese is surprisingly expensive), a £10 hot and sizzling main course dish. It is not quite pizza standards but getting there. Obviously the more expensive the ingredients, the more difficult it is to make money. So a big fat bit of fillet might look overpriced at £35 but it will not be the most lucrative dish for us.

And it doesn't take much for the GP to slide. If you get a chef who's a little bit lax and starts burning the food, or throwing the end of the carrots away, peeling too much off the celeriac, leaving flesh in the bones of the fish, you can suddenly find your GP slipped back to 65 per cent without you really noticing. Jean Christophe Novelli famously checks his bins every morning to see what is being thrown away, thereby making sure no one is being too profligate with his profits. You *have* to be on it all the time. Otherwise you suddenly find that lamb prices have doubled since the spring and the rump you've had on the menu all year is costing you twice as much as it did, and you haven't changed the price on the menu. You've got to be in and out of the kitchen and all over the books like a Ritalin-fuelled nit-picker. I am sure that's one of the reasons why large companies such as Gordon Ramsay Holdings find it tough to keep such a great big show on the road. It's hard to be hands on and abreast of the goings-on in all your kitchens when you're on the other side of the world watching a Lakers game with David Beckham.

I walk through the back of La Restaurant's kitchen to have a quick look in the fridges. I don't want Oscar turning up and opening the large walk-in to find raw meat dripping on cooked meat, or dripping on the floor as I'd found it last week before going totally mad and throwing the whole lot out onto the kitchen floor. Or an army of revolting Pharaoh ants like I found last month. They are horrible little bastards. Protein eaters, they feast on spilt blood or any bits of meat left on the floor. I was straight on the phone to Rentokil to get them out. We've got a contract with them to come and deal with our rats, mice and cockroaches. If we are going to keep our star, cleanliness is all part and parcel of the package.

Fortunately the ant army is nowhere to be seen and the meat is neatly stacked. There is a large shelf of T-bones, then a couple of racks of lamb chops that are waiting for a trim. They're on different shelves to indicate which day they came into the restaurant. On another shelf there's a large pancetta curing, a huge tub of giant green Cerignola olives, and a large bucket of par-boiled artichokes, plus a stack of baby pink rhubarb, chicken liquor and some more blood oranges.

I am just closing the door when I hear a terrible scream.

'Ma-a-a-an! Fuck off, ma-a-a-an, stay away from me, ma-a-a-an!'

There's a clatter of knives and some screaming and shouting and, as I walk back into the kitchen, I hear the back door slam.

'What's going on?' I ask. I look from one commis chef to another. They are standing there, opened mouthed, staring at the recently slammed door. 'Where's Sean?'

'He's gone,' says Barney, stating the obvious.

'Gone where?'

'He started freaking out about the cauliflower,' Barney continues, glancing across at the chopping board covered in white florettes. 'He said it was like chopping brains, people's brains, mad people's brains. It completely freaked him out and he ran out the door. D'you want me to go after him?'

'Yes, but be quick about it, we've got two head chefs turning up in three minutes – as if that's not going to be enough of a shit storm, without being two commis down as well.'

8–9 a.m.

Barney comes back a few minutes later to tell me he found Sean quivering, whimpering and snotting near some bins belonging to L'Italiano, the cheap and cheerful E. coli trap along the street. He'd apparently found some leftover Ketamine in his wallet while sitting out the back and had decided to finish it off before service. I have to say the logic of that defeats me, but then I'm very much the wrong side of forty and don't really see the appeal of disappearing down a K-hole. Unfortunately, or indeed unsurprisingly, it seems that horse tranquillizer and veg don't mix and he came up, or fell down, or whatever you're supposed to do, doing his *mise en place*. Apparently he'd been able to cope with the puntarelle – it's an innocuous if high-maintenance vegetable – but it was the cauliflower that sent him over the edge.

Any affection I had for Sean has now completely evaporated.

The brigade is a man down and I have the double-headed ego of Andrew to massage and, quite frankly, my own hangover to deal with. I don't expect to see Sean again. And I'm hoping he'll be too mortified to come back and pester me for his wages. He's only on £16,000 a year, but as they say, every little helps.

'Morning!' Oscar pokes his head in through the back door. 'OK to come in?'

'Oscar!' I grin broadly as he walks in swathed in a thick, blue, chunky duvet coat, with a rucksack on his back and his brown leather knife roll tucked under his arm. 'Great to see you!' He unzips his coat and takes it off. 'You look well!' I lie.

He looks bloody terrible, especially under the warts 'n' all strip light that bounces of the white wall tiles and illuminates backstage. Last time I saw him he was a plump-cheeked cherub, with blond curls, fat forearms and dimpled fists like a toddler. He loved his grub and obviously sampled quite a lot of it. Two years in France seems to have taken it out of him. He's clearly been working his moobs off, his gut and half his body fat. He's aged about six years.

'How was France?' He raises a pale eyebrow, as he looks around for somewhere to hang his coat. 'Robuchon?' He raises both his eyebrows. 'Hard work?' I hazard a guess.

'You could say that,' he says, running his hands through his thinning curls.

'Over there,' I say, pointing to the row of pegs in the corridor. 'How long did you last?'

'Almost a year.'

40

'Impressive. That's about ten months longer than Gordon and a few weeks less than Tom Aikens.'

'And not quite as long as Richard Neat,' he adds.

'Indeed, but then he was a self-proclaimed psychopath.'

'Great chef, though,' nods Oscar.

'Where's he now?' I muse.

'Costa Rica,' comes the swift reply.

'Have Robuchon still got the one employee to one client ratio going on?'

'Isn't that how you maintain three stars?'

'God, I remember hearing the old stories about Robuchon, the twenty-one-hour days, the three hours' sleep and the endless cleaning. You'd bleach your boards, you'd bleach the floors, you'd bleach the sides, the stairs, the fridges, the walls, you'd bleach your own bloody hands off. Christ, no chef left the place stinking gently of garlic and thyme – they stank of Cif and fucking Toilet Duck.'

Oscar smiles. 'It hasn't changed much; he trained as a monk, what do you expect?'

'I think it has to be one of the toughest and one of the best kitchens in the world.'

'True,' agrees Oscar.

'D'you remember Jean Marc who worked here for a while?' Oscar nods. 'I remember him talking about the headaches he got working there. By Thursday he'd had so little sleep and so much coffee his head used to throb. No amount of Solpadeine or bloody Nurofen was going to crack that mother. He never ate because he was no longer hungry. He lived on air and adrenalin. He said he'd seen several guys have fits because their bodies couldn't take it any more and others who'd deliberately cut themselves to get time off.'

'Yup,' nodded Oscar. 'There's nothing like a bit of self-harming to get you off work.'

'But you survived!'

'I did.'

'How was Michel Bras? A walk in the park after that?'

'Put it this way, the hours were a little better. The lifestyle was little kinder and I saw daylight.'

'Practically a holiday then?' He smiles. 'Well, we're delighted you came back to us! I can't wait to work with you.'

'I am excited,' he nods. 'Very excited.'

'Why don't you get changed over there,' I point back to the corridor. 'And I'll meet you in a minute in the dining room. We've got a lot to get through . . .'

'Perfect. Over there?' he quizzes, looking back over at the minimal changing facilities in the corridor, where the boys, the girls, the chefs de partie, the commis and the KPs all slip into their Denny's work gear.

In the old days the head chef wore a grand toque hat with a hundred pleats, which supposedly represented the hundred ways he knew how to cook an egg. The colour of your trousers denoted your seniority in the kitchen, with the darker shades reserved for the most important sous chefs and the chefs de partie. The white jackets were made from heavy-duty material to protect you from spills, burns and stabbing yourself in the chest and they were also doubled-breasted and reversible so you could hide those stains. However, in recent years things have changed. Despite being around for some four hundred years the toque hat is in decline and is really only used on cruise ships, in provincial hotels, and in all-you-can-eat buffets. Any stylish head chef worthy of his own photo shoot in *Observer Food Monthly* usually wears gel, some well-teased Harry Styles locks, a ponytail, or in the case of Andrew, a white Zandana – which, like all good chef headgear, releases humidity and absorbs the sweat. The hats were, and are, never about keeping hair out of the food and all about the sweat. The pouring, stinking, dripping sweat. So our commis chefs wear black skullcaps, my chefs de partie don white and the KPs have a nice black and white check.

There's the sound of a throbbing engine roaring around the back of the mews, then a screech of tyres and the loud sounds of Eminem.

'That'll be Andrew.' I smile. 'I'll see you both through there in a minute.'

Quite why Andrew James feels the need to drive a Ferrari, I don't know. I do know how much I pay him. He gets around £90K a year when all his bonuses are factored in, so I don't really know how he affords it. I suppose he's got it on HP, but I don't get the appeal myself. I think Andrew wants a fast car because Gordon has one and his old mate, the very talented Mark Sargent, also had one. Maybe it's a chef thing. A sort of contagion they got from footballers. Perhaps he perceives it as a mark of his success? Or the sort of thing you have to acquire once you've got a star. A star, a car and a taste-testing slot on

MasterChef, and you've made it. Or so Andrew clearly thinks.

'All right?' he says, about five minutes later, loafing into the dining room and chucking his leather jacket over the back of one of the chairs. He puts down his beige, perforated leather driving gloves and plonks himself down in front of me, stinking of fags and attitude.

'How are you this morning, Andrew?' I ask.

'Not bad.' He stretches both his hands above his head and yawns in my face. I am half expecting him to break wind but we are all fortunately spared that delight. 'Tired,' he pronounces.

And he looks it. He's unshaven, his long dark hair is greasy, his hands look like he's been shovelling tarmac and he's in the same grey T-shirt he was wearing yesterday. Andrew's a good-looking bloke, lean and long, easily over six foot. The ladies love him, but today he'd have a job pulling anyone. They'd have to be at least two pints of Gavi de Gavi down before they'd give him a second glance. But that's usually how he likes them, drunk and brief, so he can get back to his wife without too much hassle.

'Well, thank you for agreeing to show Oscar the ropes for the next few days,' I start. 'It is extremely kind of you and well beyond the call of duty.' He says nothing. 'Um, I was wondering if we might have a look at the menu to start off with to see if Oscar here has any ideas.'

'Nothing wrong with the menu,' says Andrew, swinging back on his chair. 'I didn't hear any complaints when I got my star.'

'No, no,' I agree, very quickly. This is going to be much harder than I thought. 'Um, would anyone like any water?'

I wander over to the small bar area we have in the corner by the entrance to Le Restaurant. It is not the sort of bar designed for people to prop up for hours at a time, but it's quite a good place to park a customer if his table isn't quite ready. The bar itself is simple, black with a silver-polished mirror front; it has four cream leather stools for perching on, and a couple of silver bowls of skinned and hand-fried almonds. Behind are a load of glass shelves weighed down with premium whiskies, fat bottles of expensive brandy, and a collection of obscure liqueurs. Below the bar are a few bottles of Speyside chilling in the fridge, one of which I help myself to.

By the time I get back to the table Oscar has taken a large notebook out of his rucksack and is leafing through it, licking his fingers with enthusiasm. Meanwhile Andrew sits stubbornly, picking the fluff off his jeans. You could cut the atmosphere with a Global knife.

'What have you got in there?' I ask Oscar, sitting down and pouring the water.

'Just a few bits and bobs that I picked up in France,' he replies.

'Have you got the Chocolate Fondant pudding recipe?' I ask.

'Of course he's got the Chocolate Fondant pudding!' snaps Andrew, the front legs of his chair landing back down on the floor with a thump. 'Everyone's got the fucking fondant recipe. Anyone who's ever employed anyone who's ever set foot near Michel Bras's Laguiole has taken the fondant recipe and made it their own. Gordon's done that, everyone has. It's like the Basil Sorbet from Robuchon: we've got ours, Hartnett's got hers, it's in Nobu. Christ, even Jamie sodding Oliver has done a basil sodding sorbet! Everyone's "inspired" by someone – it's just that some of us are more subtle about it, aren't we, Oscar?'

'Yes,' Oscar thankfully agrees.

'I mean, the lemon tart recipe everyone uses is Marco's. But I'm pretty sure Albert Roux or Pierre Koffman "inspired" it. Unless you're Noma or even Heston, I suppose, there's only so many times you can reinvent the wheel. There are only three or four genius chefs in the world – Ferran Adrià at the dear departed el Bulli, René Redzepi at Noma, and I suppose Jean-Georges Vongerichten in New York, but he's doing French fucking Asian bloody confusion and I *hate* that shit.' He swigs his water and belches the bubbles. 'I can't stand fucking coriander.'

'I was thinking sardines,' says Oscar.

'They're a lot cheaper than turbot,' I enthuse.

'Sardines? Who the fuck wants to eat sardines? They are itty and bitty and full of bones—'

'And flavour,' adds Oscar. 'With cucumber, beetroot and razor clams.'

'Great,' I smile.

'If you're a fucking dolphin,' says Andrew.

'Robuchon does it,' says Oscar.

'Robuchon . . . Robuchon.' Andrew's head is moving side to side slightly like a chicken. 'Are you sure you've got it down properly?' He can hardly contain his sneer.

Although some chefs are famously generous with their recipes – and Gordon is one of them – there are others who can be a little bit more devious, withholding vital ingredients or specific techniques, just to fuck you up at the final furlong. But the world of top-drawer chefs is so small, most of them at some stage have cooked in each or everyone's kitchen. Gordon trained with Marco, Jean Christophe trained with Marco, Marco trained with Raymond and Albert, Heston trained with Marco and Raymond for about three weeks in total, and then Jason Atherton, Marcus Wareing, Angela Hartnett and Mark Sargent *all* trained with Gordon who also trained with Albert. And so it goes on.

'Of course I've got it down properly!' Oscar looks indignant. 'I didn't spend a year sweating my bollocks with Robuchon to learn nothing! What else do you think I have been doing for the past twenty-two months in France if it wasn't going from kitchen to kitchen, looking at the way they do things, watching how they work, how they plan, how they manage, picking up tips, writing them down?' He slams his hand down on his notebook, the tops of his ears bright red with anger.

'All right, fucking Ratatouille, what else have you got?' Andrew nods at the book. 'Go on . . .'

We are, obviously, like every other place blazing any sort of trail, a 'seasonal' restaurant, and we try and update our menu according to what is available and fresh, but you have to be careful. It's not so much we have that many 'signature dishes' but there are certain things that people expect to see on the menu when they come here. We've always got a bit of pigeon, a loin of venison, and a beef shank, and then you've got to have some fish for the ladies because they are much more likely to order fish than anything else, plus a couple of stalwart puds. Equally, you want to keep the thing fresh and looking alive. There is nothing worse than a totally moribund menu that looks like the chef's been churning out the same old shit for months. It needs to feel like an old friend with some interesting news. You've also got to keep your eye on the weather. There's nothing like a couple of hot weeks in May when you've still got a heavy wintery menu to completely ruin the GP. Equally you don't sell many salads when it snows. But changing the menu can give you all sorts of problems. You can't overtax the kitchen with too many new moves and ideas because the chefs won't thank you for it. So you have to move relatively slowly, much like you're turning around a heavily laden tanker, rather than a slick and well-oiled machine.

'Hello, ladies!' I look up to see Jorge waving both hands at me as he strides towards the back table with shiny shoed purpose. 'Lovely day for it.'

'For what?' says Andrew, staring hard at Jorge, his lank hair hanging in a centre parting.

'Whatever you want, darling,' smiles Jorge. He goes over and gives Andrew a kiss on his cheek. Andrew hates it when Jorge kisses him, which is, of course, the reason why Jorge continues to do so.

Jorge is my maître d' and has been ever since we opened. He is camper than a *Strictly Come Dancing* judge and loved by everyone – except Andrew. Slim, dark and handsome, with hips as narrow as a pencil, he can work an Armani suit better than any straight man I know and he comes from southern Spain.

'Jorge, d'you remember Oscar?'

'Of course I do!' He claps his hands together with delight. 'I took him to his first gay club!'

'No you didn't,' says Oscar, his ears pinking again.

'Don't tell me you'd been to the Shadow Lounge before?' Jorge whispers, putting his finger to his lips. 'Well, I never, you naughty thing.' He looks Oscar up and down. 'It is always the quiet ones!'

'Jorge, you are incorrigible,' I say.

'If I knew what that meant, baby, I'd thank you,' he says, walking through the swing doors into the kitchen. 'All right, ladies?' He greets the brigade in the same manner he greets everyone.

'Morning, Jorge,' comes the mumbled reply.

Andrew knocks back his water and slams his glass back down on the large round table. 'So just the sardines . . . ?'

'Well, I have a few other things,' suggests Oscar. 'A ceviche—'

'A ceviche?' Andrew yawns. 'You went to France and came back with a *ceviche*?'

'I was thinking of adding some foie gras to your pigeon.'

'There's nothing wrong with my fucking pigeon!'

'Snails with morels?'

Andrew rolls his eyes. 'Let's stick to what we've got, shall we?'

Oscar closes his book. He is smart enough not to push it. Andrew has one week left before he hangs up his whites in this kitchen and it's simply not worth the tantrums and tiaras to pursue his own agenda just yet. I am not sure where Andrew's going, but no doubt he'll turn up somewhere. People like Andrew always do. They get given jobs on past glories, although how long they last in them is a different matter. But then London is littered with chefs who move from one job to another, some through disagreement, some because they want to try something new. It is not an industry that hands out carriage clocks and gold watches. If you stay ten years in a place people think you are a little odd. It's good to move. Although few walkouts were quite as spectacular as Ben Spalding's recent departure from John Salt; despite garnering great reviews for his twelve-course tasting menu, he marched. And he marched citing 'creative differences', in a manner not dissimilar to Johnnie Mountain huffing off after being humiliated by a rather smug Marcus Wareing on *Great British Menu*. There is nothing more flouncy than a chef with his nose out of joint.

'Oh my God!' exclaims Jorge, coming back through the kitchen door. 'I can't believe it! Sean!' he says simply, and shakes his head. 'Who would have thought it!'

'I can't say I'm surprised,' I reply.

'What?' asks Andrew, looking from Jorge to me. He hates not coming to gossip when it's piping hot.

'Sean came in off his nuts on Special K and had a shit fit in the kitchen and has had to leave. He found the cauliflower terrifying!' Jorge ticks each element off his slim fingers and then raises an eyebrow. Given his fondness for the local botoxeria, I am amazed his still can.

'Is he OK?' asks Oscar.

'Does that mean I'm a man down?' says Andrew.

'Yes.' I nod at Andrew. 'And who knows?' I reply to Oscar. 'And before anyone says anything I am not getting any agency drones in at short notice. I'm pretty sure we can pick up another commis chef by tomorrow and, in the meantime, you can manage.'

'Manage?' Andrew gets up and walks past me like some sort of surly teenager in search of his games console, his shoulders hunched, his lank hair hanging like curtains either side of his face. He looks like an unkempt Afghan hound. And he's got BO. The acrid wave follows after him, turning the air sour. God knows how he gets laid so much. It's completely astonishing. I'll never understand women – but with two divorces under my belt at the age forty-five, that's a given.

Oscar follows on afterwards. I have a feeling this is going to be a day from hell. I need a really strong cup of coffee, something that will kick me hard in the kidneys to keep me awake. That, and at least a cigarette.

'Oh my God!' exclaims Jorge. At the other end of the restaurant, I jump. 'Nooo!' he continues with a long loud sigh as he pores over the front of house computer system. I stare down the restaurant at his hunched silhouette, backlit by the weak wintery sun, as he slowly drags his fingertip across the screen. 'What a total cunt!' His head rolls to one side. He puts his hands on his hips. 'A total *cunt*. Why do people do this? Why? What is the point of it all?' He throws his hands in the air with exasperation.

'What's the matter, Jorge?'

'I cannot believe it! Some shit has given us a terrible review on TripAdvisor.'

'TripAdvisor? How bad?'

'One star.'

'One! The cunt. Let me see!'

9–10 a.m.

Jorge and I huddle around the computer reading the review from 'Moleman' on TripAdvisor. The man is clearly a tosser. He describes our décor as 'outdated', our service as 'rude and surly'; he even goes so far as to say that Jorge himself was 'aloof and patronizing'. Needless to say, Jorge is outraged.

'I'm sure I know which little bastard did this. He was fat, with small eyes like a little pink pig,' he says, as his nostrils flare. 'He complained about everything. He sent back the wine.'

'I hate it when people do that,' I sigh. 'Like they have any idea what corked wine actually tastes like? It is quite unusual these days for wine to be corked, mostly because the stuff this sort of cheapskate arse orders comes with a screw top! But this is the worst bit.' I scroll down the review. ' "I was shocked",' I read out loud. ' "They didn't have tongs for the bread. This is a Michelin-starred restaurant and we had to pick the bread out of the basket with our hands!" Not their bare hands! Honestly, it's like being in the seventies. Who has tongs for the bread? No one, except bloody First Class bloody British Airways and The bloody Hilton?'

'What do they want? Gloves!' Jorge joins in.

'Well . . .' I turn to look at him. 'No tongs.'

'Tongs!' he repeats, with a look of contemptuous disgust.

You'd be amazed how much we take bad online reviews to heart, and you'd also be surprised at how much they can affect business. All you need is a couple of snide ones on Toptable, or the *Time Out* website, and people start calling a little less frequently. Then suddenly you find your sales slipping – and all because some idiot wanted tongs for his sodding bread. I bloody hate those websites. And unless the reviews are libellous they won't take them down. At least in the old days you knew who the critics were. You could grab the spankingest freshest fish with the brightest eyes (like some vacuous beauty queen banging on about world peace) the moment you saw Jonathan Meades rolling through the front door in search of a free lunch and some fine wines. But everyone's a sodding critic now and everybody takes bloody photos of the food.

Adam came back from a weekend in Denmark about a fort-night ago, having managed to squeeze his slim behind in for a dinner at Noma. He said the whole experience irritated the tits off him. Firstly, he was forced to eat a symphony of onions as there was bugger all to be foraged in the Danish countryside in deepest, darkest November and, secondly, the place was full of 'Japs snapping their bloody food'. He'd moaned a lot about it. 'Why can't they just eat the stuff instead of photographing it? Who's interested in a photo of food that someone else is about to eat?!' But then again, he's Australian, and clearly not a bloke of the Instagram age. Although he's not alone in his hatred of food bloggers. Michel Roux gets very huffy if people start taking snaps of his creations, insisting that they should ask the permission of the chef. It is also banned in many restaurants in the States. I'm sure they'd cite creative reasons or something like culinary copyright, although no such thing exists, but really it's because it is extremely bloody irritating. And talking of irritating, anyone who follows what people are saying about their restaurant on Twitter is insane. You need the skin of a rhino to put #yourplace into the Twittersphere, because what comes back will make you want to weep.

'OK, that bloody does it!' I declare, my jaw clenching and my blood gently coming to simmering point.

'Oh no!' Jorge leans in closer. 'Is that an actual *photo* of the bread basket?'

'Yup,' I nod. 'A bread basket with no tongs.'

'It looks good,' announces Jorge. 'Nice selection.'

'Of course it's good! This is a bloody Michelin-starred fucking restaurant! It was handmade by Giovanna that bloody morning. It could not be any fresher or any more delicious if it shagging tried.'

'But no tongs,' shrugs Jorge.

'No.' I reach in my back pocket and pull out my mobile. 'That's it. I'm calling Caroline.'

'Good idea,' nods Jorge.

Caroline is my very blonde, very pretty, very well-connected PR. She's been on my books for three years, ever since we got our star, and she costs me £3,500 a month to retain on a print and social media basis. She has about another twenty-five clients on her books and spends her whole life eating out in restaurants. She never normally answers her phone before nine thirty, but this is an emergency.

'Caz here,' she drawls down the phone in a voice dripping with fags, fun and a £35,000-a-year private education.

'Morning, Caz.'

'Hi, daaaarling, how are you? I was just thinking about you. We're coming in to see you this morning, are we? Is it ten or eleven? I was just cranking up the old BlackBerry to check.'

'Eleven.'

'Great, fabulous, just one thing, da-a-rling, I'll be on my tod as Ev's got to go to this new place we're looking after around the corner. They think they've got bloody Adrian bloody Gill coming in for lunch today and they've only got three other bookings. So it's an all-hands-on-deck moment, and half the office are going down to pad out the tables and make the place look super popular.'

'Really? Don't you think he'll think it's weird that most of the diners are thin, blonde and in their early twenties?'

'You're shitting me, right?'

'Er, no.' What is it with posh girls and swearing? It's like a form of Tourette's with them. They feel compelled to put at least three naughty words into every sentence.

'He's a bloke, da-a-arling. He'll just be delighted he doesn't have to look at Jeremy Clarkson for the whole of lunch.'

'Every cloud,' I reply.

'I know, darling,' she laughs. 'And you know we'd do the same for you. Only we'd never have to,' she adds quickly, 'because you're the hottest ticket in town. Right up there, darling, with Dabbous and Balthazar.'

'Not quite,' I say. 'One you can't get a table at until hell freezes over, and the other you wouldn't *want* a table at even if hell did freeze over.'

'Actually,' she corrects, 'I had a fabulous dinner at Balthazar just the other day. Jude Law was there, as was Cara Delevingne—'

'I always find the food tastes so much better when there are famous people in the room.'

'Totally,' agrees Caroline, sidestepping my attempt at sarcasm. 'Anyway, darling . . . ?'

'We have a bit of a problem.'

'Right?'

'Some twat has give us a bad review on TripAdvisor.'

'How bad?'

'One star.'

'Ouch.'

'It goes on and on, picking us to pieces, and there is a picture of our bread basket, without tongs.'

'What's that got to do with the price of anything?'

'Just read the review and you'll see.'

'So, TripAdvisor?'

'Yup.'

'Leave it with me. I'll get the office to deal with it.'

'What will you do?'

'Bury it, darling, bury it. We'll give you so many five-star reviews from the office it'll be pushed down to the next page by eleven thirty at the latest. See you in a bit.' She hangs up.

I think I love Caroline. She's the best £3,500 investment per month I've ever made. She is the same price as my second wife and a lot less hassle. I pat Jorge on the shoulder as I walk towards the kitchen. I need a cigarette out the back to celebrate my minor victory over the world of tosserdom.

My delight and small victory over the world of idiots is short lived. I walk through the surprisingly quiet kitchen. Both Oscar and Andrew are on the pass, making sure all the chopped herbs, spices and garnishes are in place. You'd be amazed at how many 'seasoning' options a chef needs. In the left-hand corner there are small silver containers of parsley, chives, chervil, dill, ginger, lemon purée and capers. Next to them is another selection including pistachios, walnuts, smoked almonds, shallot confit, toasted pine nuts, bread-crumbs and sea salt; there are doilies for wiping down each plate as it goes out and a bowl of water to dip the doilies in. All of these ingredients are supposed to be made fresh before service but some, I suspect, hang around for a day or two or three. Although some of them don't ever make it through a whole service, as everyone helps themselves to the smoked almonds throughout the day.

Outside I bump into Emmanuel, or Manu, who is sorting

through piles of stinking rubbish. A gentle giant from the Congo, he's worked with me ever since Le Restaurant opened. I stole him from Chris Bodker's old place, The Avenue, where Manu and I were working together before I set up on my own. We have both been around the block a few times, and there is little he has not seen. He works an eight-hour shift for me, arriving to scrub down the kitchen at seven each morning and he leaves at three in the afternoon after he has washed and cleaned every single plate, glass, pot, pan, knife and fork in the place. He then does a shift for London Transport, driving a bus, which he finishes at around eight.

Manu is a quiet, charming bloke who's raised three daughters on his own and I often think he is the perfect response for those who argue against immigration. He works twice as hard as anyone I have ever employed and he's legal and been living and paying taxes in this country for the past seventeen years. Granted, he is a bit of an anathema in the industry that has survived and thrived on illegal immigration for years. Although the days of employees using fake names and working off emergency National Insurance numbers are more or less over. Restaurants and hotels used to be rammed to the rafters with cowering monoglots of interchangeable origin, who were used, abused, paid about £2 an hour, and who barely ever got home to sleep. Most of the time you never quite managed to catch their name. In fact, you didn't care what they were called, just so long as they did their job and didn't annoy you too much. They were regularly baited just to amuse the senior staff. I remember one poor Algerian bloke who worked as a *plongeur* in a large kitchen I worked in being forced to eat a whole orange, peel and all. What he didn't know was that it had been laced with Tabasco. He ended up in hospital because he couldn't stop vomiting.

Thankfully, things have changed since then. It's much more difficult to employ people illegally these days, mainly because Immigration like to pop in for a little bit more than a cup of tea, on a regular basis.

Working hours are also radically different from what they used to be. The old double shift, seven in the morning to midnight, six days a week, meted out by most of the top joints, is unsurprisingly not that popular with the new sort of softer, gentler, metro-chefs who are coming through. The old *cojones*-of-steel approach, needing less sleep than Mrs Thatcher, drinking nothing but espressos, doesn't go down well with the under twenty-fives. So most places, like mine, use a rota system where you do four full days, so eight until midnight, and then have three days off. It doesn't cost dramatically more, my books just about balance, but I don't pay overtime and I don't get extra staff in to cover holidays. You step up to the mark or you piss off. It works out as a little bit longer that the thirty-five hours a week dictated by Europe, but thank God for the opt out.

Travel through France these days and it's hard to find a restaurant that is fully operational seven days a week. Joel Robuchon obviously is, but there plenty who are not. Thousands of them find it hard to stay open for more than three or four days in seven. Some of them, particularly those in the countryside, only open for a long weekend. Others no longer do lunch. It is hard to keep costs down when your workforce is only allowed to work a full two and half shifts a week.

'What's all this?' I ask Manu, lighting up a cigarette and inhaling like an oxygen-starved deep-sea diver.

'Oh,' he says, shaking his head, 'those stupid bin men.'

He doesn't need to say any more. Our love/hate relationship with the fine bin men of Westminster Council is one of life's long-running sagas. They are supposed to come twice a day, every day, to take away our rubbish, which is rather plentiful. And it is not nice. It is the sort of stuff that rats and mice gravitate towards and, given half a chance, they'd move into at the drop of a bin lid. So we pay our business rates which is about a third of our rent (£60,000 a year), our refuse collection fee which is another £800 or so, plus we pay £64.50 every couple of days for fifty refuse bags, then we give the nice boys from WC enough whisky to drown a shipload of sailors at Christmas, plus endless tips, the odd £50 here, the odd bit of beef there, a bottle of vodka . . . Frankly, they could open their own bloody off-licence the amount of treats we give them. And *still* they refuse to collect our rubbish.

Either our bags are too heavy – anything over five kilos is too much for their delicate backs to contend with. Or we haven't sorted it properly – they've got this new thing where they recycle food waste but we have to divide the meat from the veg, and the fish, and the bones. It is one of the top jobs in the restaurant; a pleasurable thing to have to do after a twelve-hour shift at the coalface of culinary excellence. And then some other restaurant or business decides, as they have today, to dump a whole load of shit in our backyard. And unless we sort through it, we're the mugs who get fined.

'What did they say?'

'One hundred and fifty pounds on the spot unless we bag this up properly,' Manu replies, sifting through a bag full of old plate scrapings.

'Where's that from?' The sweet smell of rotting food is making me feel nauseous and my cigarette taste revolting.

'L'Italiano, I should think,' he says. 'Plenty of spaghetti.'

'They're a bunch of bastards, that lot. We are always giving them milk and bread and butter when they've run out. We're *nice* to them.'

'Not always,' replies Manu. 'Andrew told them where to go the other day.'

I roll my eyes. That man can't leave soon enough. What he fails to realize is that the restaurant world is a small community, which is also part of the greater community. If we live and work in Mayfair then we have to be part of Mayfair. We help each other out when we've run out of stuff. We give leftover food to the local Christian charity group, and we also leave stale bread outside the back door for the couple of local tramps whose faces we know. What we don't do is pick fights with the local Italian, particularly if that Italian has been on the street for over twenty years and has no visible clientele. It is clearly a front for laundering something, because that place can't be doing any real business. You'd need to sell a hell of a lot of carbonara and garlic bread to cover his £200,000 a year rent.

'Do you need any help with that, Manu?' I ask, inhaling the last of my cigarette.

'Don't worry, Boss,' he says as he pulls out a handful of what looks like chicken bones. 'They're a man down in the kitchen already. I'm sure I can cope.'

'If you're sure,' I say, feeling more than a little guilty about not putting a pair of gloves on and helping him myself.

'No worries,' he replies.

I hesitate for a second, but then my phone goes. It's Adam from Le Bar.

'All right, mate,' he states, rather than asks. 'Just calling to say the toilets are fixed. The big-bird basin is back on the wall. You can use it, but not sit on it just yet because the putty's got to dry.'

'Good work.'

'Shall I put a no shagging sign on it just in case someone else fancies a go?'

'I don't think that's necessary, do you?'

'You never know!' he laughs. He's been in this business far too long. 'The cleaners are on the water so we should be OK to open.'

'I'll come over and check in an hour or so.'

He hangs up and I step back inside the kitchen. Everyone is hard at work. We have five main sections in all: meat, also known as sauce, fish, larder, veg and, of course, pastry. Each of these is headed up by a chef de partie. Matt is on meat sauce.

The most senior of the chefs de partie, he has the most important section. He has been with us for just under six months and came to us via the three-star Michelin chef Hélène Darroze at the Connaught. A Kiwi in his late twenties, he is brilliant, organized, unflappable and rather overqualified for us, but I think he is enjoying himself. Although it's hard to say as he's not a Chatty Cathy type. He's in, out, and back on the tube to Barnet every night. He's not a bloke who likes to hang around. Alfonso, who's on fish and been with us for two years, is brilliant with salmon. He can fillet the whole thing in just over five minutes, which includes removing the pin bones.

We have Davide on the larder, which is effectively anything cold – confits, terrines, salad. He's Andrew's Gallic sidekick with a vicious temper and a face full of sweaty blackheads. I fully expect him to walk when Andrew leaves next week and I have to say I'll be quite chuffed to see the back of him. His attitude stinks as much as his breath, and his teeth are black from the amount of coffee he imbibes on a daily basis.

Giovanna, our pastry chef, is as delightful and as charming as she is round. And there is Barney on veg, the lowest position in the kitchen hierarchy. He is legumes. But he is a nice legume, an enthusiastic legume, who has the kid charm of Jamie Oliver.

As well as the chefs de partie we have, or should I say *had*, three commis chefs. Stacy, straight out of college and a nice, jolly girl from Bristol; Andrea, a taciturn Italian from Bologna, and there was Sean. These three are supposed to float around the kitchen helping the chefs de partie and doing what they are told. But what usually happens is that Stacy spends her whole day making ravioli or fettuccini and popping them into the boiler. Andrea is usually on sauce or jus, and Sean spent most of the time putting small bits of cabbage into blanch or purée-ing the potatoes, parsnips or swedes. I am not sure I can see Oscar filling in for him.

'Everything OK?' I mumble as I walk through, hoping for the path of least engagement.

'Um, excuse me,' pipes up Oscar. My heart sinks. 'Can I have a word?'

'Absolutely, whatever you want,' I lie. Fortunately, thankfully, my phone goes. It's Pippa over at La Table. 'Sorry.' I nod to Oscar. 'I've got to take this.' I step through into the dining room.

'Hi there?'

'Morning,' she replies. She is sounding a little circumspect and not her usual ebullient self. 'Um. I have a girl here,' she says. 'Her name is Gina.'

'Gina?'

'She says she knows you and she says that you offered her a job?'

'Oh! Gina! Right, shit! *That* Gina.' I pour myself the remainder of the bottled water at the round table.

'Yes, that Gina,' continues Pippa who is perhaps not quite as au fait as Jorge, or indeed Adam, with my management techniques. 'Well, what do you suggest that I do with her?'

10–11 a.m.

I can tell that Pippa is less than impressed with my peccadil-
loes. Every one of my helpful handy serving suggestions as to
what to do with the delightful Gina is met with a stony silence.
Waitress? On reception? Cleaner? Nothing. So I talk to Kim,
the maître d' at La Table. Even she's not terribly impressed and
she's worked for me for a while.

'Maybe Adam could use her in Le Bar?' she finally suggests
down the phone, her voice dribbling with sarcasm, like golden
syrup running off a spoon.

'No, no, that's a fate worse than death,' I laugh. Silence.
'Send her over here then,' I say. 'I'm sure Jorge can think of
something.'

'I am not sure he bats for her team,' replies Kim.

What a humourless bunch. I think I am going to rethink my
unusually radical move of employing as many women as

possible. What's the point of being at the vanguard, if the vanguard is so bloody grumpy and deeply ungrateful?

I mean, I have always been very pro-woman (probably a little too pro) and I have always thought they had no problem cutting it in a professional kitchen. In fact, most of the time they are better organized, more creative, more charming and a hell of a lot tidier than their male counterparts. In short: a joy. Pippa would never dream of turning up for work stinking as if she'd spent the night in a Soho latrine the way Andrew does more frequently than I care to remember. Cleanliness aside, some of the best food in London is being cooked by women at the moment – Hélène Darroze at the Connaught, the fantastic Angela Hartnett at Murano, Clare Smyth at Restaurant Gordon Ramsay and the pulchritudinous Florence Knight at Polpetto. But according to the Office of National Statistics, of the 187,0000 chefs currently working the UK today, only 20 per cent, or some 37,000, are women. That's a slightly higher percentage than female directors of FTSE companies but not much. And listening to some of my colleagues chew the cud on 'girls in the kitchen', it's easy to see why. It's like the seventies' women's lib movement passed them by. I remember Marco once saying that women 'lack the physical strength of men and men aren't going to work for a woman, are they?' Like it takes bulging Arnie biceps to chop parsley and sear a scallop? Granted, they might find it tricky to butcher the hind leg off a donkey but I am sure they could always ask a nice bloke for some assistance.

In the olden days Gordon was equally as enlightened.

During the glory hours of Aubergine, where the working conditions were so tough, so steamy and so butch it was once described as 'Vietnam', he was in a quandary about what to yell at the young Hartnett. He shared that he couldn't call her a 'cunt' (which is what he called everyone else) as she had one. So in the end, after much umming and ahhing, he decided to simply refer to her as 'bitch'. Amazingly, they are still good friends, so it must have all been 'banter in context'.

Anyway, I could do with a bit more humour in my employees this morning, and for them to be a little less judge-mental. As if I haven't got enough to worry about without the good opinion of Pippa also being on the agenda.

'Was it fun, ladies? Was it fun?' quizzes Jorge, as he walks over to meet and greet the slowly arriving gaggle of his front of house staff. There are a few ladies on the team. And pretty gorgeous ones at that.

Well, I only employ good-looking people in front of house. There! I said it out loud. We *all* do, and anyone in the industry who tells you otherwise is lying. They'll deny it until they are blue in the face but all you really need to do is take a look around the gaff/caff to prove them wrong.

Personally, I always ask for an up-to-date photograph on the CV, otherwise they don't get a look in. It is illegal, but who cares? Good-looking people flirt. Good-looking people are up for it. Good-looking people engage, they get eye-contact, they are more extrovert, they are more confident and, most im-portantly of all, they make me more money. If ugly people made me more money, I'd employ them. But you are much more likely to buy another bottle of wine or order the over-priced champagne cocktail if it's suggested to you by a pretty waitress. I remember one of my wives accusing me of only employing good-looking women during some annoying row and I told her she was wrong. I employ good-looking men as well.

Your front of house has got to be fun, it's got to look attractive, it's got to lure people in, make them want to hang out, spend some time there. It has also got to sell all that food your fabulous chef has been working his or her arse off to prepare. No one is forced to eat out. No one *must* go to a restaurant as a matter of life or death. It is discretionary spending. It is a luxury, and in times of austerity, luxury has to be worth it. So the staff have to engage with the customer, make them feel special and get them to spend their money. It's a dance. It is not hard, but so many places get it wrong. They're hot – and then they're not. It's quite easy to get someone into your place once, but getting them to come back is a different matter.

When I interview my staff I am not that interested in their experience, or what they've done before; I want to know their hobbies, what they can talk about, what they like doing, and what they are actually like. Some of these Russian Natashas look fantastic, but do you really want to spend any time with them?

Equally, they do have to be able to do the job. But I often find that a certain amount of staff self-selection goes on. They have to work as a team, so if they're not good enough at their job and everyone else ends up carrying the shift, it doesn't take long for them to be 'moved on'. If you're not bringing in the tips, they'll get rid of you. If you're not nice to work with, they'll get rid of you. If you piss people off, they'll get rid of you. The team can and does find itself and its own sort of equilibrium.

However, it is very difficult to find the right people. I remember when those wise bastards Ian Schrager and Steve Rubell opened Morgans, the Royalton and Paramount hotels in New York, they recruited as many attractive out-of-towners and wannabe actors as they could. They wanted an energetic, vibrant staff, with a positive, upbeat and friendly attitude, which are clearly not the outstanding qualities of your average New Yorker. So they made a terrific effort to look elsewhere, and it paid off. They had the shiniest, happiest, most beguiling staff in town.

I have to say us Brits, especially Londoners, are also not greatly in demand in the service industry. Large companies like Soho House have been forced to look as far afield as Australia, sending their recruitment team out to Sydney in order to get their charming, easy-going staff.

Most of mine at Le Restaurant come from eastern and southern Europe. In Le Bar it's mainly Aussies and Italians, but that is obviously due to Adam and his Antipodean connections. La Table is almost entirely Polish.

'So was it fun?' asks Jorge, as the gang of seven gather around the bar to the tune of Berocca plink, plinking and fizzing into their glasses of water. 'Wow,' he says, watching the bright orange vitamin C pills dissolve in a flash of bubbles. '*That* much fun?'

'Nothing a vitamin won't cure,' smiles Anna, a very pretty blonde Ukrainian girl who's been on my front desk for just under a year. Slim, clever and twenty-seven years old, she has a linguistics degree from Kiev University. In fact, I am fairly sure it was her arrival that sent Sketchley over the edge. Not that I've got to any base with Anna, although not through lack of trying, I assure you, but she is engaged and has been for five long years.

As they chat and drink their orange fizzy drinks, I gather they all went dancing last night after work, and it turns out that Mikus, one of the Polish waiters, pulled the girl that Luca, a slight, sweet-looking chap from Naples, had his eye on. Discouraged and disheartened, he'd drowned his sorrows in vodka and fallen over outside the club. Nice. It sounds as though they all crawled home at about two, which is not something I am particularly pleased about. The only person who behaved himself was Michelangelo, the sommelier. But then he's not a great drinker. He loves wine, he really does, but only in moderation. He'd much rather nurse a big Barolo all night than chug back six vodkas and a jägerbomb. God, I feel a little nauseous, what on earth was I doing drinking one of those?

'Morning, Michelangelo,' I say, walking past the front of house team as they slowly disperse.

'Morning, sir,' he nods. He is standing behind the bar, checking on the stock.

'Did you have fun last night?'

'It was OK, sir, not really my thing.'

Michelangelo is obviously not his real name. He was given it by Jorge about two years ago and it stuck. I think his real name is Paolo, or something quite ordinary, but Jorge was teasing him about being 'a true artist when the rest of them were mere piss artists' or some late-night gag like that, and that, as they say, was that. The poor sod now has it on his name badge next to his little bunch of golden sommelier's grapes.

Michelangelo bends down and starts counting his bottles. Unlike the majority of restaurants, we do have some of our wine stock on show. Mostly, if you see racks of wine lining the walls of a packed bar, the bottles will be empty. What is not pinned down will be pinched by the customer. You'd be amazed how many bottles get half-inched, popped inside a jacket or slipped into a handbag, as someone staggers out sniggering into the street. They're invariably drunk. Actually, they are always drunk. The power of alcohol to turn seemingly pleasant people into kleptomaniacs, pyromaniacs and sex maniacs should never be underestimated.

But I am ever hopeful that our slightly more up-market client base would not resort to such lows. Alternatively, if you ever see those racks of booze lined up on their side, lit from above with spotlights, like some art installation – don't drink the wine. Those poor bottles of red have been sitting under those warm lights stewing away for months, if not years, and if they are not actually fizzing and off, they are not far away from it.

So we keep some choice wines out on show and a few less

choice ones below the eye level at the bar. So if someone asks for a glass of house wine they might think they're getting a Petrus but they're usually having a Rioja instead. We always use Rioja, as it stays freshest the longest when open to the elements.

'Ah, Jorge!' I say, walking towards the back of the restaurant. 'Can we go through last night's book?'

Like most restaurants, we keep a small book in which incidents or rudeness or disagreements or any other problems are recorded, so that we can discuss them the following day. We also note if anyone famous/well known/important has been in, so if they call again we can make a table available to them, or remind them of their last visit. Our system is called the Little Black Book, but with international outfits, like Nobu, the whole thing is computerized. So if you have behaved like a cock in New York, they know about it in LA and Budapest before you've popped an Advil and had your breakfast. And they don't really stand for cock behaviour in Nobu. They don't have to; they've got reservations coming out of their backside and celebrities falling over the paps to get in. But they won't tell you to your face. What suddenly happens is those eight o'clock bookings that you used to get just by emailing your PA become seven o'clock, or worse, six thirty! They'll be terribly nice on the phone, but there really is nothing they can do. If you have a D (meaning dreadful/difficult) or a W (meaning watch) by your name on the Nobu computer, there is not much they can do for you ever again. They run such a slick operation that each restaurant in the chain (I am afraid it is really a chain

– twenty-two restaurants is a chain) informs the others who has been in the night before. So when Lindsay Lohan pops into LA, having been at her favourite middle table in Nobu Berkeley St, London, only the week before, the staff can ask if she had fun last week and how was the black cod? It is slightly Big Brother creepy but slebs lap that shit up; they think everyone is interested in their every bowel movement, so the fact that the waiter knows what you ate seven days ago in London is water off their skinny backs.

'So did we have anyone in last night?' I ask, sitting down opposite Jorge while he opens the Black Book.

'Lots,' he replies facetiously.

'You know what I mean,' I sigh. 'Anyone *anyone*.'

'Not civilians.' He grins. 'We had Graham Norton and Nigella Lawson. Not eating together, of course.'

'Was Scott's full?' I ask. He looks at me quizzically. 'Nigella only ever eats at Scott's. Just as Simon Cowell will only ever go to his local Italian, Edera, Mr Chow and the Cipriani – oh and occasionally The Ivy if he wants to be photographed with someone.'

'I don't know,' shrugs Jorge. 'I thought it was her husband who insists on Scott's. Anyway, she was with a girlfriend.'

'Right. Good.' I'm slightly regretting my evening out now. The prospect of Nigella Lawson, without her husband, is a little too exciting for a hungover bloke at ten thirty-five in the morning. 'Anything else?'

'Right, we did ninety covers and the average spend was about £80–£85 a head.'

'OK.'

'Well, it's in the run-up to Christmas. I want to turn all those tables at least twice.'

'True,' I nod. 'Up the booze. It would be good to get the average spend up to over £100 for the next few weeks.'

'OK,' he nods.

'Anything go wrong?'

'We had a walkout.'

'A walkout? Smoking?' He nods.

I have to say I am a little shocked. We occasionally get a walkout, but we're not the sort of place that you'd book if you wanted to stuff yourself and then run, also we're not packed like an overrun zoo, thereby making your escape much easier. However, the smoking ban has definitely added to the number of walkouts. It's just made it that little bit easier to slip out, although quite often they've left their credit card behind the bar so it is more usually a drunken amnesia than anything particularly malicious. We do miss the smokers, though. Obviously I am one of them, so I was less worried about the terrible stench and how your hair used to reek after a long night's service. But we miss them because mostly the big smokers are/were also the big drinkers. They would sit around the table and chat for hours. They'd drink and chat, drink and smoke and chat and they'd shift brandies and cognacs. Poire William. Kummel. No one orders a Poire William these days. It's sad: all those delicious digestives sitting on the shelf, costing me money, gathering dust since the smokers were pushed outside under a street lamp.

'Big bill?'

'Not huge. £135 for two.'

'Do we have their number?'

'It was an email booking.'

I hate an email booking. I have to say I must have been one of the last places in town to set up a website that allowed customers to book online. There are two things that are sublimely irritating about online bookings. Firstly, they often book quite a few restaurants on the same night, to see how the mood takes them, and they are much more likely to be a no show. Secondly, they also tend to be the computer-literate type who like to review online afterwards or, worse, have some sort of annoying blog. So as a result, we are terribly nice to people who book online even if we loathe them. You have to be so careful. Having said that, I am much more likely to give away a table from someone who has booked online, my limit is about twenty minutes. Twenty minutes late and I'll give it away. And thirdly, what's so hard about calling? You're about to spend, hopefully, £100 a head in the place – wouldn't you be interested in calling up to see what they sounded like? Fourthly and finally, there are no comebacks with an email booking. You can send email request after email request for payment after a walkout but they will simply go unanswered.

'That's annoying,' I continue. 'Anything else?'

'We had a fabulous table of Arabs who drank the best part of two bottles of forty-year-old Highland Park whisky in teacups so as not to alert their wives sitting on the next-door table.'

'How much is that a shot?'

'£160.'

'And how many shots?

'Nineteen.'

'Not bad. That makes up for the walkout.'

'Yep,' he smiles. 'And then Mr Riordan was mugged for his phone, just as he left.'

'No! Mr Riordan, he's a nice bloke. Were they waiting for him?'

'The police were not sure. But it would not be the first time.'

We're fortunate not to have had too much passing crime through our place. There is always the odd snatched bag or purse, but because of where we are, in Mayfair, we are not like, say, The Ledbury who are, despite all their Michelin stars, right on the front line. I remember during the summer riots a couple of years back, the whole restaurant was held up by a gang who stole most of the customers' bags, phones and jewellery. They were eventually seen off by the kitchen staff wielding rolling pins. Another time, round the corner, at the trustafarian hangout E&O, one terrified bloke ran into the restaurant shoving a gun in his back pocket, while being chased by a gang of youths. He hid, shivering, under a table for a few minutes before being pulled out by his feet.

'Linen!' shouts the huge, burly Trev as he hurls a massive clean bundle of napery through the front door. 'Laters!' he yells, closing the door.

Jorge and I walk over to inspect it. There is something quite delicious about soft linen, hot off the press. I mean, really irresistible. So irresistible, in fact, the favourite place for staff sex is in the linen cupboard. I had a mate who worked for a wine bar chain and there was practically a staff race as to who could shag on the linen while it was still warm. I can't say I have ever managed it myself, but I can totally understand the appeal. It's something about the smell and the fact that it is so very clean. And expensive – it costs me £500 a week to get all my laundry done, and that's just for Le Restaurant. All in all, it's over a grand for the group.

Luca and Mikus pick up the heavy bundle and drag it to the back of the restaurant. All the tables are already covered and in the process of being laid, so they'll put the napkins and cloths away for this evening's service.

'We've got a full house for lunch,' announces Jorge, walking through the tables, looking at the reservations list. 'So we need to get a move on.'

The noise of the loud vacuum cleaner drowns him out as the two cleaners, dressed in navy blue all-in-one overalls, give the place the once-over before service. Both men are Kenyan and they come for a couple of hours every morning to polish the mirrors, wipe down the bar, dust the shelves and make sure the lavs are presentable.

'Oh my Lord!' screams Jorge at full volume, his splayed hands resting either side of his face in ostentatious shock. 'What the hell!'

His cry is enough to make the cleaner turn off the vacuum. The whole of front of house stops and turns to follow Jorge's gaze. Standing by the mirrored doors to the His and Hers lavatories is the other cleaner, holding a bog brush in his hand. Dangling off the end of the brush, damp and crumpled and clearly made of rather expensive silk, is a pair of tiny panties. The cleaner can hardly hide his delight. Neither indeed can anyone else.

'I just found them.' He shrugs. 'In the toilet brush.'

'Ah, thank God!' comes a very loud very posh voice behind. '*There* they are!'

11 a.m.–12 p.m.

It's quite surprising for Caroline to be on time. She normally turns up in a whirlwind of chaos and extraordinary excuses, which usually involve a litany of celebrities and expensive modes of transport. Today, however, she seems remarkably organized. Dare I say, 'on it'? Dressed in skinny, spray-on jeans, high-heeled boots, with a barely buttoned white silk shirt and a neckline loaded down with more gold chains than Mr T, Caz is not your low-maintenance, blend-into-the-background kind of girl. In her mid-thirties, she has been living with her very compliant boyfriend for the last six years. She strides across the room, chucks her camel coat over the back of a chair and, with a huge, exhausted sigh, slams her ludicrously expensive croc bag that undoubtedly has some girl's name down on the table and places a large folder next to it.

'Darling!' she says, pulling me towards her with her

whippet-thin arms. She hugs me so tightly I can smell the toothpaste on her breath and feel the individual vertebrae of her spine. For someone who spends their whole time eating out in restaurants, Caz is remarkably, perhaps worryingly, thin. She drinks like a fish so must eat less than a humming bird. How she can work in my industry and be so obviously nil by mouth is one of those delightful PR oxymorons. 'So have you checked?' She grins, pushing me away as firmly as she grabbed me towards her.

'Checked what?'

'The review!' She quite rightly looks at me as if I am a total idiot.

'Oh no, sorry, not yet.'

'Well, it's toast.' She smiles, sitting down and double-crossing her legs over each other. 'On the second page already. Christ, you're now so bloody goddamn Five Star brilliant, you should have all the fucking foodies over you like herpes before the end of the day! Can I get a coffee? I'm parched!' She looks around the room for someone to take her order. Her skinny claw waves in the air, rattling with gold. 'Jorge! Darling! A double macchiato, milk on the side, no sugar? Thanks, sweetie, I love you, you're such a star!' Caz also has this habit of sounding as if any waiter bringing her so much as a Diet Coke is actually physically, completely and utterly saving her life. There's effusive and there's Caz.

Jorge grins across the room at her in total adoration (they've been on a few Martini benders together) and nods briskly at Mikus to get on it.

'OK,' she says, turning to fix me with her turquoise gaze. 'Before we get Oscar out here, I just want to run through a few things with you.' She opens up her file and pulls out page after page of paper, including a two-page plan. 'So, we are going to do a duel campaign, personal PR for Oscar – so *GQ*, *Observer Food Monthly*, *Style*, *Style List* – that sort of stuff. He's good-looking, right?'

'Hmm,' I hesitate. I am not really sure what to say. I suppose he could scrub up. 'Not bad,' I say.

'Good. It's much easier if they are good-looking. Gordon, Jean Christophe Novelli, Giorgio Locatelli – they are all handsome,' she says, looking up. 'I mean, Marco's career was practically made by those fantastic Bob Carlos Clarke photos of him with the meat cleaver. He looked like Michael Hutchence.'

'That and a few Michelin stars,' I suggest.

'I can't get you photo shoots if you're a munter,' she says, 'no matter how many bloody stars you've got, darling.'

Jorge arrives with a tiny cup of extremely strong coffee with a small jug of foamed milk and two little brownies, fresh from the oven, all on a small silver tray.

'Oh Jorge!' says Caz, her shoulders hunching with so much pleasure that they touch her earlobes. 'You are an angel! And a lifesaver! Thank you!' She picks up the small cup, ignores the milk, the sugar and the brownies and knocks it back in one. 'Darling,' she says, looking at him through lowered Princess Diana lids. 'Could you be a poppet and get me another one?'

'And can I have one?' I suggest. It is only my place, after all.

'Of course!' replies Jorge, immediately. 'Two doubles.'

'If that is at all possible, darling, thank you.'

'I should hope so,' I reply. 'This is a restaurant. So?'

'Yes, right, so,' continues Caz, looking back down at her plan. 'I've been thinking about La Table and Le Restaurant and how to pick things up a bit. So a social media campaign to go alongside the print media campaign and a sales and marketing campaign. So that is B to B, B to C and quite possibly C to C.' She looks up. 'How do you feel about giving a free glass of champagne to everyone who has over three thousand Twitter followers just so long as they Tweet about dinner at Le Restaurant afterwards?'

'How would I feel? Fleeced?'

'It wouldn't be that many. All you need are a few big names coming in, India Knight, Caitlin Moran, those sorts of people, Richard Bacon – he's got over a million – and then they'd tell all their followers.'

'Would they do that?'

'Perhaps not those three exactly, but I can get others to do it.'

'And after they have told their followers, what do the followers do then?'

'Retweet – that sort of thing.'

'Retweet?'

'Yup.'

'But would they come? Book a table?'

'Oh, we can't guarantee that, but it would generate interest. And traffic. Lots of traffic. We might even manage to get you trending.' She smiles and nods vigorously, as if that would be a brilliant idea. 'It's good to be trending.'

'Back to the B to B and B to C?' I have to admit I am a little confused.

'Business to business, business to consumer and consumer to consumer, which is the hardest. We could get everyone in the office to "Like" you on Facebook – we haven't done that yet, I don't think. Gosh, that's bad, sorry!' She pulls a little face. 'You are on Facebook, aren't you?' I nod. 'Good – I'll get that sorted straight away. We're always "Liking" and "Forwarding" on Facebook. We've got over forty thousand friends between us.'

Thankfully, Jorge arrives with another shot each, while I consider the concept of having over forty thousand friends. We both down the doubles in one this time. The coffee is strong and a little bitter. My body gives an involuntary shiver.

'I was thinking of a pop-up?' she says, looking at me quizzically. 'A pop-up?'

'I know what a pop-up is.'

'Well, a pop-up. Everyone's doing them and they don't last long, obviously, because it is a pop-up, so it's a good way to maximize the PR without much outlay. I have a friend involved in Freeze. Freeze? The art fair? And we could do a Le Restaurant pop-up there. The place is crawling with media desperate to fill their pages with stuff so it's a good place to be. Also, you've got a good crossover from your art clients who drink at Le Bar, so it would be good to get them in here as well.'

I have to admit that Caz is probably right. It is not a stupid idea. Freeze could be good for us. Although I have to admit I find the idea of a pop-up rather loathsome. I never really understand the point of them. They only appeal to hideous food bores who want to wang on about how they've been somewhere that was so hip, so cool, so transient that it is no longer there. It's disappeared up its own culinary rectum in a puff of dry ice.

'Good idea,' I say finally.

'Leave it with me and I'll speak to Ev,' she says. 'Now.' Big smile. 'How do you feel about drunch?'

'Drunch?'

'It's very big, very now, very much the new brunch. It's very French and La Table is French, very French. Well, it's a brasserie.'

'Yes?'

'So how about a drunch menu on Sundays?'

'But we're closed on Sunday. It's one of the few days off the staff have and, anyway, what is drunch?'

'Well, it used to be a drunken Sunday lunch – so drunk plus lunch equals drunch. But now it means a late lunch that could be dinner – so dinner plus lunch equals drunch. So it's all-day menus in brasseries, that sort of thing. So someone could come in, say, to Balthazar, say at four thirty, with their mates, and order the duck shepherd's pie for a late lunch, with a few beers, or even a bottle of red, and stay till nine, rather than only be able to have a coffee and a pastry because the kitchen is closed and leaving half an hour later.'

'Right,' I nod, trying to work out the labour on such a logistical nightmare as having the kitchen open all day and especially on a Sunday. Were there even customers on a Sunday afternoon wandering around Soho after a goat's cheese salad and fries? 'Leave that one with me. Ah!' I say, looking towards the kitchen door. 'Oscar! Come over here and meet Caroline King.'

'Any relation to Jeremy King?'

'What Wolseley? Delauney? Colbert? Sadly not.' She smiles. 'Very lovely to meet you, Oscar. I hear you cook like a bastard!'

'I am hoping that's a compliment,' he replies, his ears going pink.

'That's as good as it gets from Caz,' she says.

He smiles. She laughs. Perhaps he is better looking than I thought . . .

They both sit down and spend the next ten minutes running through a list of people they know working in the business. Like a conversational establishing shot at the beginning of a film, this minutely detailed exchange of information is designed to decode who you are, who you know and who your friends are. Sitting between them, it manifests itself as a name-dropping ping-pong match.

'I bumped into Nick Jones the other day.'

'Such a nice man.'

'Didn't you used to work for the Soho House group?'

'I was briefly at Cecconi's.'

'No! I *love* that place.'

'I saw Maureen Mills in there the other day and that Jo Barnes—'

'What? Best Restaurant PR in town – after me, of course.'

'Do you know those nice girls at Bacchus PR? Anouschka?'

'So nice. Is she looking after Gordon these days? He's such a cunt.'

'Oh, I really like him. He taught me so much when I worked at Restaurant Gordon Ramsay.'

'Oh, when I said cunt, he certainly used to be, but he's much nicer since he was caught Paddy Pantsdown with that professional mistress coming out of the Dorchester. Very suspicious all of that. Gordon, such a family man, so obviously caught. Do you think he's gay?'

'Who?'

'Gordon.'

'No. Do you?'

'I don't know. Anyway,' Caz finally pauses for breath, 'what are we going to do with you?'

'Me?' Oscar pulls himself up in his seat, smooths the front of his whites and places his elbows on the table. She has his undivided attention.

'Right.' She clicks her pen. 'So I'll speak to Dylan Jones at *GQ* to see if we can get a photo shoot, that sort of thing. It really helps that you've been away in France, so you can come back "having learnt stuff". Then I'll try to get you holding half a hog or something in the *Observer* – they tend to go for the earthier angle – and maybe an interview with *ES Magazine*; they've got pages and pages to fill. How do you feel about telly?'

'Well,' he says, running his hands through his not-so-blond curls, 'I always thought that Jamie and Gordon were kind of like the roadmap that we should all follow.'

'Have you met Pat Llewellyn?'

'No.' He scratches the back of his neck.

'Optomen TV, *Naked Chef*, *Boiling Point*, *Hell's Kitchen*, *Two Fat Ladies* – all hers. She is basically the chefs' kingmaker. If she likes you and sees something in you, then you're made. She spotted Jamie at the back of Rose Gray's kitchen when they were filming a thing on the River Caff, and she saw all the shouty, sweary potential in Gordon all those years ago. I'll set that up,' she says, jotting something down. 'It's hard to sell books if you're not on the telly. And it's got to be proper telly. You've got to be Gordon, Jamie or Nigella, even Hugh Fearnley-Whittingstall, otherwise it's hopeless. A slot on *Great British Menu* wouldn't make that much of a difference. It does if you were, say, Paul Ainsworth. D'you know him?'

'Not personally.'

'Well, when he went on *GBM* his place in Padstow was booked out for months. But in London they need more media saturation. D'you know Michel Roux?'

'No.'

'Shame. *Food and Drink* is doing well.' She clicks her pen again. '*Saturday Kitchen*? *The One Show*? You could do something there. Very big numbers. Jay Rayner name-checked a client of mine three times on there last week.'

'Jay Rayner?'

'Let's not go there?' She smiles.

'I'd quite like to be Rick Stein,' Oscar suddenly pipes up.

'What? And have a fish restaurant on the south coast?' I look at him. This is news to me, I am not sure it was such a wise idea to drag him back from France if he's only going to bugger off south as soon as possible.

'No!' Oscar laughs. 'I just quite like the way he is on the telly. Sort of serious and good and not gimmicky. I like Angela Hartnett as well,' he adds.

'Yeah, well, she has a USP, doesn't she?' says Caz.

'She does?' asks Oscar.

'She's a woman,' replies Caz.

Andrew comes bursting out of the kitchen like some escapee bull from Pamplona. His head is down, his nostrils are flared and he is exuding fury. He marches towards the table, carrying a rice pudding soufflé in one hand and a pumpkin tortelli with sage and chestnuts in the other.

'Call me old-fashioned,' he snarls, his face red and steaming, as he slams the plates on the table, 'but I tend to have a run-through of a few dishes before service, just to see if the kitchen is on its toes.' He looks up. 'Darling!' he says immediately, his whole body language changing as he spots Caz. 'I didn't know you were here! How long have you been here? How are you?'

Caz gets up from her seat and wraps herself around him, giving him a kiss on both cheeks. As I watch them embrace, a rather disturbing thought springs to mind. Could they? Have they? Surely Caz is not one of the Gavi de Gavi gang?

'This looks great,' says Oscar, cutting the tortelli in half.

'Moist, firm and,' he pops it into his mouth, 'well-seasoned.' He moves on to the rice pudding. 'Er,' he says.

'What?' Andrew spins round to look at him.

'Well, it's—'

'What?'

'Not risen properly. You either need more egg white or longer in the oven.'

'He's right,' I say, before Andrew has chance to inhale.

'I should get back into the kitchen,' Oscar announces, getting swiftly out of his seat. 'It's not long before service. Do you want me to do another soufflé, chef?'

Andrew is slightly taken aback by Oscar's compliancy. 'Yes, great,' he says, before getting up from the table and giving Caz's hand a squeeze. 'See you soon.' He kisses her again, clipping the edge of her mouth as he says goodbye. Yes. I think the answer to my question is: Yes. Poor Caz. She's joined a long rather inebriated queue. 'Here,' he says, handing her the deflated rice pudding.

'No, thanks.' She recoils as if the plate might actually make her ill which, for someone who has obviously not had a carb since Tony Blair was elected on 1997, might well be the case.

'It's good, I promise.' He smiles at her. She nods away, almost unable to swallow, before she slowly reaches for her pen.

'So, back to La Table.' She smiles at me and pushes the pudding a little further away.

'The takings are not good enough. I need more traffic, I need to turn my tables and get some people in. It's quite simple.'

'OK. How much are you willing to give away?'

'Booze, food, the lot.'

'Because, you know, you have to give a bit away to get things going. Nick Jones is always very good at that. He does a lot of soft openings to get the word of mouth. He's always very generous with his product. And it works.'

'He can afford to be generous – he's got a whole bloody empire to be generous with.'

'We have some options.' She sounds sweetly optimistic. 'We can have a new brunch menu? Or a drunch menu? And we can fill the place with fab people and get that going? Or we can have a new cocktail? Or a free Bloody Mary before twelve, that sort of thing? We could do a Matt Roberts carb-free lunch for the ladies in January, post-Christmas bulge, that sort of thing? You've got that posh school near you. That might work? How about celebs?'

'I like celebrities,' I confirm.

'Enough to pay for them?'

I hesitate. 'How much?'

'There are levels. Some will come for a free lunch, and they'll let you pap them on the way out.'

'What? You tip the press off?'

'Of course. Those Spotted slots are always good for that. *Daily Mail Online*, that sort of thing. Some you can give a free birthday party for, and then they bring their friends and you pap the lot in and out, and, although it costs you more in the long run, you'll get a better spread in *Hello!*, or *OK!*, or something afterwards. And there are others you provide transport for. So a cab there and back plus a free night out. Or more expensively a cab there and back plus free dinner and a two grand appearance fee.'

'Two grand!' I lean back in my chair. 'Who would I get for two grand?'

'Oh, you know, a couple of models. An X-Factor winner – they're about two grand. You can go higher. We could involve specialist celebrity bookers, if you want.'

'How much higher?'

'I heard the other day of one skinny model who now needs two First Class flights back from New York for her and her friend, as well as another twenty grand for her to pop in.'

'Is she that very pretty, very thin model?'

'Yeah,' she nods. 'She probably wouldn't eat you out of house and home either, there's always that bonus!'

'There's that. How about getting some actual critics in to review the place? People who know about food!'

'I can suggest it,' she smiles. 'But they're tricky bastards. They're like bloody horses: you can take them to a restaurant but you can't force them to review it. I used to think alcohol was the answer. I'd take them to lunch and get them plastered, but it almost never worked because they were too pissed to remember what they ate anyway.'

'Didn't that happen to Giles Coren?'

'At Royal Hospital Road? Well, so Jan Moir says. I think he rang up to check on some details of the ingredients in the twelve-course tasting menu he was writing about. It was before they had it all online.'

'I love his stuff. He's my go-to critic.'

'And mine.'

The door to the restaurant swings open and in comes a massive flower arrangement, of white orchids with bamboo twirls.

'Oh, thank God you are here!' declares Jorge, running to get the door. 'I thought we'd lost you, Suzanna.'

'What, dead? No. The traffic is bloody awful,' comes a quiet voice from behind the arrangement. 'Is everyone Christmas shopping already? It's chocker out there.' She plonks the large, very modern, very edgy-looking display on the bar. 'Hi there,' she continues, turning around to find me. 'This OK?' She gestures towards the bar. 'I thought I'd hold back on the holly and the ivy and all that red until a bit closer to Christmas? You lot are too classy to go off too soon. I'm thinking 16 December? Is that OK for you? Or would you rather I did it sooner?'

Suzanna, the florist, is one of those expenses that you forget to factor into your business plan, but who is, of course, essential. You can't have a restaurant without flowers. You need the big display on the bar and something on the tables. These need changing at least twice a week, otherwise they droop and look sad and so does the restaurant. Suzanna is charming, not hugely expensive (I pay her £52,000 a year to do all three of my places, although Le Bar only has a large bar display – no one really cares about the florals when they've had a few drinks) and extremely hardworking. She's up at three every morning and trawling through Covent Garden market getting the best hydrangeas when the rest of us are crawling home. She does at least another four places around Mayfair and, amazingly, always seems to come up with a different style and form for each.

'Perhaps next week for Christmas?' suggests Jorge, mindful of the profits. 'We always sell more champagne when we're closer to Christmas.'

'OK,' nods Suzanna, with a sigh. 'Can someone help me get the table decorations out of the van?'

While Mikus and Luca help Suzanna with her arrangements, Caz packs up her papers and puts on her camel-coloured coat.

'So, lots to think about,' she says, hurling her handbag over her shoulder.

'Absolutely,' I reply.

'Oh, by the way,' she smiles, 'I've got this.' She hands me a piece of paper with a telephone number scribbled on it. 'Don't ask me how because I won't share.'

'What is it?'

'Only Marina O'Loughlin's husband's mobile number!'

'No!' We both look at it as if it were gold dust.

Well, it is actually gold dust. Restaurant gold dust. Marina is one of London's top restaurant critics; she used to work for *Metro* and has recently moved to the *Guardian*. And the most irritating thing about her is that no one knows what she looks like.

'Apparently she always uses this number.'

'You're brilliant!'

'I know.' She smiles. 'Also there's a new boy at the *Standard*, d'you know that?'

'Who?'

'Stone. Jason Stone. I am having someone get a photo for you so you can add it to your collection. Expect it sometime today.'

We have collection of crit-shots sellotaped under the front desk, so should anyone try to slip into the restaurant having booked under a false name, hopefully Anna at the front desk will spot them. That's the theory, anyway.

I escort Caz out into the street. The pavements are busy. The Christmas shopping mafia are out in force. It is still a grey day but the fog appears to have lifted.

Caz leans in to kiss me, smelling this time of coffee and her recently applied lipgloss.

'Question?' I say.

'What?'

'Have you and Andrew, ever . . . ?'

She takes a step back and looks at me with a mixture of surprise and irritation. She opens her mouth to reply, but is interrupted by the arrival of a tall, leggy, long-haired blonde.

'Gina!' I exclaim, practically electrocuting myself with my own surprise.

'I was told I'd find you here,' she replies.

'No need to ask you the same question!' declares Caz, pulling her coat collar up and marching off down the street.

12–1 p.m.

Gina is a lot taller than I remember her to be, but then I suppose it was dark and we were both sitting down and really rather drunk.

'Very nice to see you again,' she says, pursing her pink lips and flicking her long blonde hair. Wearing black trousers and a black polo neck, with a long leather coat, she looks a little edgier than my usual sort of girlfriend and surprisingly good in natural light. Not that she is a girlfriend, obviously, having only met her last night.

'Yes, likewise,' I hear myself saying, like something straight off *Austin Powers*. I open the door. 'Come in.'

Inside, the room is ready. The tables are laid up, the fresh flowers are in place, the carpet has been hoovered, and there is a sense of anticipation in the air; the show is about to begin. I look around at the team. Each of them deals with their pre-performance nerves a little differently. Luca is polishing glasses, Jorge is fussing behind the bar, Mikus is straightening the chairs, while the other three are shuffling from one foot to the other at the back, staring somewhat vacantly at the revolving door, waiting for Jorge to open up.

Anna is the only one who's still really got her head down. Dressed in a dark red shirt and tight black pencil skirt, she is sitting at the front desk, manning the phone. Having spent the last hour or so confirming the reservations for lunch today, she is now dealing with callbacks explaining late arrivals or emergency cancellations.

Despite our calling to confirm policy, we'll still get a few people who won't show up, or who cancel at the very last minute. Mostly their excuses are good. A birth. A death. An accident. Some dull transport problem or a business meeting that's gone awry. Mostly it's business.

The business lunch is our bread and butter. We're the sort of place that people book when someone else is paying. And we're good at it. We're impressive enough to soften up a client but not too hugely expensive for their accounts department. The only problem with business lunches is they all want to start and finish at the same time. Everyone's keen to be in at one and out by two thirty at the latest, which puts a massive strain in the kitchen. So we try and stagger the arrivals, offering a twelve forty-five booking here or a one fifteen there, but typically we'll just keep you waiting at the table. So the waiter will dither about getting you the menu and he'll spend a little extra time talking you through the specials. He'll have a joke about the table: who was here last night, what they did, how often they come – anything to keep you entertained so you don't notice you've been sitting on your plump arse for fifteen minutes without anyone taking your order. If only you'd taken the suggestion of a one-fifteen table, you could have saved yourself, and indeed us, all that bother in the first place.

It is at lunchtime, in particular, when the maître d' comes into his own. Because of the huge time constraints, he has one eye on the room and the other on the kitchen. He knows how many orders have gone in, and how long he has to wait before he can hit the kitchen with more. He'll pop over, he'll chat, he'll tell you some story, he'll remember when you were here last time. What a blast you had. A good maître d' is worth their weight in gold, frankincense and myrrh. And they are hard to find, so once you've got a good one you are not keen to let them go. The salary isn't bad, £40,000–£50,000 a year plus tips, but for a maître d' with a reputation, a following, it can be an awful lot more.

There's a reason why long-serving pros like Jesus Adorno at Le Caprice since 1981 end up running the place. Or why Sebastian Fogg holds so much sway at The Delaunay, or why Richard Caring shelled out for Byron Lang, formerly of The Wolseley, The Ivy and The Savoy Grill, when he needed a safe pair of hands to help open up Balthazar. Forget the décor and the killer menu; these are the people who become the life and soul of the place. They make it run smoothly and, most important of all, they make the customer feel special. Greeting them by name, remembering which table they like, what wine they prefer, how they like their steak. There are many ways of doing this.

If you are a big swanky place like The Wolseley, your maître d' not only has *Hello!* and the *Sunday Times* Rich List tattooed in his brain, recognizing the rich, the famous and the influential, despite their new haircuts, their dramatic weight loss/gain or their sudden change of husband/wife, he's also a dab hand at the computer. Minutes before you arrive, he pops your name through Google-images, just to make totally, completely, exactly sure who you are. There's nothing worse than pointing all those shiny eyes and teeth in the wrong direction. So no matter that you haven't been there for a while, because your name is stored in the computer and your face is checked on the internet, you'll still get the best service around.

We are, obviously, a little smaller and a little less showbiz, but our clientele tend to be the loyal returning types, coming a couple of times a month, or as much as twice a week, and it is our job to remember who they are, and treat them as if they are the stars of their own lunchtime.

Getting customers to return to your restaurant is all about redelivering their previously good experience. When you book to go somewhere, you have committed in your mind to pay the money, and for that you have certain expectations. Say you've decided to go to Scott's. You have committed to spend around £70 a head, it's a treat, and when you are paying that kind of money, a certain level of anticipation sets in. It is not a canteen; you expect good food, good service and Charles Saatchi and Nigella Lawson to be sitting outside, smoking. If Scott's deliver on the food and the service (perhaps not on Nigella and Charles) then you will be coming back. If they don't, then you have been let down, your expectations will not have been met and you will not return. It is that simple. You give them the chance and if they blow it, you won't go back.

So our job, Jorge's job, is to fulfil your expectations and more. The first of which is that we remember who you are, and that you are made to feel very special. Jorge is brilliant at this and to see him in action is like watching a master at work. He told me once that it was all about the open-ended question. He explained to me that with correct probing you could get all the information you needed out of someone without ever putting your foot in it. The customer, as he said, would naturally fill in the blanks. Mainly out of our very British politeness. And the conversation would go something like this:

Jorge: 'I saw a friend of yours the other day . . .'
Customer: 'Jean?'
Jorge: 'That's right, Jean, she had just . . .'
Customer: 'Been to the British Museum.'
Jorge: 'That's right and she was with . . .'
Customer: 'Dave.'
Jorge: 'Of course, Dave, her . . .'
Customer: 'Son.'
Jorge. 'Yes, son. Such a nice chap.'
Customer: 'They said they'd come in and had a very nice time and you were very kind to them. They couldn't believe you remembered them.'

Jorge. 'Oh, I remember everyone. That's my job. Here's your table . . .'

Customer: 'Simon.'

Jorge: 'Of course it's Simon. I know that! I was talking to Jean about you just the other day. Welcome back. Glass of champagne?'

Simon: 'Gin and tonic.'

Jorge: 'Your usual, of course.'

They will, he said, eventually, tell you everything you need to know.

Equally, it is important for Jorge to know exactly when to keep quiet. He says you can see it in their eyes as they come through the door. The blind sense of panic, the rictus grin, the speedy way they walk with their head down through the place, desperate to get to the quiet table at the back. It screams: 'This is my mistress. I am with someone I should not be. And please shut the fuck up.'

Jorge has perfected a neutral face and a smart nod for these occasions to which he adds a simple, 'How lovely to see you.' No 'again', no 'since last week', no nothing. It is basically his all-encompassing, arse-covering comment for every tricky occasion.

Just before the first customers arrive, Jorge claps his hands together and gathers his troops. He goes through the amount of covers we are expecting, what VIPs we have, if any, which regulars are coming in and if there are any difficult customers. He'll also go through the list of 'specials'.

'Specials' are a culinary double-edged sword and it is the waiter's prerogative to sell them. Sometimes things are genuinely 'special'. For example, the fishmonger has arrived with some fantastic razor clams that the chef has just not been able to resist. Or say the River Caff hasn't pinched all the partridge before we put our order in and we've managed to get our hands on a few plump little critters for the table. Other times the 'specials' are only 'special' because we are desperate to get rid of them. We've over-ordered on the beef, we've got some lamb about to go off, or we've got a few sea bass looking a little worse for wear after three days in the fridge. The rule of thumb I have worked out over the years is that if the main ingredient appears somewhere else on the menu, like there's a double beef option, then the special is perhaps not that special at all. However, if it is genuinely something a little left of field, a little bit of King Scallop, then it is probably something the chef was keen to get his hands on, and is perhaps worth sampling.

Today, so Jorge informs the front of house team, we are down to fifty-five covers (not enough) since the phone check; there is one VIP who is something to do with motor racing – everyone's face goes blank – and a family with an elderly grandpa in a wheelchair, who Jorge is proposing to put in the corner table so that the wheels don't get in the way of service. The special today is venison, which I know is new and fresh because I saw it out the back in its box a couple of hours ago. And turbot. Possibly one of the most expensive fish in the market, so I am hoping it's been hanging around for a while. Otherwise Andrew is deliberately racking up the bills before he hands over to Oscar. This would of course be a low blow, but nothing is too low for Andrew.

'Jorge,' I say, and he looks up from his list, as the others go back to their stations. 'This is Gina.'

'Hello.' He smiles broadly, clearly not sure if she is a customer. 'How are you?'

'Very well.' Gina smiles. His Spanish charm is working.

'Gina is going to do a couple of shifts,' I say.

'She is?' His attitude changes but he is smart enough to cover his tracks. 'Good stuff.'

'Do you have a spare uniform anywhere?' I ask.

'What, right now?' He looks shocked.

'I don't see why not. Gina, you've worked in a restaurant before, I seem to remember you saying.'

'Yes,' she says. 'In Copenhagen.'

'Not Noma?' asks Jorge, his dark eyes widen slightly.

'No, Nandos,' she replies. 'And also in a couple of bars.'

'Nandos!' Jorge spits under his breath.

'I thought you were Dutch?' I say.

'No, Danish,' she replies.

'Brilliant. Dutch or Danish, she has bar experience. She can work behind the bar, can't she, Jorge?' I nod towards the bar. 'See if you can find a spare white shirt and waistcoat. If you're short of a shirt, she can always go to Marks and Spencer round the corner.'

I leave Jorge to come to terms with the nubile Gina and walk through to check on the kitchen. She might be fabulous, I think to myself – well, she certainly looks fabulous. And she's only working a couple of shifts behind the bar, so how much damage can she do?

In the kitchen, I'm immediately hit by the heat. There is so much steam in the air; it feels like a sauna. I can feel the pressure, smell the tension; you can almost hear the clock ticking. Well, actually, I can. There is large black and white one hanging on the wall bang opposite the pass. Underneath is a sheet of paper, or Call Away Sheet, on which are marked various columns – Table, Starters, Main Course. The waiters use it to write down the precise time each of the courses goes out. Not only does it help to keep track of what has been ordered and sent, it hopefully makes it easier to see how the kitchen is keeping pace. Ideally, if things are working, there should be twenty minutes between the starter and the main course. If the time between the starter and main starts to stretch beyond that, the kitchen is swamped. If it slips to thirty minutes then it's in the shit. And if this happens at lunchtime, where there is so little room for error, then it is deeply in the shit.

Each time a waiter comes in with an order it's given to the head chef to call out. When the order is called, the chef waits to hear a positive affirmative response, usually a 'Yes, chef!' or if you're feeling French, a 'Oui, chef!' Although this sounds a little poncy, it is really only so the chef knows he's been heard above the clatter, steam and banter in the kitchen. The dishes are then cooked and delivered to the pass.

The pass is potentially one of the most political areas in the whole restaurant. Obviously it depends on the kitchen, but in the first place I worked in London, the head chef wouldn't let anyone get anywhere near it. If he'd been a dog, he'd have cocked his leg on it every morning by way of marking his territory. Come to think of it, he probably did. He was a filthy bastard. And having claimed his territory, he guarded that pass as if his life depended on it. It was a border between the kitchen and the restaurant and relations between the two were about as matey as North and South Korea. The waiting staff were never allowed to cross the pass and the chef was never allowed into the restaurant. It was war, but a cold, seething war of attrition.

'What the fuck is this?' Oscar suddenly shouts from the other side of the pass. The kitchen comes to a dramatic stop and watches as Oscar slowly pick up two plates of crab salad and brings them over to the pass. Andrew saunters over, wiping his wet hands down the front of his whites. Oscar places the two plates under the hot lamps and Andrew leans in to inspect. The two crab salads are identical, right down the scattered baby leaves around the edge of the plate and the two purple violas placed on top.

'Good,' nods Andrew, tucking his lank hair behind his ear. 'Good. Well done, Davide. Nice work.'

Davide smiles across from the larder section, displaying two hideous rows of brown-coated teeth. I can't wait for that man to go. He reminds me of a commis we hated so much when I worked in a one-star place around the corner from here that we used to put pigeon hearts and fish eyes into his coffee. He wouldn't notice until he'd drained his cup and he'd go mad, picking bits out of his teeth while swearing at us and clipping us about the head.

'Nice work?' Oscar is stunned. 'What's happened to this kitchen? It's supposed to have a star? I don't get it? When I worked here before everything was made *à la minute*? Fresh? To order? Like it should be? You can't have crab salads sitting here already made up, pre-seasoned with herbs on them?' Oscar starts shaking his head, as he picks up the plates and starts moving over to the bin.

'Don't,' says Andrew, looking Oscar so straight and so firmly in the eye it stops him in his tracks. Everyone stares at Oscar, standing in the middle of the kitchen with a crab salad in each hand. How is he going to react? He takes a step towards the bin. Andrew continues to stare. He doesn't flinch. It is the most bizarre form of Mexican stand-off I've seen in a while.

'Here,' I say, walking between the two of them and taking the salads out of Oscar's hands. He looks relieved. Unlike Andrew, he is not a confrontational soul but, having made a stand, it's rather difficult to back out of it. 'I agree with Oscar that it should all be *à la minute*, that is what our customers are paying for. But seeing as Davide has so kindly made up six crab salads in advance we should use them rather than throw them away. However,' I smile, looking at the two chefs, 'I think it is perhaps best that he doesn't do it again.'

I place the two dishes back on the pass and briskly make my escape while I can.

'All OK in there?' asks Jorge, reading my pained expression.

'Tense.'

'There will be violence before the end of the day. I can smell it,' he replies, before pirouetting round to greet the family of four with the elderly grandfather in the wheelchair. 'Good morning!' he says, touching his black tie as he strides towards the front of the restaurant, the light catching the shine of his highly polished shoes. 'Let me help you with that,' he adds, taking the wheelchair off the younger of the two sons, and deftly weaving it over the carpet and between the tables towards the corner of the room. 'Are you well, sir?' he leans in and asks the elderly gentleman.

'What?' asks the old boy. Straining his head forward like an ancient tortoise, he places his shaking, fleshless hand behind his ear. 'I can't hear!'

'Are you well?' Jorge ventures again.

'By taxi,' he replies, with a nod as he places one hand, speckled like a hen's egg, on top of the other.

'He's ninety-two,' says the slim, rather elegant-looking mother.

'And deaf,' shrugs the eldest boy, pulling his chair out.

Jorge already has the menus; he is keen to move this table through quickly while there is still plenty of room in the kitchen. Out at the front, Anna is chatting and smiling at a couple of businessmen who have just arrived. Through the window I can see a couple more smartly dressed middle-aged men casually using one of the two olive trees either side of the door as an ashtray. Gina is looking rather good, if underoccupied, at the bar, opening a bottle of fizzy Speyside.

We don't sell much of it these days, not since bloody Giles Coren, followed by bloody Fay Maschler, kick-started their parsimonious, irritating, penny-pinching, tight-arsed, un-necessary kick-the-restaurant-industry-in-the-balls campaign about bloody tap water. The pair of them have ruined the very lucrative, very handy, very-nice-thank-you bottled water market almost overnight. Up until about four years ago every-one, and I mean everyone, ordered a bottle of water for the table. Fizzy, flat, whatever. It was a given. It was almost the equivalent to a cover charge. But now everyone thinks it's OK to order a 'jug of tap'. Actually, they probably think it is very environmentally cool, hip and on-it to order a 'jug of tap'. So the money's gone.

And it was good money. The mark-up on a bottle of water is quite useful. We buy our water for 45p a bottle and sell it at £5. It used to be a little something for the restaurant, some-thing to keep the hungry wolf from the door, and now we don't have that revenue, restaurants are resorting to a cover charge. All over the West End they're charging something like £2.50 a head for you to just sit there, which adds another £10 to the bill if you're a table for four. Quite a lot, I think. Well, you have Giles and Fay to thank for that. And if they're not dish-ing out a cover charge, they're making you pay for the bread. No decent restaurant should make you pay for the bread. Only a chain can really charge for bread, but you'd be surprised who does. We absolutely don't. We give a lot away for free: bread, butter, olives, nuts, and it would be nice to make it back somewhere else. I do miss the heady water days. Not that I can taste the difference between any of them. I did hear of a couple of water sommeliers plying their wares in the States but that, I am afraid, is where I draw the line. There, and importing ridiculously distantly sourced bottled water like the Fijian water they have at Nobu. Granted, Nobuyuki Matsuhisa has shares in the company, but it does seem rather a long way to fly the stuff, especially when they produce something quite similar in Malvern.

'Boss,' whispers Jorge in my ear.

'Yes?'

'Table Six.'

I turn to look at the corner table with the family and the old boy in the wheelchair. They have their starters already. Two crab salads, one scallop, one pan-fried sweetbreads and one beef carpaccio; they all seem to be eating away quite happily.

'The old man,' Jorge hisses. 'I think he's dead.'

1–2 p.m.

Jorge and I spend the next five minutes staring at Table Six, trying to work out if the old man is sleeping or if he is, in fact, dead. His head is slumped back in the chair, his chin is pointing towards the ceiling, and his mouth is hanging open. He looks like he's awaiting a root canal in the dentist's chair, except the flesh on his cheeks appears sunken and hollow. Could he be asleep? You never know. Catching flies? The skin is looking a little greyer than before, as if the pink tinge of life has ebbed away. And his chest is neither rising nor falling. In fact, he is not moving at all. But the family don't seem unduly perturbed. They are noshing their lunch, tucking into a nice chilled bottle of Chablis Première Cru, chatting away, and apparently enjoying themselves.

'What d'you think?' asks Jorge, completely transfixed. His body is rigid with tension; he appears to be enthralled and a little terrified at the same time. 'Will you go?' He narrows his eyes and gives a little shiver. 'I don't like it. I have never been near a dead body before.'

'Really?' I look at him. I am completely surprised.

Working in this business the law of averages dictates that you must have come across a couple of corpses in your time. I've seen two, up close and personal, and heard of quite a few more. Right at the beginning of my career I remember an old man collapsing in the restaurant I worked at just outside Stratford-upon-Avon. I had just done a St John's Ambulance life-saving course, so I was straight in there with mouth-to-mouth, which was a terrible mistake, revolting; he was bringing up all sorts of stuff, which was dribbling and burping and bubbling out of his mouth. Anyway, the ambulance crew finally arrived and took over the pumping. They firmly con-gratulated me on saving the bloke's life and I have to admit I was rather pleased with myself. I told my parents, who told their friends, and I was quite the hero. It wasn't until a month later when the same crew tipped up again after some customer had fallen over, pissed, in the car park and broken his leg that I found out the man was dead even before they got him into the ambulance.

I remember also a rather large elderly granny keeling over when I was working in a hotel one long, miserable summer holiday in Brighton. We had coachloads of grannies turning up for an all-inclusive afternoon tea and a dance. They'd arrive, bus-fresh, a symphony of pistachio-coloured slacks, pale purple bubble perms and soft beige shoes, exuding an odd aroma of Blue Grass, talcum powder and dust. They'd have a cup of tea and then dance to music blasted out of an old giant tape recorder sitting on a table in the corner of the room. All the women would partner each other because, or so it appeared, all the men were already dead. They'd then tuck into a cream tea before being ferried off again. Anyway, I recall a large lady making an odd squeaking noise before falling head first into her scone and another waiter and I having to haul her out of the dining room into the reception area. It was quite an odd experience, because after we'd cleaned the cream off her face we were told just to leave her there, lying on a sofa, and go back to serving the tea. By the time I had finished with the cream and scones, the body had gone.

I had a friend who worked at Bibendum a while back when some woman collapsed in the cloakroom. She was lying on the ground, on the verge of death, being attended to by a couple of waiting staff, while someone kept a lookout for the ambulance, when another couple came in demanding their coats. My friend tried to explain the situation, asking them to hang on for a few minutes. But they were having none of it. They were in a hurry, they insisted. No time to spare. So, stepping over the body, they collected their coats, claiming they simply couldn't wait any longer.

'I am sorry to sound a little weird,' mumbles Michelangelo out of the corner of his mouth as he walks past with a bottle of Atal Sia, Chateau Ollieux-Romanis, 'but I think that old man is dead.' He nods over his shoulder towards Table Six. 'He hasn't moved for ten minutes.'

'We were just thinking that,' agrees Jorge.

'Your wine, sir,' exclaims Michelangelo loudly, bringing the bottle to a nearby table.

'Shall I go? I should go, I should really go. I'm the maître d'. But . . .' Jorge turns to me, a pitiful, pleading look on his face. 'Can you?'

I pat him on the back. 'Don't worry.'

I approach the table just as they are finishing off their starters. Needless to say, the plate in front of the old man has not been touched. They all watch me as I arrive, the mother smiles.

'Everything all right?'

I am not exactly sure what to say. Is he dead? Sounds a little brutal. What's up with Granddad? Sounds a little crass.

The mother replies with a wide smile on her face. 'It's delicious, thank you so much. Absolutely delicious.'

'My sweetbreads were fantastic,' says the father.

'Where did you get the crab?' continues the mother. 'Is it Dorset? We used to spend a lot of time in Dorset.'

'Yes, it is Dorset crab.'

I nod and smile. There's a pause as we all look at each other, waiting for someone to say something, broach the subject of Grandpa sitting there, with his head back, his eyes closed and his mouth wide open.

'And your father, did he enjoy . . . ?' I look at the husband.

'*My* father,' interrupts the wife, as she leans in and lowers her voice. 'Sadly, he didn't manage to eat any of it before he died.'

'So he *is* dead.' I glance briefly over at the body.

She nods. 'Before the starter.'

'Shall I ring for an ambulance?'

'Isn't that for people who are still alive?' asks the elder boy.

The mother leans further over. 'We don't want a fuss, honestly. We've been looking forward to this lunch, all of us together, for quite some time. He used to love these pre-Christmas treats. And it would disturb everyone else's lunch to move him now. We don't mind, if you don't. We don't want a fuss, you see. Nothing worse than a fuss.'

I stand for a second, not sure what to say. She is perfectly right, of course. It would be a right pain to move him in the middle of lunch. The ambulance would have to be called and the tables moved to get the corpse out. It would be a palaver. And put the other diners right off their lunch. But I am not sure I could possibly sit there eating my crab salad with my expired father sitting next to me.

'OK,' I say, rather weakly. It is hard to think what to do in this situation with jägerbomb brain.

She nods at me. 'When it all quietens down we can move him.'

'If that's what you'd prefer.' I turn a little hesitantly.

'Excuse me,' says the mother, leaning her head to one side. 'Yes?'

'Could you clear his plate?'

I pick up the untouched crab salad, trying not to get too close to the rapidly chilling corpse. The idea of his cold, dank skin gives me the shivers, but I still can't resist a look. His eyes are not completely closed, they hover a few millimetres apart and underneath, between his short sparse eyelashes, you can see the drying whites of his eyes. His mouth is ajar, but weirdly silent, and alongside his worn yellow teeth lies his long, grey motionless tongue.

'Jamie!' the mother says to her son, picking up her fork. 'I can't believe you've left one of your scallops! Hang on.' She nods at me, before popping a scallop into her mouth and handing me the plate to clear.

Never have I been more grateful to get into a steaming hot kitchen in my life. I walk though the doors, lean flat against the wall and exhale. I just need to take a moment, before getting out there again with my best service-industry smile back in place.

'I hear we've got a dead body,' says Andrew on the pass.

'Anything to do with your cooking?' jokes Barney, from the far corner of the kitchen.

'Fuck off,' quips Andrew.

'When they said lunch was dead, I didn't think they meant it literally,' laughs Matt, as he chucks a rabbit loin into a small blackened frying pan. He looks up; half the kitchen has turned to stare at him. 'What?' he says, looking a little worried. It's honestly the first joke he's cracked since he's been here.

'Funny,' says Barney with an appreciative nod.

And true. Lunch is dead. Well, not completely *Grandpa* dead, but certainly not as lively and perky as it once was. It depends where you are, obviously. In the West End you can still get a full lunch service in places owned by Richard Caring

and Chris Corbin and Jeremy King, Dean St Townhouse, Polpo
– all Russell Norman's places – Brasserie Chavot, Angela
Hartnett's Murano, and fabulous tapas places, like Fino, have
them queuing round the block. But even in those places, which
are packed and bustling, lunch is not what it was. As business
cuts back on expense accounts and we worry more about our
waistlines, so the three-bottle lunch for two is no more. The
long, languid afternoon boozathon that ended in brandies and
stickies and a couple of puds is now much more likely to be a
salad and a jug of bloody tap. The tables are booked, the bums
are on the seats, but no one's really getting stuck in. The
leisurely drunk lunch is a distant memory, it's like smoking
inside, we've forgotten how to do it.

Out of the West End, there are little pockets of lunchtime
success around. Notting Hill and Chelsea somehow manage to
keep their end up during the week. Bill Grainger on
Westbourne Grove is rammed to the rafters with blow-dried
women in skinny jeans, who merrily queue up to build their
own stacked salad for £16 and spend the next hour and a half
flicking it around a plate.

But as Will Ricker once said, 'It's all about the women.' And
out of the West End he is completely right. His restaurant
E&O has been a ladies lunching favourite since it opened in
2001. Patronized by the likes of Claudia Schiffer, Stella
McCartney, Kate Moss and Sadie Frost, it is always full. There
used to be a gang of girls who descended there every Friday for
a 'naughty girls' lunch' that would go on and on until the early
evening. Their children were collected by a large Addison Lee

minibus and dropped off at the restaurant, lest the school run interfered with the cocktails.

Design a menu for women with plenty of salad and fish and naughty fried bits that they can eat alongside the salad and the fish, and shove in a couple of bloke dishes, and hopefully the girls will come. And where the girls go, the boys follow. Or at least their husbands do, because women are much more likely to book the lunch or indeed the night out than the men. They decide the social life and where to go, they make the call and the bloke usually does what he is told. So if you capture the female market and cater with them in mind, you get the men as well.

We're trying to get women in here at the moment. We've got a table of six of them arriving in about five minutes as one of Caz's promotional ideas. She's organized a series of PA lunches in the last few weeks where we've invited PAs from local companies for a free lunch so that when it comes to booking a table for their boss, they'll suggest us over anywhere else. It is hard to see if the strategy is working just yet, but a table full of women is always preferable to one groaning with blokes.

Women are also easier to sell to. I remember when I was learning the front-of-house ropes, I was taught to sell to the girls rather than the boys. 'Women,' so Spencer, the maître d', told me, 'are the weakest link.' He was giving me a lecture on how to get the profit up on a table when people aren't ordering. They've ordered their main course, but it's steak and sea bass and the inevitable jug of tap. The GP on that is useless: too many expensive ingredients and not enough margin. 'So,' he said, 'you target the women and try and sell them stuff. They'll always pass on a pudding, but you can probably get a cappuccino in there and, with one cappuccino, at least another three mint teas follow. And once you've got the mint teas, go back to the pudding. They've committed to sit there longer, there's at least a "one to share" to be slotted in there. Or even a little something. If they've had a drink, you can usually persuade them to have a glass of something on top. Champagne is always good, so suggest it, let them think they're getting it for free, on the house, and then pop it on the bill.'

Spencer was a whizz at popping things on the bill. He'd chance anything – an extra bottle of wine here, a starter, some coffees, a couple of extra cocktails. He always said that no one ever checked their bill properly and he's right. They really don't. There are those who will give it the quick once-over while deep in conversation, but mostly customers don't. It is almost like it's too grubby or embarrassing to check, a little bit bourgeois, so they wrap the bill around their credit card and hand it over, like a turd on a stick, without even looking at how much they're about to pay. We could have added three bottles of claret for all they care. And with Spencer in charge, we had. Occasionally you get a retentive with a pencil who goes through the lot, totting it up on his mobile phone, and he is usually accompanied by a table of losers who 'didn't have a starter'. Spencer's philosophy for that was simple: if they noticed and he got caught out, all he needed do was turn on the charm and apologize profusely. He'd whip the bill away, take the offending item off immediately, offer you a small, sickly shot of limoncello and charge it all to someone else who was too pissed to notice.

Woe betide anyone who asked him to come up with recommendations when ordering their food or who asked him to bring a few 'bits and pieces' along, 'for the table'. He'd take this as carte blanche to load your bill up with as many 'bits and pieces' as he thought he could get away with, and charge you accordingly. But the customers loved him because he was the life and soul.

We are right in the heat of service at the moment and judging by the Call Away Sheet, the timing in the kitchen is beginning to slip. There's currently twenty-five minutes between the starter and the main, with one table having slipped to thirty.

'What happened here?' I ask Luca whose table it is as he comes through the door.

'Oh.' He rolls his eyes, as he stands at the pass, loading his tray. 'Table Four, there is a man who does not stop the bloody talking. He takes a rest in the middle of his starter. Telling some great long story, so long that Alfonso has to recook a bloody fish.'

'Cunt,' says Andrew. 'Waste of fucking turbot.'

'Turbot? Cunt,' I agree.

There is nothing like someone taking too long over their starter to knock the kitchen off course. As soon as your starter goes out, the kitchen is 'mains away' or, as they say in the US, 'fire the mains'. Say the sole takes ten minutes, they start the pasta, the meat is resting, the garnish is being heated, someone's on the burrata – they all have to come up to the hot plate at the same time and go out. But if you're not finished with the starter, the meat can sit, as can the pasta (for a few minutes) but the fish can't go cold. And unless the waiter gets back in the next few minutes the stuff has to be binned and then the kitchen is another ten minutes behind, because the sole takes ten minutes.

You can always tell when the head chef is losing his timings and control of the kitchen. Like an air-traffic controller who's lost the plot, they'll stand at the pass and do a slow 360-degree turn, and come back to the same plate they were holding in the first place, having done nothing. Fortunately and somewhat surprisingly, Andrew is nowhere near the spinning stage. Perhaps he is trying to out-focus Oscar, to prove to him because of the crab salad moment that he is so on the ball he could probably out-manoeuvre Rooney at Wembley.

Standing there, with his head down, he has four plates in front of him, which he is loading all at the same time.

'Rabbit?' he shouts.

'One minute,' replies Matt.

'Hurry it up.'

'Yes, chef!'

'Halibut?'

'Here, chef,' replies Alfonso, delivering a small, perfectly cooked square of halibut to the pass on a silver tray.

'Garnish? Veg?'

'Here, chef,' says Barney, coming to the pass with another small silver plate with five savoy cabbage leaves perfectly cooked, a small pile of baby carrots and some peas in a cream jus.

Andrew starts to load the plate. First he places the halibut in the middle; next he layers the cabbage, eating a leaf on the way through just to make sure it is cooked thoroughly. Next the carrots are laid like a small log-pile, slightly to the side of the fish, and finally he spoons the pea jus over the top. He uses a spoon taken from his back pocket and tastes the sauce just before he puts it on the fish.

'These peas are shit,' he pronounces. 'When were they cooked?'

'Yesterday, chef.'

'Yesterday?'

'Yes, chef.'

'Fucking yesterday! They're dry and fucking old. Fucking chuck 'em and fucking don't do that to me again.' He turns to eyeball Barney. 'Fucking useless cunt. What are you, Barney?'

'A fucking useless cunt,' repeats Barney, sloping off to his station.

'A fucking useless cunt, CHEF!' shouts Andrew.

'A fucking useless cunt, chef,' Barney barks straight back.

Andrew turns back to his dish. The spoons goes into his mouth and back into the sauce, then back into his mouth and back into the sauce, before the sauce gets ladled on to the plate. Next comes the rabbit, placed on a small silver plate with a pan of jus.

'Thank you, Matt,' says Andrew, wiping his nose with the back of his hand before he picks up the rabbit loin and squeezes it to see if it's cooked, before putting it back on the plate. 'Veg!'

'Yes, chef.'

Barney comes running, with a copper pan of cauliflower purée. In goes the spoon, back out it comes, straight into Andrew's mouth, back it goes into the rabbit jus and back into Andrew's mouth and finally into his pocket.

'Good, good.' He nods, taking the spoon back out of his pocket and putting it into the cauliflower, before smearing the purée like a cream skid-mark across the middle of the plate. He picks up the rabbit, places it on top and then lines up seven green beans in a small pile. He then pops his spoon in and out of the sauce one more time and back into his mouth, just to make sure, before covering the rabbit and the cauliflower.

'Service!' he shouts, shoving the tray towards the other side of the pass. 'Fucking go!'

Luca picks up the tray and, smooth as silk, reverses through the swing doors and straight into the dining room. I wonder if the diner would tuck in with such relish if they knew exactly how their food had been put together. You only have to take one look at Andrew to retch at the idea of one iota of his saliva in your food. But he has tasted and sampled, picked and tweaked, gobbed and regobbed into everything on your plate. He is not alone; every chef has their spoon and occasionally a bit of cross-contamination occurs. Only the other day sixty-three customers left Noma with a full belly and the norovirus, which was probably a little more foraging than they'd banked on.

It used to be worse when presentation was at its height and

every little tiny weeny bit of garnish was placed on the plate. We used to call it 'lick and stick' cooking. How else was that little violet flower petal ever to stay on the plate? It was like laying out postage stamps. A curl of cress? Lick and stick. A slither of radish? Lick and stick. A salad leaf? Lick and stick. I always thought it was style over substance, and I always knew it was presentation over hygiene. Talking of filth, my mobile rings. It's Adam.

'Mate? Got a minute?'

'Yes.'

'Can you pop down the road? I need to show you something.'

'Give me a minute to do the tables and I'll be there.'

2–3 p.m.

It takes me a good ten minutes to get out of Le Restaurant as I give the place a quick table-hop on the way through. There is an art to this, which I am still trying to perfect. It takes years of practice, as the last thing you want is to get caught at the table and be forced to sit down and have a drink. Jeremy King is perfection in motion – all those years at The Ivy have paid off and he's like a knife though butter at The Wolseley as he skewers the stars in the inner circle and then moves on to the agents and publicists around the edge. I have watched Nick Jones do Dean Street Townhouse a few times with slacked-jawed admiration: a slap on the back here, a hug, a shoulder squeeze and he's out on the street off to another meeting. Gordon always used to do it in his whites, whether he'd been cooking in the kitchen or not. He'd pop on the jacket and walk through, making his presence felt, mainly so everyone could say they'd had dinner at Claridge's/Restaurant Gordon Ramsay and they'd seen the great man himself.

I walk through saying hello to a few regulars. Tony and Bill, a couple of sixty-somethings who always have the same lunchtime corner table of a Friday. These two are the last of the lunchers. They'll have a couple of stiff gins before they move on to the wine, but even these two have cut back on the liqueurs. There's Stephen, an entertainment lawyer who works a few streets away. He entertains in here a few times a week, always at his client's expense. Opposite him, and always with his back to the room, sits a rather rotund plastic surgeon who lunches here a couple of times a month. He is obviously very good at his job because the women are invariably pneumatic and he is never with the same lady twice. I check up on the family with the dead grandpa; they appear to be happily ordering pudding. I say hello to the table of PAs and offer them a bottle of champagne; it's the least I can do since I am also comping their bloody lunch.

This little scheme of Caz's had better work. I do trust her. She does know her job and she's up there in the top five or six along with Maureen Mills, Anouschka Menzies at Bacchus PR, Tanya Layzell-Payne, Jo Barnes and Jori White. But I could really do with a little less outlay on my publicity just at the moment. I am not sure I can pull my metaphorical belt much tighter.

I have a brief chat with the Formula One bloke and his three other companions. I have to say I'd be very surprised if the brunette with the lips and the off-the-shelves tits was in fact his wife. However, he introduced her as his 'Mrs' and it's amazing what sort of woman a thick, fat wallet can attract.

Finally I am out into the street, for a fag, some fresh air and a brisk stroll to check up on Adam and Le Bar. I must also pop in to see Pippa and La Table at some stage today because there are so many things I need to discuss with her. I turn left out of the door and pass two of the PAs who are now using my olive trees as ashtrays. I would put some of those silver ash stands out by the trees, only the last lot we had were pinched. They lasted five days, four more than the ones we had before. Quite why anyone would want to pinch them is beyond me, but there is, in my experience, zero logic in the mind of the drunken klepto; they appear to have all the sartorial sensibilities of a magpie.

The weather has perked up. The sun has managed to claw its way through the clouds and it's turning into one of those bright blue winter days that make people think it's practically summer and they can sit and drink wine outside. Were it not for the endless Christmas tunes being piped out of the snow-smeared windows of every retail outlet I pass, you could mistake this half-out sunshine for the first early days of spring. The street itself is mainly full of middle-aged woman with their heads down, credit cards at the ready, focused on shopping. By some weird migratory force they are drawn to Fenwick, with a list, an agenda and a train to catch by five at the very latest, otherwise the commuter supplements kick in.

'What do you think?' grins Adam, meeting me with a fag in hand at the door of Le Bar.

'What?'

He waggles his wrist in front of me; the bright shiny new watch face flashes, catching the sun.

'Cartier,' he sniffs, exhaling out of the side of his mouth. 'Fucking A.'

'Very smart.'

'From the bloke whose office party we did the other day.'

Talk to anyone who runs a hot bar, or who is, more importantly, the maître d' of a hot restaurant, and you'd be amazed by the amount of stuff they get given. As guardians to the coolest places in town, they get their palms so regularly crossed with little gifts that they've got drawers full of stuff. An old mate of mine who was maître d' for a number of years at one of the capital's swankiest establishments has a box full of Mont Blanc and Cartier pens. He's also got four designer watches, three Gucci key rings and two Prada bags and he used to get invited absolutely everywhere. Royal Ascot, Wimbledon, Silverstone – he gave me a couple of Cup Final tickets once because, being a single boy in the restaurant trade, football wasn't his thing.

Stay running one of these places long enough and the celebs who frequent them cease to become clients whose numbers you recognize on the restaurant phone system; their digits find their way into your own mobile and they become your friends; your number becomes the secret number. They call you instead of the restaurant when they want a last-minute table for them, plus six of their friends. They give you their George Michael tickets by way of a little thank-you, or invite you to meet Madonna at a private gig she's doing downtown. It's presents for access. It's a case of Dom Perignon at Christmas. It's a lovely bottle of claret on a Wednesday and occasionally it is a weekend away on someone's yacht. Sometimes it's cash. But not that often, a £50 here, a £100 thank-you, a £200 tip, although a pal was offered £5,000 the other day to book a table for eight on New Year's Eve. They have a restaurant that faces the river with a good view of the fireworks. He says he didn't take it, but I don't see why not. Your celebrity moment in the sun can often be quite brief. If the restaurant loses cachet, they stop calling. Somewhere else hotter opens, they don't come. Worst of all, you lose your job, they employ someone else, someone younger and more glamorous, and then no one calls at all.

The trick is not to get too caught up in it. The temptation is to grab the ride, take the drugs, burn the candle at both ends. You always end up doing drugs. Drugs are what keep you going. Drugs are what keep it interesting. Drugs are what bind you all together, partners in crime. Invariably, you end up snorting coke around a kitchen table, while some desperado celebrity talks endlessly about themselves till dawn, and while they roll over and curl up in their duvet, ignoring their agent's calls, you have to go home, shower, get dressed and pull another twelve-hour shift at work. I know of guys who've got so involved in the celebrity night-owl culture that they used to regularly not go to bed for days at a time. Then, Saturday night, they'd crawl into bed only to wake up on Monday morning, having missed a whole day to sleep. But you can see the allure. Everything is fabulous and fabulous fun and you are at the fabulous epicentre of it all. In fact, so much at the epicentre of it all that my mate was offered £25,000 by the *National Enquirer* just to confirm that Kate Moss was pregnant. He didn't take it, more fool him I say, but he stayed loyal to his friend.

Except they are not really your friends, although perhaps he and Kate still might be. Mostly they move on and so do you. Neither of you are that useful to each other any more. I remember once being invited to Cannes, as part of some massive piss-up freebie. I was working somewhere hip and happening and very film at the time and I was invited along to make up the numbers. Now, if you think we are debauched in the restaurant world, then you've never been to a film party in Cannes. There was so much champagne and cocaine it was de rigueur to walk around with your nostrils frosted like a margarita glass. Rather wonderfully, a gang of errant boys couldn't be bothered to go to the lavs to take their coke, opting to chop out on a tree outside in the garden. You could tell who they were because the rest of the evening they had small, furious, little black ants crawling out of their nostrils. Fortunately their noses were numb with drugs so it was only the ants who were at all put out.

But I know a few who have played hard and fast with the A-list and ended up, not in rehab, but in Wormwood Scrubs. There is an inherent problem about living a champagne lifestyle on lemonade money and that's the cash. This old friend of mine was a lovely chap who was pretty and fun and easily led and just wanted to keep up, so he started to rip-off the place where he worked to keep paying the bills and scoring the cocaine. Naturally, he was discovered, and they prosecuted. I think it was too much money to ignore, and off he went. For over a year, I think. None of his glamorous so-called friends came to see him behind bars. He's come out the other side of it all now. But you can understand why he was so tempted and beguiled by the bright lights in the first place.

Adam takes a swig of what I presume to be a Bloody Mary and admires his watch. 'It was a good night,' he grins.

'Excellent.'

'We've got a big one tonight. The second Christmas party of the week.'

'Who is it?'

'Some computer company – you should come down.'

'Not if I can possibly avoid it. Anyway, was it just the new watch you wanted to show me? Only I've a dead body to deal with back at Le Restaurant and I really should try and see Pippa at some point.'

'Obviously the watch, but I wanted to talk through this party and how much you want out of it?'

'Right,' I nod. My phone goes in my pocket. *Mission Impossible* again. I am ditching that after today, I can't bear it any longer. I look down. It's Le Restaurant calling me. 'Hello?'

'Hi,' comes a very quiet whispering voice down the line. 'You need to . . .'

I can't make out what she's saying.

'Anna?'

'Yes?'

'You've got to speak up.'

'I can't,' she whispers. 'He's right here!'

'Who is?'

'Caz sent the photo.'

'What photo?'

'The photo.'

'What fucking photo!' I am now shouting.

'The new restaurant critic from the *Evening Standard*, Jason, Jason Stone!' She hisses it so loudly I presume half the restaurant can hear.

'Five minutes!' I hang up. I look at Adam, who sees the panic in my eyes.

'Laters,' he says and nods towards Le Restaurant up the street.

I set off at a brisk pace and am met two doors up by Anna, who comes towards me, wringing her hands and biting her bottom lip. She looks immaculate in her red shirt and black skirt, almost a little overdressed for the street.

'He asked for a table, said he hadn't booked, but I told him I could squeeze him in, then he says he heard that Oscar was starting today, which I thought was a little odd. So I checked the critic photos but he's not there, and then I remembered Caroline's email at midday and there he was. It's him! The new critic, Jason Stone, from the *Evening Standard*.'

'Did you tell him that Andrew is still cooking even though he's handing over to Oscar?'

'No, because I thought I wasn't supposed to know who he was. And if I did, he would know that I know, if you see what I mean.'

'What table is he on?'

'Three,' she says.

'OK. On his own?'

'Yes.'

I am furious; the critics always do this. They're like bloody teenage boys: they come far too early. They are always so desperate to be ahead of each other, ahead of the bloggers, or whatever bloody curve they want to be ahead of, so they're always reviewing in the first week, when the service is shit or the kitchen hasn't found their feet. It's very unfair. It's like being a bride: all that work, all that effort, all that planning, only to be caught with your pants down having a pee. Some of them are so bloody keen they review even before the place is open. Charles Campion and Fay Maschler are famous for it – they like a soft opening. I always think it's like a theatre critic turning up before the first night and telling everyone how crap the play is, before it's even had its premier.

In the old days critics were eminently corruptible. The stories about who was in whose pocket are everywhere. Certain magazines and organs were easier than others. Indeed, organs often played a part. There was one chap who used to boast that if the PR took him out to lunch and gave him half-decent drugs, and sucked his cock in a hotel room, he'd happily give the place nine out of ten for the food and a possible ten for the ambience, although he would need a receipt to claim it back on expenses.

Others were less keen on being noshed off and more keen on

free nosh. There were some restaurants that kept their legendary five-star status by basically wining and dining the critics for free. They could turn up whenever they fancied and scoff down a three-course lunch with 1948 Petrus just so long as they mentioned it was their 'favourite place to dine' whenever they were quizzed by any magazine or newspaper.

One of my favourite stories is about one top chef accusing a hack of accepting a £50,000 bung from his arch-rival. It's an interesting idea and a generous amount of money, although in the grand scheme of things, not quite enough. It's not worth losing your job for £50,000 – and what was the £50,000 buying? Good press? You could probably get that for £5,000. Journalists are always broke, that's why they fiddle their expenses.

I know of two who lost their jobs because of false accounting. With one, it was the classic double-invoicing scam. This journalist was invoicing his paper for hugely expensive restaurant meals which he had the receipts for but wasn't actually paying. So he was making money on his free meals as well as getting paid for doing the job.

The other scam was a little more problematic. The critic booked to stay in one of those posh country restaurants with rooms above the shop and his wife called up and demanded extra rooms and extra days for their children and the nanny. The small country place said it was rather a lot, what with two double suites and everything, to which the wife replied, 'Do you want a good review or not?' Needless to say, the country place called the newspaper to complain about being bullied and the critic was fired forthwith. We all know that it's standard practice for the critic to drive to the place and charge the newspaper for taxis, earning a quick £3,000 a year extra, but threatening a place with a bad review for not shelling out on free hotel accommodation is something else.

All of which begs the question: just how powerful *are* the critics? Restaurateurs always say not at all. We always say that they are leeching pariahs with no charm or palate who know absolutely jack about food. And yet, give us a few drinks and we can tell you verbatim what so-and-so said about our place, or how many stars we were given, what our score was, how sustainable we were, what our service was like, how many sodding little knife and fork symbols we got. Not only that, we can also tell you exactly what everyone else got. We know exactly what they said about the competition and, at the same time, we all avidly read what they said about the big boys as well. The reviews of Balthazar, The Colbert, Brasserie Chavot, Jason Atherton's Social Eating House, The Clove Club and Story were finger-read with moving lips in every kitchen in town.

Fiscally, critics can make a huge difference. I heard one bloke complain that Giles Coren was a total turd the other day and that the shitty review he gave his place south of the river cost him over £250,000. Equally, Chris Galvin always says Coren put his children through private school because his glittering review of Galvin at Windows meant he had to hire another three staff to answer the phones and the place was booked solid for the next three years. And just ask Ollie Dabbous how powerful the critics are! He was lauded from the skies as the new Heston and you can't get a butt-cheek in his place on Whitfield Street for the next ten months.

That's not to say there isn't a whiff of the old boy network about the scene. It's a small industry and it's an even smaller group who go around reviewing. We bump into each other, we become friends, we go out, we get drunk. Christ, I'll be the first to admit critics can be excellent company. Some of them are right pompous bores who I'll actively cross Old Compton Street to avoid, but the likes of Coren, Gill and Matthew Norman are as witty and amusing in the flesh as they are on paper. But there is a problem when everyone lives in everyone's pocket: some people's pockets are tastier and more glamorous than others, so they become untouchable. No one is ever going to give Chris Corbin and Jeremy King a bad review: they own The Wolseley, The Colbert, The Delaunay, Brasserie Zédel – and we all want to eat there, the critics most especially. On their days off, they want to get tables, they want the good service; in short, they want to be their friends. In fact, let's be honest, everyone wants to be Chris and Jeremy's friend!

'Which one is he?' I ask now.

'There.' Anna nods. 'Small and dark in the corner.'

I turn around to take a good look. Thank God for Caz, because Jason Stone looks more like an accountant than he does a restaurant critic. Wearing a blue and white striped shirt tucked into his jeans, he is hunched over the menu, laboriously checking each dish and jotting things down in a notebook. A notebook! The only critic to use a notebook is Jay Rayner. Oh, and Matthew Norman. Michael Winner used to bark into a dictaphone, but then he loved everyone knowing he was there. The others try to blend in as much as they can. Staring at Jason Stone, I have to say he is making me more than a little irritated. There is something rather annoying about his stealth tactics and something deeply irritating about his coming here right at the tail-end of a lunchtime service, when everyone is more likely to be a little irritable and off their game.

I walk through the room, passing Luca with a tray of nicely risen rice-pudding soufflés and Michelangelo trying to tempt a table of businessmen with a super dessert wine. The family with the deceased grandpa are on to coffee and petit fours, which is where most of the diners are at. I can't believe Mr Stone has just turned up expecting to be served.

'Morning,' I say, breezing into the kitchen.

'I think you'll find it's the afternoon,' corrects Andrew, whose normally waxen face is bright pink.

'Do you want the good news or the bad news?'

'The bad news?' says Oscar.

'The bad news is we've had the new *Evening Standard* food critic just turn up,' I say slowly enough for even the likes of cloth-eared Barney to hear. 'But the good news is, he is on his own so he is extremely unlikely to go for the full five courses.'

'You're shitting me, right?' asks Andrew slowly, taking his spoon out of his mouth.

'No,' I reply, raising my eyebrows. 'I shit you not.'

3–4 p.m.

Fortunately for Jason Stone he doesn't order the full five-course lunch, as there's no end of bodily fluids that could have ended up in his food. I am not joking, I have seen it done. The most extreme version of which was when I worked on the larder section in a restaurant near Stratford-upon-Avon. There were two very pretty girls on the front desk and one of the perks of their job was that they were allowed to eat a proper lunch in the restaurant at the end of service. Well, firstly all the chefs fancied them and neither of them would ever put out, and secondly, there is nothing more irritating than having to cook another couple of bloody lunches after doing a full and crippling service. And thirdly, they were so goddamn smug about it.

So the chefs would take the two to three day-old smegma from under their foreskins and wipe it on the food. They would wipe it over the chicken after it was cooked. You can put almost anything anywhere before it's cooked as any bacteria is killed during the cooking process. Fried food is the safest; nothing can survive the blast of a deep fat fryer so if you are ever in doubt about the food the safest thing to eat are the chips. Anyway, they'd put their fingers up their arses and stick them into the mash. They would gob and snot on the food. Sometimes you could actually see the snot on the plate, especially if the KP had been asked to contribute. The deal was that if they ate in the restaurant the girls had to clear their own plates. So we'd all sit out the back, sucking on a fag, waiting for them to finish. If they didn't like what they were given, they'd pop their plate by the sink, but more often than not they'd eat the lot and come back and express their compliments to the chef. And what was weird, the more we dicked about with their lunch, quite literally, the more they seemed to like it. We did stop short of shitting in it, but only just.

Not that any of my boys would stoop so low, but I wouldn't put it past Andrew not to give the steak a gentle, spur-of-the-moment sneeze on the pass, just to prove a point. It really isn't the done thing to come and test the kitchen right at the end of a shift.

I can sense their fatigue as well as their seething fury as I leave the kitchen. The restaurant is emptying quite rapidly now. Only Tony and Bill are left in their Friday corner, considering the possibility of a brandy to go with their espressos and petit fours. The PAs are beginning to get a little giggly on their free champagne and the Formula One bloke is just settling up the bill. The Andersons, with their dear departed grandpa, have suggested that, having finally finished their lovely lunch, they are ready to shift the corpse. Although now, with the arrival of the media in the restaurant, I am less inclined to want to take the old boy through the restaurant and, after a short conversation with Jorge, we decide that it is far better for all concerned if we take the body through the kitchen and out the back. Jorge has already put the call in to the ambulance crew and has asked them to park up in the mews. My job is to distract Mr Stone while everyone else forms some sort of human shield.

I am about to plonk myself down, with my brightest smile, when Jason suddenly gets up, patting his pockets like he's about to pop outside for a cigarette. So I follow him, carefully placing myself between him and the window.

'So you own this place?' he says immediately, pulling out a Silk Cut.

'Yes,' I confirm, slightly taken aback.

'Good crab salad,' he says.

'Thank you.' I light his cigarette for him. Suddenly Gina appears from behind the bar. Her borrowed waistcoat is a little tight over her rather fecund figure.

'Gentlemen,' she smiles, 'I have brought you an ashtray for your addiction. I think the olive trees have had enough nicotine for today.' It is not quite the sort of Michelin-starred service I am after, but fortunately Mr Stone is so distracted by her backside that he doesn't see the ambulance crew arriving at the back of the restaurant.

'She's new.'

'I like her style,' he replies, blowing his smoking after her.

'So how long have you been in the job?' I ask, a little distracted by the action behind. It is taking four men to shift Grandpa and they're moving all the tables and the chairs.

'What job?' He looks at me, a little surprised.

'I am afraid we know who you are, Mr Stone,' I come clean.

'How?' He's looking annoyed.

'It's our job to know who everyone is. That's what we pay a PR for.'

'Right.' He rolls his eyes. 'How come no one knows what Marina O'Loughlin looks like and she's been doing it for nine years?'

'She's made it her mission to be incognito.' He doesn't respond. He looks down and is about to turn around and see the body being hoisted into a trolley. 'How are you enjoying it so far?' I blurt. 'It must be a very interesting, very entertaining, very exciting job?' They've got Grandpa on the stretcher, covered in a blanket, and are heading towards the kitchen.

'It's fine,' he says, taking a long lug of his cigarette. 'This the third place I've done.'

'Great,' I enthuse, as the late Grandpa's feet disappear through the double swing doors. 'Well, best of luck to you! And do please be kind to us.' I move to walk back inside. He flicks his cigarette into the path of an oncoming taxi and follows me in.

'I'll speak as I find,' he says. 'Steak next.' He rubs his hands. 'Rare. Let's see if they can do that.'

I smile stiffly at him and make a mental note never to accept his booking again. The man's a git. A short git, to boot, and he's wearing a hideous pair of rubber-soled shoes. Looking at him, creeping back to his table to tuck into his bloody steak, you can understand why chefs suddenly see red and ban critics from their restaurants. Nobu banned Michael Winner, as did Anthony Worrall Thompson, Nico Ladenis banned Fay and Gordon banned Adrian – or at least asked him and Joan Collins to leave his establishment in a fit of feather-spitting high dudgeon. Mr Stone will sadly never find a reservation here. Unless, of course, he gives us a five-star review, then he'll be welcomed back with free Veuve Clicquot-popping joy.

My phone goes.

'All right, mate!' comes a jovial male voice speaking cab-Cockney. 'Phil Crammer. I'm right outside.'

I look up to see a black BMW double-parked between the two olive trees. There's a loud honk of the car horn and a sky-blue shirtsleeve shoots through the sunshine roof and gives me a wave. Phil Crammer is indeed parked outside.

An affable porky fellow with a fine-dining paunch that is barely contained by his shirt, Phil occupies a lucrative subset of the restaurant business – buying and selling properties. They are a small, eclectic group who include great characters like Frank the Yank, who deal solely in restaurant real estate. Phil spends his days eating in establishments (hence the paunch), chatting up owners and persuading them either to sell or expand their businesses. He's been badgering me for weeks to come and look at this 'jewel of a place', or so he says, just on the edge of Covent Garden. Obviously I don't have the money at the moment to buy anywhere, but good spots come up so rarely in the capital that even if you're not in the game, you'd be a fool not to investigate.

I have a quick word with Jorge to make sure the Andersons are looked after. He thinks I should comp them the wine. I am not sure it'll help their grieving process but it's good to look generous under the circumstances. He's also promised to give Mr Stone the full-beam maitre d' service and to keep me updated on his progress.

'Ready?' asks Phil, revving his engine and turning down Kiss FM. 'It's not far from here and I tell you, mate, you're going to fucking love it.'

With the heating turned up high and the roof down low, we head off towards Seven Dials.

'This part of town is hot right now, mate,' Phil says, burning down the road. 'I mean Soho is hot right now too. Hot. So hot. Ten years ago it was rocking, then later you couldn't give any-where away and now, in the last two years, it's buzzing. Everyone wants a piece of it. Rents are up. I am selling leases here for over a million. I had two in the last week that went for £1.1m and another for £1.2m. A couple of years ago that was unheard of. Depends on what side of the street, obviously. Dean Street, it's the left. Greek, it's also the left, Old Compton it's the right as you stand with your arse facing Wardour. But it's gone crazy, I tell you, crazy.' As we drive up Garrick Street, the heating in his car is beginning to freeze-dry my face.

'I love that club,' he says, nodding over his shoulder. 'You been in there?'

'No.'

'You should, it's amazing. It's a proper club, not like some of the places round here.' We move along Floral Street and into Catherine Street. 'Not far now,' he adds. 'It's rocking round here. Balthazar's around the corner – did you hear about the fist fight for that place?'

'A bit,' I say.

'Extraordinary. You know Corbin and King, Rex Restaurants, thought they had the place sown up? Well, they were planning to open The Delaunay there, were practically measuring up the fucking curtains, when Richard Caring swooped in at the last minute and said to the landlord, "I can bring you Balthazar." Like it was the Holy Grail with a heavenly choir attached. Balthazar!' He does jazz hands over his dashboard. 'A proven brand, all the way from America!' he laughs. 'Poor old Rex were kicked into touch.'

'That's a bit tough,' I say.

'But that's restaurants for you, isn't it? Dog eat dog, although hopefully not *actually* dog. Mind you, in some of these places in Chinatown you never bloody know, do you? Filth!' He throws back his chin collection and laughs.

I'm not sure he is right about the dog, but he's right about restaurants being a tough business. Location is everything and when a good place comes up there's always a fight and it's nearly always the same blokes going for the same spots. Caprice Holdings, Rex Restaurants, Ricker Restaurants,

Russell Norman is now in the mix with his ever-growing collection including Polpo, Polpetto, Da Polpo, Spuntino and Mishkin, as is Arkady Novikov, owner of the hugely success-ful Novikov, who is said to be keen on getting a larger foothold in London, having recently lost out to Rex Restaurants in the fight over Brasserie Zédel, which was formerly The Atlantic Bar and Grill.

The competition between these guys is stiff. Getting the site involves a protracted and expensive beauty competition of bid and counter-bid, with each company promising more and more. The leaseholder is in an enviable position with everyone falling over themselves to get their foot in the door. Move out of Soho, Covent Garden and Mayfair and the situation is a little different, although there are pockets such as Notting Hill and Westbourne Grove where rents get up to £450,000 a year, and Marylebone and Borough, which is catching the lucrative fallout of the Shard, where the big boys still want to play. There are prestige sights like the recent Rex victory for the twenty-year-old Oriel's site in Sloane Square. But every-where else is lot trickier to sell.

You have to be so careful because you may find yourself a fabulous-looking site but if the area is not right you can end up killing yourself trying to make it work. I had a mate who had a restaurant near Hammersmith, which didn't work. He said it was caught between two zones, Chiswick and Notting Hill, and the clientele wanted to be more glamorous than they were. He said that people prefer to travel into town to eat out, they very rarely travel out – the River Café being one of the few exceptions. But it was an awful thing to see. It's crippling to have a restaurant that's not working because they are so expensive to keep going. But if you are not busy and your takings start to slide, it is very hard to get out of the shit. Punters don't like eating in empty restaurants, and if they won't come in it is very hard to drag them in.

And the costs of setting up a place have spiralled out of control. I think you need about two million to get yourself off the ground these days. It's insane. Half the battle is to get the site, then you have to think up what you're going to do with it, then you have to execute it, build it within budget, then you have to find the staff, get it all right, then you have to open it, publicize it – and then Adrian Gill walks in and says it's shit and that's that. It's a mug's game really. Although if you get it right, and occasionally someone does, then it's a licence to print money. I hear Novikov is raking it in, something like £600,000 turnover a week. I sadly can only dream of such things.

The market is sensitive at the moment and it's not a great idea for me to spread myself too thin. When the recession hit in March 2009 and everything fell off a cliff, my business halved over night. It's picked up a lot since then, but it has made me a little wary of expansion. However, talk to anyone in the business and they'll say the opposite, that it's all about expanding, getting a brand, and rolling it out. Everyone is on about 'roll out'. The smart chefs are always trying to get themselves out of the kitchen; they do a bit of telly, get themselves a reputation, and then they can't drop the tea towel fast enough – they start up a few places and they'll do the menus, chat to their chefs and call themselves a businessman. Marco and Gordon used to be everyone's pin-ups with their shining collection of fine dining establishments, but these days it's Jamie Oliver.

Jamie did it all slightly the other way and managed to irritate everyone who had ever been to catering college while he did it. Everyone was jealous, green, livid, they kept on thinking why did Pat Llewllyn spot that lisping knob? What's he got? Which was another way of saying: Pick me, Pat, pick me! But Jamie was smart, very smart, he did the books, the TV shows, he worked hard – and he's a nice bloke, actually. He did Fifteen and then he did Jamie's Italians. The Holy Grail! A brand! That works! Which he has rolled out all over the country. He's got over thirty of them now and he owns, so I'm told, about 70 per cent of the company. Apparently he was turned down by various investors, so he thought, sod this, and put his own money in. You see, smart chap. Raymond Blanc has done the same. He's got his Brasserie Blanc brand all over the UK, in Bath, Bristol, Oxford, Leeds. The Soho House Group, apart from expanding internationally, is also 'rolling out' their Chicken Shop and Pizza East brands. And of course there's Carluccio's. What I wouldn't do for a brand!

'So, what do you think?' Phil slows the car down to a gentle kerb crawl as he passes a small, blue-fronted restaurant. 'It's Greek. I mean, Christ, no wonder it's failing. Who wants to eat Greek? When was the last time anyone said to you, "Hey! Let's go out and have a Greek? D'you know what, I'm starving, I could murder a Greek"? Feta? Retsina? I ask you! You never want to eat that shit, not even in fucking Greece!'

He rocks with laughter, and slaps my thigh, encouraging me to join in. Yet all I can think is, poor sod, he's probably been here since 1972 when everyone loved a Greek. They'd chow down moussaka, smash a few plates and have a right old laugh dancing in a circle with their pals. And now he's sitting here, much like the bowler hat makers of Great Britain, wondering where all the customers have gone.

'But the spot rocks, don't you think?' says Phil, mounting the pavement with his car. 'Look,' he nods up and down the street, 'theatres, plenty of offices, literary agency around the corner and plenty of tourists. Top spot.'

'I agree.'

It *is* a good spot, very good, in fact. I can feel my heart beating in my chest. I hate it when that happens because it usually means I want to spend money that I don't have.

'What are the figures?' I ask, getting out of the car.

'Not bad,' he says. 'It's seventy covers, basement kitchen, they're looking at an £800,000 premium, negotiable obviously, and the rent is £90,000 a year and your rates are a £27K. It's good. It's right for round here. You can have some tables in the street, get those hot lamps out. Little bar inside . . .'

'Who else have you shown it to?'

'A few. No one as, you know, as top notch as yourself.' He pauses on the threshold. 'Shall we go in?'

Once inside, I realize I am completely correct. The place must have opened around 1972 and no one has redecorated it since. The walls are painted a turquoise blue that is peeling around the edges. The dark bentwood tables and chairs are covered in matching turquoise check tablecloths and cushions, the small windows down the side, encaged with black metal bars, are swathed in matching check curtains. On the walls there are a few old posters from the Greek Tourist Board in cracked, yellowing Perspex frames. Next to the posters are some twisted hanging ropes and a few large, green, glass fishing floats. The ruby carpet is sticky underfoot and the place smells of bleach, fried food and stale cigarettes – which is a feat, since no one's legally been allowed to spark up in here since July 2007. At the back the nautical theme continues with smaller glass floats hanging from the bar. There are three bottles turned upside down – of gin, vodka and whisky with brands I have never heard of. Behind the optics is a collection of curled, faded postcards pinned to a corkboard, depicting various scenes from the Greek islands.

Phil shakes hands with the owner who must be about a hundred and five years old and comes up to his armpit. Dressed in a white open-neck shirt and black slacks, he has a large Saint Christopher nestling into his grey chest hair. We exchange smiles and pleasantries and he escorts us through the restaurant. Somewhat optimistically all the tables are laid for supper (or perhaps they were laid for lunch) and, in the middle of each, sits a bevelled beer glass full of breadsticks, sealed in white, waxed wrappers.

He takes us down some thin, narrow stairs, past the toilets and into the basement kitchen. It is a minute, airless dungeon.

How they manage to get any food out of here is a miracle. It doesn't look as if there's a plate lift either, so I presume anything that comes out of here has to be hand-carried up the stairs. It must be so hot during service, sweat flying all over the place. The white walls shine with grease and the equipment is all very much past its sell-by date – as, I imagine, are half the ingredients in the fridges. The surfaces themselves are relatively clean; someone is trying to look after the place, but just one look at the back and I can see the seals on the fridges are gone and I'd lay money on the ancient extractor fan not working. In short, you'd have to be insane to cook or indeed eat here.

'It needs a little updating,' says Phil, nodding his way around the room. 'A few bits, a few bobs. A refit here, there. But can't you just smell the potential?'

What I can actually smell is rancid cooking fat, along with all that potential, but still, for some reason my heart is beating. I don't know why I am so excited. The place is a hell-hole. But it is a hell-hole in an excellent location.

Back out in the street in the blinking bright sunshine, Phil gives me one of those hearty slaps on the back that forces me two steps forward.

'So? So? So?' he asks.

'So it looks interesting.'

'So it's fucking great, isn't it?' He grins.

'So it's good.'

'It's more than good, it's *fucking* good.'

'So who else have you shown it to?'

'Russell Norman's had a sniff but it's too small for him.' He pauses. 'And I've mentioned it to Big Pete.'

'What? *The* Big Pete?' My heart sinks.

'There's only one,' he says, opening the door to his BMW.

'Yes, and he's a complete shit.'

4–5 p.m.

Big Pete is one of the less savoury characters on the restaurant scene. I've heard some fairly unpleasant things about him and I really don't fancy him in my orbit. He is an investor, a backer of restaurants who likes to follow his money about and get involved. I think he is lured by the glamour and fancies himself as a player, a culinary Charlie Big Potatoes, but in reality he's a boorish thug no one likes.

I remember hearing something about him kicking some young guys out of the bar they were renting from him a couple of years ago now. Apparently they were having some problems with their services – the power and the water kept cutting out, two things which are just a little crucial if you are trying to run a place. Anyway, they complained to Big Pete who did nothing; they asked again and again and he continued to do nothing. In the end they said they would withhold their rent, they'd place it in a holding account, so he could see they had it, but they wouldn't release it to him, until he'd fixed the water and the electricity. When they came to open up the bar on Monday morning, they found the locks had been changed on the building and all their stuff was chucked out in the street, being picked over by passers-by. When my friend complained to Big Pete, telling him that perhaps he was being a little harsh, Pete looked him in the eye and said: 'When you see a cockroach you stamp on it; when you see it wriggle, you stamp on it harder still.'

I shiver. I am not sure any place is worth going head to head with Big Pete. But it is a good spot, right in the heart of Covent Garden, which is as rare as rocking horse shit. There's something about it that's piqued my interest.

'I do like it,' I say to Phil as he drops me off outside Le Bar. 'Let me think about it.'

'Don't think too long,' he says, clicking his teeth and giving me a wink. 'You know what they say about the early bird.' I smile. 'Laters,' he says before shooting me with his right index finger. He pops on his mirrored shades, pumps up Kiss FM and roars off down the street.

I am just about to walk into another meeting I've got at Le Bar when I am engulfed in a cloud of dope smoke. I check my watch, it's just gone four – it's spliff o'clock outside L'Italiano and indeed half the cafés and bistros in town. If you walk around Charlotte Street and parts of Soho at this time of day you'll find most of the kitchen staff on their break and the mews and alleyways will reek with the heady sweet smell of hydroponic skunk.

I remember when I was a lot younger I'd combine my spliff break with a couple of lagers down the pub. It was never worth going home for the hour or so we got off, and we'd all go to the pub, have a drink, shovel in a couple of packets of crisps, and then crawl back to the kitchen coalface. Quite how I managed to get through another six hours of work I don't know. The dope wasn't quite as strong as it is now, that's for sure. The stuff they smoke out the back of L'Italiano always smells lethal. I remember one restaurant I worked in where we'd all gather outside the kitchen door and skin up. Unfortunately, one afternoon there was something wrong with the extractor fan and the wind blew all our smoke back inside the kitchen. The head chef came steaming out. He'd been given the blow-back of a lifetime and was furious. Thankfully the whole of his brigade was puffing away on the stoop so he couldn't fire the lot of us at once.

'Christ,' I say, walking into Le Bar. 'I am practically high on next door's supply.'

'Not the L'Italiano stoners again?' Adam grins. 'It gets so bad during the summer I have to close the window in the office at the back, otherwise come four thirty in the afternoon I can barely see straight.' He laughs. I am not sure whether Martina from Drinks Inc believes him either, but she smiles and laughs along anyway. 'You remember Martina,' he says.

I can't imagine many people forget Martina. She is gorgeous, clever, smart and gives away lots of free money and booze. No one forgets that delightful combination in a hurry.

'Hi,' she says, getting out of her seat, running her hands through a mass of thick, dark curls. I had forgotten quite how pretty she is. 'Happy Christmas – well, nearly!' She laughs. She has a trace of a Spanish accent, which makes everything she says sound sexy.

'Happy Christmas to you!' I hear myself laughing like a fool. I'm supposed to be negotiating with her; I had better get a grip.

Martina works in the drinks business for a small but perfectly formed company called Drinks Inc who specialize in bespoke vodka, gin and rum. Drinks Inc is part of the massive UK alcohol industry, and when I say massive, I mean truly enormous. It's worth around £40 billion a year and it pays just over £16 billion into the Exchequer, which is tantamount to £316 per adult in the country, or double the UK overseas aid budget. Although there are some small players like Drinks Inc, the booze market is more or less carved up by the big boys, which include giants like Diageo (over £13 billion turnover, 25,000 employees, quoted on the FTSE) who owns Smirnoff (the world's bestselling vodka), Johnnie Walker (the world's bestselling Scotch whisky), Baileys (the world's bestselling liqueur) and Guinness (the world's bestselling stout). Another big chap is Bacardi Ltd, which has a portfolio of some two hundred brands including Bombay Sapphire, Martini, Dewar's, Bacardi Rum and Grey Goose Vodka (which they acquired recently for a cool £1.1 billion). Pernod Ricard has big hitters like Absolut Vodka, Jameson Whiskey, Malibu, Beefeater Gin and Chivas Regal. And then there's First Drinks with another fifty brands including Hendrick's Gin,

Cointreau, Tia Maria and Piper Heidsieck Champagne.

These are all huge companies with huge brands and products that are household names, and which, because of their alcoholic content, are rather difficult to advertise on mainstream TV. So they have to go about it in a very different way if they are going to reach their audience.

If you are the proud owner of a cool bar, in a cool part of town, with a cool clientele, with cool cash and cool friends, then the drinks companies are falling over themselves to get their bottles into your place – and they'll pay you for the privilege of stocking their stuff. Not only do they pay, but they will also provide the stock for free. And we are not talking a small amount. If a small, hip restaurant in Notting Hill can get £30,000 a year from one vodka brand, you can see why big groups can trouser up to £2m for the privilege of stocking one spirit over another.

These sweeteners are called listing fees, and for a place like ours they can be worth about £250,000 a year, which is, as you can imagine, rather helpful. The listing fee means that the drinks company gets ownership of the 'house pour'. The house pour is the bottle of vodka they have behind the bar in the 'well'. House pour is what the barman will use when you ask for a 'vodka and tonic'. House pour is where the big money is in the UK as most of us, some 90 per cent, don't ask for a 'vodka and tonic' by brand. In the USA, it is absolutely the opposite, with 90 per cent of customers using 'brand call'. So unless you ask for a spirit by name you will get the house pour. If a bar has been 'listed' by a drinks company, the barman might suddenly suggest a few brands to you by way of a serving suggestion: 'Would you like Grey Goose? Or something else?' That's a very good way of suggesting you might want a Grey Goose. But if you stick to your guns because you know that once they put the tonic and the lemon in it doesn't really matter what brand you are drinking, then they will serve you up the house pour. In the US is it the cheapest, most cheerful vodka they can get away with. It will be poured below your eye line and it will probably be a brand you've never heard of.

In the UK the house pour is supposed to be a reflection of the bar, so if it is a swanky, swinging place full of swanky, swinging, expensive people, then the brand they use should reflect that. And if you're charging £15 a drink then you shouldn't really have mass-market brands like Smirnoff or Gordon's as your house pour. Obviously, many do. But they are supposed to be offering up something else. So if it were a Grey Goose, Bacardi Ltd-listed bar, then something like Eristoff would probably be the house pour.

When shelling out listing fees, drinks companies also hope to come away with ownership of the 'back bar'. It is not guaranteed and it rather relies on the powers of the rep's – in this case, Martina's – persuasion. Personally I have never taken a listing fee without giving away the back bar.

The back bar sets the tone of the place so you try and pack it with as many expensive, glamorous-looking bottles as possible in order to tempt your drinkers. Your glamorous and expensive customer is supposed to cast their eye over the back bar and have their tastes reflected back at them; they are supposed to be reassured that they are in the right place. So if you ever want to know what sort of customer frequents some-where, check out the bottles on display. The Imperial Collection Fabergé Egg full of vodka on display at Nobu Berkeley Street, which sells at £2,600 for the coloured enamel egg, or £5,600 for the gold and silver one, wouldn't really go down well at Le Bar. It is also a brilliant example of what Martina calls the 'escalation of filtration'. Imperial Collection boasts that its vodka is 'distilled five times through birch charcoal, then several times more through quartz sand and finally through an algae whose micro-structure guarantees this rare purity'.

Adam and I are obsessed with collecting filtration techniques or obscure marketing ideas behind shifting bottles of vodka. My current favourite is a Canadian brand, Iceberg, that pro-fesses to harvest genuine icebergs in order to source the purest water available to humanity. You can have a lot of fun with vodka. I also quite like Roberto Cavalli's vodka, which comes in a tall bottle with swirls, either frosted or black, and is marketed as 'fashion on the rocks' – and Roberto opines: 'Fashion vodka . . . because "black" is fashion . . . sexy and mysterious . . . Just like the women I love.' Yours for just under fifty quid a bottle.

Talk to anyone in the drinks business and they will tell you that vodka is vodka and gin is gin. You can play around with it, add colours and flavours and filter it as much as you like, but it is distilled in a closed still and requires no maturing or nurturing at all. So unlike whisky or dark rum, which are matured in vats and as varied as the brands there are on the market, different brands of vodka or gin are extremely difficult to tell apart. So much so that they are mostly referred to in the trade as simply 'the liquid'.

When I first met Martina she talked me through the marketing of drinks. Rum is apparently the new big thing. In the seventies and eighties we were mad for gin and then we had an obsession with vodka but now, apparently, it's all about rum. I have to say we have noticed some customers starting to order rum but only in the last few months. Anyway, she talked me through this new rum they have which was apparently delicious but was in a bottle that looked like a 'cut-price olive oil bottle that only its mother could love'. The label was black, white, green and orange and look very retro but not in a good way. The rum was only selling two hundred cases (twelve bottles in each) a year. Smirnoff sells something like seven million cases in the UK alone. So it really wasn't singing for its supper and they decided to give it a makeover. They kept the liquid, changed the bottle, updated the label and now they shift four thousand cases.

'What's the difference between a rat and a squirrel?' Martina smiled. 'Marketing.'

Bottles are crucial. Tall, thin and long tend to be vodkas aimed at women. Short, fat and square are gins. Square is masculine, round is feminine. A tall bottle is modern, clean and sophisticated, whereas short and squat is robust, traditional and full of heritage. And glancing at the bottles she has lined up for Adam and me to have a look at this afternoon, she is right. The gins are short and fat and the vodkas are all pretending to be triple-filtered supermodels, so pure and elegant, I am amazed they contain alcohol at all.

Martina is pitching for our cocktail list. We are currently in bed with another drinks company, but Drinks Inc have some very cool brands which I think our customers would like. It is a constantly moving market and in order for us to look as if we know what we are doing, we have to keep ahead of the others; the last thing we want is to look like we are behind the curve.

We shift a lot of cocktails – we have an eight-page menu with ten cocktails per page and Martina is keen to get in on the action. Drinks companies pay to get their brand on these lists and, depending on the bar, it costs between £50 and £250 per cocktail to get a name check. So cross my palm with £200 and suddenly my Moscow Mule, when sponsored, turns into an Absolut Mule. Give me another £200 and my normal straight-up martini becomes a Martini Grey Goose. And the thing about cocktails (martinis aside) is that you can charge through the nose for them but they are nearly all mixers. We are charging anything from £16 to £21 for a drink that costs us about £1 max to make.

Although quite often they cost us nothing. Along with the listing fee and paying to get on to the cocktail list, the lovely drinks companies obviously also give us stock for free. So along with our nice cheque for £250,000 we'll get given fifteen to twenty cases of stock for 'events' – whatever they're supposed to be. So instead of throwing a Malibu promotional party at the Le Bar, we'll either sell on the 'events cases' to the customer or keep them back for a staff party.

You can also get retro deals, so if you sell £200,000 worth of stock you can get 20 per cent kickback off your next order. They'll also throw in staff trips to see the liquid being made. They'll say it's 'training', but everyone knows it's a gigantic piss-up. A trip to the freezing cold Scottish Highlands to see whisky being distilled is fine, but a long weekend in Cuba checking out the rum is a very good way to incentivize the barman. And that's what they do. They befriend the barmen, they take them on cocktail courses, load them up with freebies, teach them the 'perfect pour' and then once they've groomed them, they'll follow their careers from bar to bar. Every barman you ever employ has his fingers in such and such a company, and a mate here, and a pal there. It is a very old-fashioned way of doing business; nothing is ever formalized, there are no great contracts to sign, there is a lot of mutual back scratching and plenty of room for manoeuvre.

However, the great unfathomable in all of this is fashion, taste and the fickleness of the customer. Martina told us how a club around the corner tried to delist her after three years. They were paying £28,000 a year to get one of their rums as the house pour. They were in all the cocktails and shifted a guaranteed eight hundred cases a year. But the club got greedy and decided that they could get more from selling themselves elsewhere. The only problem was that the customers didn't like the new rum, they liked the other cooler brand, as did the bar staff, and there were complaints that the £100 Golden Box cocktail didn't quite cut the mustard. So the club begged the cool rum to come back. They said they would, but this time they wouldn't pay the £28,000. The club agreed. They are not putting their rum in all the drinks, but they are shifting some three hundred and fifty cases for no fee. Or as Martina put it: 'You don't get the big apple but you get a lot of cherries instead.'

In an attempt to control the market, drinks companies used to employ young, groovy cats to go around trendy bars and clubs and order their branded drinks. These 'cool hunters' or 'early adopters' were supposed to create a buzz, asking for certain drinks by name, in a loud voice, openly demanding why such-and-such a brand wasn't stocked at all. However, these cats were just a little too smart for companies and would take money from more than one drinks company at a time. So instead of being employed solely by, say, Bacardi, they were also working for Diageo and Pernod Ricard all at the same time. Their back pockets stuffed with cash, they just went out and partied, irrespective of what branded cocktail they were drinking.

'So we have this triple-filtered vodka,' says Martina.

'Through a virgin's armpit, I hope,' suggests Adam, picking up the glass and giving it a sniff.

'Granite,' she smiles.

'Excellent,' he says, taking a sip. 'What do you think?' he asks me.

The last thing I want to do is starting drinking vodka at four fifty-two. I have eaten no breakfast, no lunch, I'm starving and the last time I did a vodka tasting with Martina we ended up sitting at the back end of the bar doing the 'dentist's chair' – mixing shots in our mouths and swallowing them back in one. That girl has a stronger head on her shoulders than any rugby club boy I have ever met. I went home feeling like I was on a cross-Channel ferry and spent the evening with my arms wrapped around the lavatory bowl like it was my best friend in the entire world. I think she carried on and went out to dinner.

'I think it's great.' I nod, giving it a sniff and just wetting my lips.

'We're doing well with it,' she says. 'It's Latvian and gone into three bars in Soho in the last week.'

'You have anything a little more left field?' asks Adam. He's never been keen on the idea of following others.

'We've got a coffee liqueur from Mexico,' she suggests.

'Don't you just love the drinks trade? Two shots of alcohol, some colour, some flavouring, stick a name on it, add some sexy girls with their tits out – no offence, Martina – and you've got yourselves a drink. Baileys? Sheridan's? What the fuck are they? Brandies, vodkas, gins? They are completely shagging made up.' He pauses and knocks back the Latvian vodka in one. 'Go on then – what are we supposed to do with it?'

She brings out a large black rather phallic-looking bottle, called Cafta. 'I was thinking Espresso Margarita?'

Adam approaches the bottle with care. 'Really?'

'It's quite sweet,' she says.

'Oi, Damon!' shouts Adam to the bar. 'Didn't you spend some time in Mexico?'

A tall blond bloke in his mid-twenties ambles over. His hair is stiff with product and his trousers are slack with attitude. Fortunately for him he is not wearing trainers. He takes one look at the bottle and laughs.

'I've had that.' He nods. 'It made me barf on the beach.'

Adam laughs. 'Barf on the beach – that's a good name for a cocktail.'

'It's not quite the image we're after,' says Martina. 'The liquid is good,' she continues. 'Try some.' She pours out a small shot in each glass and hands them out to the three of us. I take a sniff and it doesn't smell too bad so I knock it back.

'It's tequila based,' says Martina.

Too late I think: I can't abide tequila.

'Oh it's good,' says Adam with rather too much relish. He pushes his glass towards her. 'Hit me.'

'It is good,' acknowledges Damon. 'That's half the problem. The stuff is lethal!'

'I like it,' says Adam, his eyes watering slightly after he's downed his second shot. 'We could do a party with this. Sponsor an event?'

'Do you have an events manager?' asks Martina, who I notice has yet to sample her own wares. So that's her trick. To look like she's knocking it back but actually not. Although I do distinctly remember her actually being in the dentist's chair; I can't have imagined that?

'I do all the events managing here,' says Adam, leaning in. 'If Karl Lagerfeld wants to hire the place for £100,000 he has to talk to me.'

163

'We could do some sponsored events during Fashion Week? That's always good,' she says, nodding.

'The only thing is, fashion people don't have any money,' says Adam.

'That's OK. We'll pay for the party, give you the stock, and we'll get some nice photos out of it.'

'Cool!' agrees Adam. 'What d'you think, Boss?'

My phone goes. It's Caz.

'Darling! Darling! There you are!' She sounds like she's been scouring London on her hands and knees looking for me, instead of just picking up the phone. 'Pippa's rushed off her feet and we're both wondering when you're coming down to the Bring Your Daughter to Tea at La Table?'

'Oh, Christ! Is that today?'

'Fuck yes, buddy. Right here. Right now.'

5–6 p.m.

Ten minutes later and I'm walking down the street to La Table. Outside the brasserie, in the dying light of the day, I can see two freezing, shivering blondes, wearing pink glitterball head boppers, each holding a clipboard. There are two large bunches of shiny pink helium balloons tied to the planters, blowing in the breeze, and a short strip of red carpet rolled over the pavement going into the entrance.

'Hiya!' smiles one blonde, the pink glitterballs on her head waggling from side to side. She looks like she's having as much fun as the designated-driver on a Hen Night. 'Welcome! Is your name on the list?' She smiles at me; her pink-frosted lips have turned a pale shade of blue in the cold.

I must have been mad to agree when Caz suggested this as an idea. Firstly, all the pink is clashing rather heavily with the carefully chosen red leather for the brasserie banquettes and, secondly, I am not sure the idea of having two shivering women doing meet-and-greet on a door is anyone's idea of fun.

'Why don't you two girls come inside?' I suggest. 'It's far too cold to stand outside.'

'God, we'd love to,' replies one of the girls. 'But Caz says we've got to stay out here till the owner comes.'

The other one laughs. 'Yeah, just so he can see he's getting value for money.'

'Well, I *am* the owner.' They both look stunned. One of them covers her mouth with her pink-tipped nails and the other pulls an odd gurning grimace like she's got a knife stuck in the toaster.

'Darling!' comes a hiss/bark through the doors. 'Get in here, right away! Half the women are leaving! Honestly,' says Caz as her skinny, clawed hand reaches out into the street and snatches me in, 'I don't know why I bother organizing a brilliant B to C event when you can't even be bothered to show up.' She is talking out of the side of a rictus grin as she pushes me towards an explosion of pink that seems to have overtaken my restaurant. 'They've been here for an hour. The fairy enter-tainer has done her job, we've done the face painting and all you needed to do was show up . . . Here he is!' she announces in a loud voice, pushing the small of my back towards what must be at least Dante's first circle of hell, if not the second.

There is glitter, pink and princess shit all over the place. There are fairy cakes, cream cakes, a big bloody pink cake, and glasses of pink champagne scattered everywhere. There are streamers and balloons and bits of shiny pink stuff as far as my slightly screwed-up eyes can see. I must have been completely drunk when I approved this.

'Ladies!' I smile, opening my arms out wide trying to appear generous and ebullient. 'I hope you are having fun!'

For the next fifteen minutes I am passed from one frown-free skinny woman to another, as they each in turn thank me profusely for my hospitality and confess to having eaten 'far too much'. I am then introduced to an infinite and varied collection of daughters who are all entirely clad in that pink shiny material that shouldn't go near a naked flame and who all appear to be called something ending in 'a'.

'Where are the boys?' I finally manage to ask Caz, before she shoves the small of my back towards another group of women.

'It's an all-girls school over the road,' she growls in a voice laced with jaded incredulity.

'Oh.'

'Yes, fucking "Oh"! Do your homework, A-hole . . . Here he is!' she announces, smiles and shoves. I can tell she is rather enjoying herself. There is nothing that Caz likes more than being totally and utterly in the right.

And she is. This place really needs some help. It was supposed to be rather like Tom's Kitchen is to Tom Aikens's Michelin-starred place around the corner. It wasn't supposed to cost me a huge amount – we're using the same suppliers, the same laundry company, all that sort of stuff. And we are supposed to be able to turn tables all day. The takings are not what they should be and I am a little worried. I am wondering if I should replace my maître d', Kim. She is a nice enough girl.

But is she nice enough? I remember speaking to Russell Norman who is king of the packed, popular, delicious, fast-moving local, where people queue up to sit down. In his collection of six and counting (Polpo, Da Polpa, etc.) he doesn't appear to have a weak link. His secret? He said it was being nice. The key about making a good local work was having charming staff. Good food was a given, but they all have to smile, they have to look after the regulars, they have to get them coming back for more. Getting them to come back again, and again, is crucial.

Talking of nice and charming, I look around the room for Pippa, hoping she's forgiven me for foisting a pneumatic Scandi on her at such short notice. Finally I spot her, hovering just outside the kitchen. Dressed in whites, her cheeks are flushed, her face is shining in sweat and her dark hair is pulled back into a ponytail. She gives me a brief smile.

'I am very sorry,' I say, walking over and giving her a kiss. She smells of cake.

'Next time don't send me your sexual conquests and ask me to find them gainful employment,' she grins. 'Do I look like I run a lap-dancing club?'

'She's not a lap dancer, she's a waitress.'

'Says who?'

'Says her, she worked at Noma.' I lie a tiny bit.

'Noma, my arse. The only thing she's ever foraged is a tenner out of her knicker elastic.'

I laugh. 'Anyway, how's it going here?'

'Busy,' she confirms. 'Busier.'

'Really? It's Christmas, I suppose.'

'No. Caz is doing a good job. These women will come back.' She looks across the room as the skinny frown-free women all appear to be kissing each other goodbye and gathering together their pink children. 'They've crossed the threshold. They're not scared to come in. People are often wary of new places.'

'These woman aren't scared.'

'You'd be surprised.' She shrugs. 'Are you hungry? I'm just making a quick beetroot salad.'

Beetroot? I'm ravenous but I daren't tell her that I can't stand beetroot and haven't so much as let one of those purple bastards pass my lips since 1976. I follow her into the kitchen. The atmosphere back here is in complete contrast to the all-cocks-drawn tension at Le Restaurant. I am not sure whether it is because it's simple brasserie food without any critical expectation, or whether it is because Pippa is on the pass, that makes it less fraught. But it is actually rather nice and relaxing to hang out here. Four commis chefs are chopping and slicing, sorting their *mise en place* for this evening. They are slowly working their way through the evening prep list, otherwise known as 'the road to freedom'.

'You've met Alison on veg,' says Pippa. She taps a young woman on the shoulder; she turns to look at me. Her dark hair and blue eyes are stunning.

'Evening,' she says.

'Your very best beetroot for the boss, please.'

'Right away, chef,' she replies. I don't have the heart to tell her I'd rather eat a turd sandwich.

'Roberto?' asks Pippa. 'How's that new pudding idea going?'

'What's that?' I ask, feeling my stomach rumble.

'A new salted caramel ice cream with a vanilla panna cotta.'

'It sounds delicious.'

'It should be,' she smiles. 'I nicked the salted caramel ice-cream recipe from the River Café.'

Pippa worked all over London before I managed to prise her out of Jason Atherton's kitchens. She very much cut her teeth during the hot, steamy days when chefs never saw daylight and would barely be bothered to keep a flat as they spent so little time in them anyway. She did once explain to me that being a woman in what was essentially a man's world only made her work that much harder. She said you have to be tough, you have to make sacrifices, because it's rare for female chefs to fit in getting married and having children, and these are things you have to weigh up and work out on the way. You have to cope with the banter, you have to prove to those chauvinist shits that you can hold your own in the kitchen.

She always says that women are not ambitious enough. She told me the story of Angela Hartnett calling Marcus Wareing within twenty-four hours of him losing his head chef and asking for the job. 'Not enough women do that sort of thing,' she said. 'How else are we supposed to get ahead?'

But it is an industry full of contradictions. I remember hearing that Gordon used to remark hilariously that women could only really properly work for three weeks out of four and yet at the same time he wouldn't let any of the women who worked for him ever clean the stove. By far the shittiest job in the kitchen was reserved for the blokes.

'I do think it is all really rather ridiculous,' Pippa once said to me. 'All the shouting and screaming and slapping and hauling around great sides of beef and all we are really doing is making people's tea.' She laughed. 'It's just a bit of tea.'

'Here you go,' she says now, handing me a plate of beetroot and feta salad. 'Have some vitamins on a plate. KP, silver!' she shouts and Omar, the KP, brings over a knife and fork. She puts her hands on her hips and stares at me.

'Are you not having one?' I ask.

'No. I made it for you.'

'Oh, right, thank you.' My mouth goes suddenly really very dry. I pick up the fork and play with it a bit before steeling myself and digging in. I pop in a small mouthful and chew.

'Well?'

'It is delicious! It is completely delicious!' It really is. I can't believe I have been such a baby not to have eaten a beetroot for over thirty years. Like the last beetroot I had in 1976 bears any resemblance to this. That one was soggy and pale and doused in vinegar. This one is fantastic, properly sweet and delicious. 'Wow!'

'He likes it,' shrugs Pippa.

'Like it, I love it!'

'Let's put that on the menu.'

I spend the next three minutes shovelling in Pippa's food quicker than an extra in *Oliver Twist*. I can't believe how fabulous it is.

'Thank you,' I say. 'I feel so much better.' It's true, I do; my hangover is almost clearing. My mobile goes. I am definitely ditching that bloody tune.

'Hello?'

'Stay away from my site.'

'Sorry?'

'Stay away from my site if you know what's good for you.'

'What site?'

'The old Greek on Charlotte Road.'

'Is this Pete?' I start to walk out of the kitchen, giving Pippa a little wave.

'I don't know who you mean.' His voice sounds deep and wheezy, like he's just tried to the catch the bus or stubbed out his twenty-sixth cigarette. 'I am just delivering a message.'

'Or what?' I'm not sure what I am doing; perhaps the vitamins have gone to my head. But I am not a man to be bullied. I haven't worked this hard for this long to be cowed by an idiot with emphysema. 'Or what, mate? What, exactly?'

'I'm just delivering a message,' he huffs down the phone. 'Stay away from the Greek.'

'Who do you think you are? The Krays? Piss off! Fuck off! Do you hear me? Do you? Do you? FUCK OFF!' There's nothing but silence. I look at my phone and realize I've been cut off.

'So there!' I shout at the phone, only to look up and see Caz, Kim and three flicky blonde women looking at me. Fortunately my phone goes again. 'I'm sorry, I must take this.'

It is Steve, my old mate, who's invested a bit of money in the business and who rather fancies himself as the Chief Financial Officer of the company. He isn't, but every few months or so, when he's bored with working in the City, he'll ask to have a look over the books on his way home, while helping himself to a few drinks. And by the sound of his voice he's been helping Martina with her spirits.

I walk into Le Bar to find him sitting on a stool, sipping a worryingly dark looking cocktail.

'There you are!' He waves. Completely bald, with a round stomach poking out his navy suit jacket, Steve already looks pink-cheek pissed and remarkably uncomfortable perched on something so precarious. 'How are you?' His small blue eyes are a little watery.

'I'm fine. And you?'

'I'm drinking some sort of fantastically strong coffee margarita cocktail. I had a one-bottle lunch and this has just about finished me off.'

'Has Martina gone?'

'Do you mean the pretty girl with the curls?' I nod. 'About ten minutes ago.'

'Adam is sorting a few things with her, I think,' chips in Damon from the other side of the bar.

'Right,' I reply, slightly annoyed at his joining in the conversation.

'Can I get you anything? A coffee margarita?'

'No thanks,' I say. 'I think I might just have a cleansing lager. It's about that time.'

'Oh, that's a good idea.' Steve belches into the back of his hand as he pushes his glass away. 'I'll have one of those, Damon.'

'Two lagers,' replies Damon, before walking down the bar.

'You've broken twenty-five glasses this month,' begins Steve, tapping a bit of paper with his porky index finger. 'That's a lot of glass. Seventy-five pence each.'

'Not personally, I haven't.'

'All the same.'

'We haven't broken them to annoy you, Steve.'

'I know but we need to get some more money through this place. Get the big spenders in. Go after the Russians.'

'Really? I tell you, I'm not that keen on the Russians, they don't know how to behave, they click their fingers when they want to be served – I can't abide that.'

'I went to a Russian place the other day and it was amazing – they had brass at the bar!' he chortles.

'That's the oldest trick in the book getting prostitutes at the bar.'

'I know, but the place was packed. Thursday night.'

Thursday night is business night. It is the major night of the week for corporate entertainment. There are business dinners other nights of the week, of course, but Thursday's the night when the boys in suits go out and they are in the market for whores. Friday night is a friends and family night, it's not really for meeting or work, so the whores are much less in evidence at the bars of swanky restaurants. Monday night is usually quite quiet. Tuesday is always surprisingly busy, almost in a way to make up for the boredom of Monday. Wednesday and Thursday are working nights in every true sense of the word, and everyone knows that Saturday night is amateur night. It is bridge and tunnel. It is the toughest night of the week. They are the people who complain the most, the customers who question everything, and the ones who are most worried about being taken seriously or not being treated correctly, because they don't go out much. The only good thing about Saturday night? It is usually pretty brief. The men drink beer, the women have a Pouligny-Montrachet spritzer (which is such a waste of good white wine) and they usually clear off by ten thirty as they have to catch the train home.

'It's all about the Russians,' says Steve. 'Novikov is cleaning up, that place is packed. Burger and Lobster – Russian. They've just got a new place in Chapel Place, £300,000 a year rent, a hundred and twenty covers.'

'I know, that's a lot of steak and shellfish,' I humour him. 'But if you want Russians in your restaurant you have to have a menu as long as your arm. They want the lot – sushi with their spaghetti bolognese. That's why Nobu has a hard time in Moscow: they can't understand why their menu doesn't have pizza.'

'I hear you,' he agrees. 'It's just that they're the ones with the money. Them and the Arabs.'

'But do you want a table ordering £1,000 of food and no one touching it like they do at Zuma, just so they can drink whisky and show off to their mates how much bloody stuff they've got on their table?'

'If they pay I don't care!'

'I do care when they are rude to the staff. I heard an awful story about some rich tosser who ended up shouting at the coat check girl in Zuma because she couldn't find his coat. Apparently he yelled that the coat cost more than she could earn in a year. That's not charming behaviour,' I say. 'I don't think that's a great way to behave.'

'Since when have you been the litmus test of good behaviour? Two wives and more one-night stands than Barry White.'

'Did he have a lot of one-night stands?'

'I don't know, but we've all certainly had plenty to his music.'

Steve laughs as Damon finally arrives with our lagers and attacks his with all the zeal of a parched prisoner of war who's just made it out of the desert.

'Oh, that's better,' he says. 'That other cocktail made me feel quite sick.' I take a sip of my ice-old drink. 'He's a popular fellow your barman,' continues Steve.

'Really?'

'People popping in to see him all afternoon.'

'Really?'

'Well, you know, five or six since I've been here.'

'What do they do?'

'Oh, they sit at the bar, order a Pepsi or something, have a chat and then leave.'

'Right,' I say. I think Adam needs to keep a bit of an eye on Damon. 'I went to see a new site today.'

Steve looks at me, slightly surprised. 'You're not thinking of expanding, are you?' A worried return-on-my-investment look flickers across his face.

'It's a very nice little place in Covent Garden, seventy covers, something like that.'

'Covent Garden? That's a bit off-patch for you?'

'It's a good place, I am seriously considering it.'

'Don't look at me for money!' He puts his hands in the air. 'I'm skint.'

'Really skint or City skint?' He smiles. 'But anyway it's just an idea at the moment.'

'Anyone else interested?'

'A few, I think. Big Pete . . .'

'Really?' He wrinkles his short pink nose. 'I'd stay away from him. He's always trouble.'

6–7 p.m.

The restorative forces of a pint of lager and a plate of beetroot can't be underestimated, so when Pippa calls and tells me she's just heard on the grapevine that one of the new Russian players has been sniffing around and is thinking of poaching Jorge, I barely break my stride. He won't go. He couldn't possibly go? Jorge? My old pal? The best maître d' I have ever had? I own his arse, so why would he possibly want to go anywhere else?

Poaching is a regular problem in this business, particularly amongst the ever-growing number of chefs agencies. They are well known for their sneaky, back-handed ability to head-hunt chefs and pinch front of house staff, which is extremely bloody annoying. But it also goes on between rival restaurants. If someone is any good it won't be long before he, or she, will have other outfits sniffing around them. And like a lot of the manoeuvring in this business it is done with a huge service-industry smile and plenty of charm. There is an etiquette that most people stick to, because the industry is so small and god-damn interconnected. You are supposed to call the opposition and inform them that X has come for an interview, or that Y is thinking of moving across. The fact that you have been grooming, fluffing, charming the sweaty jockstraps off both X and Y for the last month or so, trying to lure them to your outfit, with incentives, financial packages and extra days off, has little or nothing to do with it. It is a bit like having an affair with someone else's wife: the poacher makes the running but then, in the end, you have to give notice, you can't just swoop in and grab them. At the end of the day you don't really want to have to cross the road to avoid someone because you pinched his or her staff. As a result, there is a wonderful sort of frenemy culture, so while we all get on so famously in public, with the back slaps and the free drinks and endless puddings all round, there is plenty of shafting going on behind each other's back.

I walk into Le Restaurant to catch the tail-end of staff supper. They are all sitting glumly at the back, on three or four different tables, clearing their plates with little or no conversation. Gina is sitting down in the far left-hand corner, staring at her plate in disgust, picking around the edges with a fork. I smile. I wonder what sort of crap Andrew's slopped out of the kitchen today.

In most kitchens, staff food is pretty disgusting. The chefs resent having to feed the troops, the owners want to keep it as cheap as possible, and everyone is keen to balance the books.

So staff meals are the first in line for any form of scrimping and saving. But when you think I have to feed over forty people every day, it adds up, and you can understand why they can get the remains of the stockpot plus some carrots.

Mostly carb heavy, with plenty of pasta, using the cheapest ingredients around, the head chef (although sometimes this job rotates between the chefs) usually cobbles something together using leftovers, grog, baloney, whatever you want to call it, maybe with a few eggs or a couple of old chicken legs he's found at the back of the fridge. Sometimes, if the chef is in a good mood, he can knock-up something delicious, as good as you would get in any nursery kitchen. Stockpot with mash and peas – but it would be fabulous mash and great peas. But if the chef is pissed off and the waiting staff has annoyed him, he's more likely to get a load of grog and cover it in a béchamel sauce, rendering the whole lot inedible.

Some places are very generous with staff grub. The Anchor and Hope in Waterloo, for example, give their staff incredible food and at the River Caff all their team have a sit-down dinner at eleven thirty with a glass of wine. Others, however, are actually quite shocking. There's a place around the corner from us that gives their staff baloney, mustard and white bread from the corner shop, while the customers, the other side of the door, dine on some of the finest freshly plucked ingredients money can buy. We try to tread a thin line between finances and keeping people happy. So sometimes they might get a bit of stewing steak or a lasagne but it really depends on what is left in the budget. Today, judging by the look on Gina's face,

Andrew's right royally pissed off with everyone and has gone for the béchamel sauce.

'Everything OK in here?' I ask as I approach the back of the room, not really wanting an answer. There is a vague murmur in the affirmative. 'Jorge?' He looks up at me. 'Can I have a word?'

I am actually not going to broach the subject of his flirtation with the Russians, I am much more interested to hear how our Mr Stone got on. Did he like his steak? Did Jorge manage to charm the pants off him? Are we going to get a shit review? Jorge replies that short of going on all fours and sucking the man off he could not have been more effusive.

'You know I would, for you,' he smiles, 'but I don't think he dances at my end of the nightclub.'

'I don't know, he didn't look that fussy to me.'

Jorge insists that he tried to give him free pudding, some wine and a little digestif, all on the house, all of which Mr Stone refused. But he left a tip and smiled and said thank you, so it was not all bad.

'I think four stars,' says Jorge, half-closing his eyes.

'What are you? A fucking clairvoyant now?'

'I just feel it.' He shrugs. 'Just as I know we are going to have all the annoying tables in first.'

You don't need to be able to see dead people to know that the the evening crowd in a restaurant are always the most irritating. Either they are coming for a 'quick bite' before the theatre or they are on some sort of bloody food deal. I don't mind the theatre crowd that much. At least they are in and out, although they tend not to tip very much, and they are not going to sink a bottle of wine and chug back nose-bleedingly expensive cocktails. Thankfully, though, they don't block the table and we can normally kick them out quite quickly and fill the space with someone else who's prepared to open up their wallet.

But it's the food voucher customer I can't bear. There are these poxy schemes all over London that discount food, which we occasionally buy into when our bookings, to put it tactfully, aren't quite what they should be. So we sign up to something like Toptable or Taste of London, or some *Evening Standard* thing, where diners can come and eat for half price, or 20 per cent off, or for £30 with a free glass of champagne. And it is nearly always something that I live to regret.

The problem is that they are always such a bunch of tight-arsed lemon suckers and they don't play the game. The idea is that we, the restaurant, don't actually lose money when taking the booking and letting them in, but we sure as hell never make any either. They are supposed to come and fill the place up a bit. We take them as early evening Polyfilla, plugging in the gaps and filling in the corners. But they are supposed to play their part. Which of course they don't. They never bloody do, and I don't know why I am ever surprised as they always, without fail, stick to the deal. They never order anything more than the sodding free glass of champagne. They will never go off the set menu. They never deviate. They only ever order their free fizz and a jug of fucking tap. You can walk past the table and see a clean mains plate, a clean pudding plate and two drained glasses of champagne. You ask them if they might want a cup of coffee, casually mentioning that you would have to charge them, and they refuse. They always bloody refuse! And they ask for the bill. They are evil and annoying and I can't tell you how much we hate them. If I can possibly avoid letting them in, I do.

I am not quite sure why we have any voucher tossers in tonight, especially this close to Christmas. I think Caz has hooked us with some deal with *Times* readers, where we give away a free drink, so I am hoping they might show a bit of class and follow up their complimentary beverage with a bottle of wine.

No doubt they'll order the second cheapest bottle on the list. Those who know nothing about wine always do. They'll sit for a second, like rabbits in headlights, bamboozled by the list, too nervous about looking like a mean tightwad to order the cheapest bottle on the list, so they go for the second cheapest. It's a given, which is why we always mark that one up higher than most. I have to say, if in doubt, go for the house. We've normally got a deal on it, which is dependent on volume, so we are usually quite keen to sell it. Hence the reasonable price. Don't go for the second cheapest bottle, because we have quite obviously seen you coming.

The psychology of a menu is fascinating. If you look at it carefully, the way it is worded, the way it is laid out, you can see what the restaurant wants you to order. We'll pop a box around it, place it in the top right-hand page, give it a longer billing so it sticks out. We'll also try and spread the suggestions across the board so no one part of the kitchen is more over-loaded than the other. If one part of the kitchen is being slammed while the others are idle then we're deeply in the shit.

The other week I was out at some groovy Spanish tapas place in Borough and I saw 'black rice' all boxed up and pretty sitting in the corner of the menu, like a sexy siren on the rocks beckoning diners over. It was a 'house special' priced at £6.80 and I thought no wonder they're keen to flog it. £6.80? It really is money for old rope/rice. The GP on that is outrageous. Equally, you can practically hear the whole kitchen weep when everyone at the table orders the black cod. It was hiding away in the menu, it wasn't boxed, we're not supposed to sell as many as that! At about £100 a kilo, you lose 40 per cent of that when you defrost it, so it effectively sets you back £140 a kilo, making it the most expensive thing coming out of the kitchen but with the least amount of mark-up. The margin on that is enough to make anyone close up shop.

Expensive wines are a similar story. Low down the list, we mark them up four or five times. So your £5 bottle of wine in the off-licence is £15–£20 at the table. But with expensive wines we tend to go for a cash mark-up. So a bottle of '79 Petrus that is £1,270 a bottle in a wine merchant would probably cost around £2,000 a bottle at the table, which is not even twice the price, but is a handy £720 cash mark-up, enough to keep the wolf from our door. So often the more expensive the wine, the better the value to the customer.

Not that any of these early birds are ever going to go any-where near a bottle of wine, let alone expensive wine. It's the set menu, the tap and the free glass of fizz. My only hope is that I can get them in and out of here as quickly as possible.

Turning tables is key to our industry and it is the most in-exact science. On a busy night most places try and have about 80 per cent bookings and 20 per cent walk-in. The thing about a walk-in table is that you can turn it three times in a night as opposed to a booked table which, in a smart restaurant, you can only really turn twice. There are some places in the centre of town where the ten-thirty dinner booking does exist and you can really keep the pressure up on the kitchen right till the very end. But here, in gentle Mayfair, outside of Soho and Covent Garden, we can only really stretch to turning a booked table twice and sometimes we don't even manage that.

However, in an ideal world, you turn the booked table twice and the walk-in three times. With the walk-in your aim is to do: six thirty to eight, eight to nine thirty, and then nine thirty to eleven. That is obviously a very tight fit and you can only get away with it if you have a bar where you can park people and a selection of tables where you can juggle an overrun to eight fifteen and nine forty-five. You also need to have a maître d' who is charm personified, plus a hot restaurant where the customers are desperate enough for you to be able to call the shots. The process is relatively simple. You astound the customer that you might actually have a table: he is so lucky there was a cancellation, what with all those fabulous reviews (despite the fact that you have six tables going begging), but you say he can have it only on one condition, that you have to have it back by eight. Usually the customer is so pleased, delighted and amazed that you can fit him or her in that they will agree to anything. This charade is repeated three times in the night, and hopefully these tables have really paid their way and made up for the table of four who were all on some sort of special needs diet and drank nothing but a jug of tap for the whole night.

Obviously there are customers who get pissed off with the idea of turning tables. We have some very privileged, very entitled people living in the capital these days who think that once they have booked a table they can do with it what they like. They can add to it, take away from it, and think it is their right to stay there as long as they like, despite the fact that when they booked the table they were told we'd need it back at nine thirty. I may be in hospitality, but it is still a business. My tables need to work for me. In most restaurants you won't get more than an hour and a half cheek-time. You don't need two hours and if you do, then the kitchen is not working properly. Restaurants are in the business of selling food. They give you a slot and if you don't like it, don't go. We can't have a guy sitting there not eating or drinking when we have other customers. What sort of business is that? You wouldn't sit in a doctor's surgery, chatting away, reading the free magazines, while a queue of people built up behind you waiting to be seen.

There are loads of places these days which won't take bookings. Polpo, Bubbledogs, Bill Grainger. Personally, you wouldn't find me queuing up *anywhere* to spend my own money, but these places are packed. Their only problem is they have to rely on the goodwill of the customers to bugger off. If you have a no-bookings policy it is much harder to get rid of the squatters or campers. There may well be a queue of snappily dressed hipsters waiting at the door, but you can't move the other table on, as no out-time has ever been discussed or agreed upon. It's at times like this that the maître d' earns his money.

Or indeed this. I look up to see two couples walking in through the revolving door, brandishing their *Times* vouchers.

'Good evening, ladies and gentlemen.' Jorge genuflects and minces his hands. I wonder if he might actually be able to kill them with kindness? 'Your table? Can I offer you a drink? A bottle of water?'

'Thank you,' replies a slim, bespectacled bloke who appears to be the designated Alpha male. 'A champagne for me.' He nods around the table. 'A champagne? A champagne?' He looks back at Jorge. 'I think we'll all have a champagne.'

'Four glasses of champagne it is,' replies Jorge, spinning on the sole of his shiny shoes and rolling his eyes. I see Michelangelo at the other end of the room silently punch the air. They have clearly got some sort of bet on, to see if it is possible to get the voucher party to go off-piste, or indeed get piste, at all.

'Do you have a minute?' asks Anna, gently tapping me on the shoulder. I nod as I follow her over to the desk. 'So,' she says leaning and clicking the mouse on the restaurant computer. 'We have the birthday man, Mr Lister, and his party at the back on Table Ten and then we have Mr Kerr with his usual table and usual time and then we have Mr Russell.'

'OK.'

'But I have a problem, because Claridge's have just called asking if we can take a pop star and his group of six.'

'Really?'

'Yes. Well, we had all the concierges from most of the big hotels in last week and they are beginning to pay us back for our hospitality.' She smiles. I am never quite sure whether Anna has the driest sense of humour of any woman I have ever met or if she is actually completely devoid of irony.

'Did they say which pop star it was?'

'No,' she shrugs, appearing completely disinterested. 'I didn't ask.'

'Why not?'

'Because at the moment we are full.'

'What, no walk-ins?'

'No.'

Sadly we are not one of those places, like The Ivy, The Wolseley, Nobu or Scott's, that regularly holds back tables in case the rich, the famous and terribly important decide to patronize us with their presence at the very last minute. Sometimes we'll get a call from Sean McDermott at Scott's or Colin Short, the concierge at the Lainsborough, saying that Scott's or The Delaunay are full and can we squeeze them in, but we are a small place; we can do it at two or three days' notice, but usually we need a little bit more than a couple of hours.

'I am trying to contact a booking that was made today but I can't seem to get through. So I have no confirmation for a table of eight.'

'Eight?' Eight is as big as we get. I try not to overload the kitchen with too many of them, as it is usually a one-way ticket to chaos. 'Shall I call and check?' She hands me the number and I dial.

'Hello there, and thank you for calling Battersea Dogs and Cats Home, I am afraid we are busy . . .' comes the somewhat nasal, pre-recorded reply.

'Battersea Dogs Home?'

'I know, that's what I got.' Anna shakes her head.

'What is the customer's name?'

'Mr Russell. Mr Jack Russell,' she reads off the computer.

'Ha bloody ha.' I shake my head, more than a little pissed off. She looks at me, a small furrow bothering her brow. It is not her fault. It is a particularly English joke to play. Although quite who would do that I don't know. 'Don't worry.' I shake my head. 'Call up Claridge's and say a table has miraculously become available.' She nods. 'And please do find out who the hell it's for!'

7–8 p.m.

I'm standing outside the back of the mews having a quiet fag, ruminating over the Jack Russell booking. It only came in a couple of hours ago and Anna confirmed the man had a weird, breathy sort of voice. But it can't be Big Pete messing me around, can it? It seems rather a juvenile joke for someone of his unpleasant standing. I am paranoid. Surely he wouldn't be sending me a message this early in the game? As far as he knows I could be backing off – he couldn't possibly have heard my mad shouting rant. After all, the phone had cut out? Hadn't it?

'Excuse me, mate?'

I look up from contemplating the lack of polish on my Church's shoes. There's a skinny, twitchy-looking bloke standing in front of me. Both he and his clothes have seen better days. His skin has got that weathered, leathered look that comes from cheap booze and a park bench tan. His eyes are small and bloodshot and have a flimsy grey film across them and his nose is covered in burst red veins that criss-cross his nostrils like the branches of some exotic tree. He doesn't look well and he persists in scratching a large, sore-looking scab on the back on his left hand. I reach into my pocket, presuming he's after cigarettes.

'Have you got any oil?' I look at him, puzzled. 'You know, oil.' He scratches. 'Cooking oil?'

'Cooking oil?'

'Yeah.' He shuffles from one foot to another. 'For recycling?'

'Recycling?' This is a new one on me. I stub my fag out and go back into the kitchen. 'Barney?' I grab the first person I see. 'There's a bloke out the back wanting cooking oil to recycle.'

'Oh, cool,' he says, appearing completely unfazed. 'We've got some here we can give him.'

'I thought the council came round and collected the stuff and sent it off to one of those plants that burns it all to make electricity?'

'They do,' he sniffs, putting his knife down. 'But junkies have also worked out they can collect it and sell it on for a fix.'

'For how much?'

'I don't know. A quid a litre, something like that. However much a fix is.'

'And you give it to them?'

'Why not?' he says, walking towards the storeroom. 'We don't want it and it's a pain in the arse.' He bends down to pick up rather a large blue barrel. 'Is he outside?' I nod. 'Great,' he says, carrying the barrel towards the door. 'He can take this. I hate the smell of old oil, it's rank.'

'Right.'

'We're just helping out the community,' he grins.

I watch him haul the barrel outside and turn to go back through the kitchen.

'Check on!' shouts Andrew from the pass. 'One rabbit, two duck, one pork belly!'

'Yes, chef!' the brigade replies.

'Check on!' shouts Oscar. 'One crab salad, one fettuccine.'

'Yes, chef!'

'Oui, chef,' he corrects.

'Oui, chef,' the brigade shouts back.

I see Andrew shoot Oscar a look; it's enough to curdle the rice pudding soufflé. Fortunately, Oscar's too busy plating his crab to notice. I feel a knot growing in my stomach; I just hope they manage to get through the next few hours.

Back out the front and *The Times* table has managed to consume their starter in a matter of seconds. Their plates are licked so clean the KP could just as easily send them back out again with their main courses. Yet, unsurprisingly, they appear to be nursing their flutes of fizz like newborn infants, gently taking little tiny sips, one at a time.

Michelangelo walks past with a rather nice Burgundy. 'Table Four,' he says, nodding over his shoulder at the Voucher Vultures. 'I have a £20 bet with Jorge he can't sell them anything extra. Jorge thinks he can get them to buy wine AND coffee.' He chuckles. 'Poor bastard! He hasn't got a hope in bloody hell. I am *really* going to enjoy this evening.'

Another person gearing up for a big night is Adam. He's got the office party in of over a hundred colleagues, which I think is going to keep him more than busy. Well, I hope it is. I am slightly relying on him making a lot of money tonight. We could do with the cash flow; it is nearly Christmas, after all.

I remember the days when I was working and training with Maître d' Spencer, we used to see the office party season as a golden time to load the bill. I remember the biggest rip-off we ever did was for some computer software company and therefore the dullest people in the world. The MD was a regular; a nice, good-looking sort of a guy who would have lunch in the restaurant twice a week and we'd give him the same table and look after him. So he decided he wanted to hold an office party in the place. He said they'd come in late for lunch, so we could do the normal lunch service and then turn the tables for him. It was a great win-win situation for us. We had a hundred in the bar before lunch and did a hundred-cover lunch for them, with Christmas pudding, the works. Everyone was really enjoying themselves and getting pleasantly pissed and then, for some reason, it kicked off. The MD got so drunk he tried to punch Spencer out. I am not sure exactly how it happened, but he went from being a nice affable soul into a drunken psychopath in the space of two hours. It was extraordinary. I had to call the police to get rid of him. They took him away, kicking and spitting into the blood wagon, and then he spent the night in the cells.

193

Next we found his PA snorting coke in the lavs. Now, there are ways of snorting coke in the lavs and getting away with it. A discreet trip to powder your nose is fine and nobody is any the wiser, that we can cope with. We expect it. In fact, we quite like it as you always drink more alcohol afterwards. I remember a mate of mine who worked at The Pharmacy (a trendy den of iniquity that sold food that was clearly surplus to requirements) used to tell ridiculous stories of rock stars and football stars chopping out lines next to the basins. He'd regularly have to go into the toilets and complain: 'Boys, is that the best that you can do?' To which they'd politely apologize and retire to the cubicle.

But being caught face down, nostrils glued to the cistern, with the door open, shouting like a leery navvy at six in the evening, is not the way to do it. She was so high and rude and had a top lip covered in smeared coke residue that Spencer decided enough was enough. He called Danny, the barman, and me over and said, 'How much have we done on these computer tossers?'

'Not bad,' replied Danny.

'How not bad?'

'Not bad. Not brilliant yet, though.'

'Can we make it brilliant?'

'Yes, we can!' he enthused like some motivational Bob the Builder.

This was the cue for Danny to notch up the cocktails and write down three drinks when he sold two. He was also to start offering out drinks that were not agreed to on the original contract – so spirits and champagnes – when they only ever asked for wine. I then followed Spencer upstairs where he asked the head waiter how many cases of wine we'd shifted.

'Four,' came the reply.

'Is anyone sober?'

'Only that bloke in the corner and he's leaving.'

'Can we rack it up?'

'By how many?'

'How many can we get away with?'

'Another three?'

'Cases?'

'Cases.'

'Do it.'

You can hardly blame him. The PA's been snorting coke like a Dyson DC35 cordless, the MD's been arrested and taken to the cells for the night, he can charge what he likes – so we hit them for £100,000. We thought £1,000 a head was pretty reasonable. They paid. But I'm not sure if the bloke ever came back.

The only other time of year when restaurants can really take the piss like that is on Valentine's Day. Valentine's Day is the gift that keeps on giving and the more commercial and hideous it becomes the more we enjoy it.

Everyone knows it is the worst night of the year to go out to dinner. People who normally don't go out to eat go out to eat, and there's all that weight of expectation and all that tension. As a restaurateur you know you can't ever really give them the orgasm they want, you're just going to give them dinner. So it's a difficult night. The boys know they have to take the girls out, and the girls expect it. We, having had a relatively lean January, need to make hay while the poor chap's bollocks are in a cupid's vice. As a result Valentine's night is all about a set menu, just like New Year's Eve, which is another mug's night out when we force you to dig deep. So the poor bloke sits there, not talking, not wanting to be there, drinking the champagne when he'd rather be on red wine, knowing he's going to be stung for £300 for two at the end of it all. And he knows he probably won't even get laid. No wonder they always look so miserable.

I go and stand outside the front of Le Restaurant and give Adam a call, just to check that he is set and fine for tonight.

'Yeah, it's all great, mate,' he shouts down the line above the loud music. 'They seem to be a nice bunch. Mind you, we're only a drink in, call me back in an hour!' He laughs.

I hang up to see three very attractive-looking girls, with high clicky heels, expensive handbags and year-round tans, go through the revolving door. One of them looks vaguely familiar, as if she might present some programme on the TV – or perhaps she's one of those women who is snapped 'flaunting her curves' or 'looking worrying thin' while going about her business, in the *Daily Mail*. Either way, I have seen her before. I watch as Jorge meets and greets the girls and places them at the front table in the window. Clever Jorge. You always put the pretty girls at the front.

Dressing a restaurant, sitting the clientele is an art form. There are good tables (facing the door with a clear view of the room, so you can see all the comings and goings and be seen). Bad tables (near the loo, behind a pillar, right in the door draught, at the back, near the kitchen). The prestige tables tend to be booths, the corner tables where you can see and not be seen. But it depends on the diner and depends on the place. In The Wolseley it is all about the inner circle, anywhere else is Siberia. At The Ivy it's the tables on the left as you first come in. At Sheekey's it's the far right dining room. At Colbert it's the corners and the left-hand corner table as you come in is supposedly the best. In Nobu Berkeley Street it's the right-hand side of the room by the window upstairs. At Le Caprice, it's Table Seven, Princess Diana's table, which everyone wants.

Some people like to be seen. The likes of Lindsay Lohan prefer a centre table, while others, like Madonna, sit with their backs to the room. Kate Moss apparently doesn't care where she's put – she's far too rock 'n' roll to mind. It is always the most insecure people who kick up a fuss. But as a rule, you put your stars/your slebs/your VIPs, or WKFs as we call them – Well Known Faces (the letters VIP always look so gauche when written down) – in the front two corners and in the two tables on the left-hand side as you come in. The pretty girls go at the front. The A gays go next to them, as they spend money and are always up for a laugh. Then it's the tables with groups and mixes. Odd numbers are always the best, as they look less formal and dull. So three blokes and two girls. Or better, three girls and one bloke. The straight fours and couples are put close to the fat Russian men, and the least alluring of all, the four Japanese businessmen, go right at the back, tucked away behind a pillar as there really is nothing to see there.

I always find restaurant etiquette rather interesting. Women are supposed to sit looking out at the room, and the bloke is supposed to have his back to the room, feasting his eyes on nothing but his charming guest/wife/mistress. But you'd be surprised how often this is not the case. Just as many men no longer pull out or tuck chairs in for their female guests, I am not sure whether it is ignorance when a bloke forces the woman to sit with her back to the room, or whether the man is just a cock. Either way, good manners are a dying breed and I have to say that when any of us see a bloke sitting like that, chest out, we do all think he's clearly a bit of a dick.

'Ah, Mr Andreyev!' I hear Jorge exclaim behind me as a brace of Russians arrive with their unfeasibly pneumatic wives/girls on the clock. 'Your usual table?'

'Of course!' says Mr Andreyev, giving Jorge a hearty hug and the sort of hefty neck-slap you generally give a prop forward as he charges off a rugby pitch. Jorge practically topples over with such immense physicality. 'This is my friend from Novosibirsk, Ivan Sergeev.'

'Good evening, sir,' smiles Jorge, still shaking from the impact. 'Novosibirsk, you say? Here's your table, gentlemen.'

There is something sublimely boring about rich people in that they always want the same thing. They want their same table and they want the same food they ordered last time. I had a friend who used to run one of those extremely expensive resort hotels who said that as your average millionaire checked out of his seaside bungalow on stilts after Christmas, he'd book exactly the same villa for exactly the same two weeks the following year. It is almost as if the richer you are, the less you like being surprised. Perhaps their real lives are so stressful, and they are so preoccupied by having all that lolly, that they find it impossible to eat anything but caviar, lobster and foie gras. I mean, we all know those things are nice enough to eat, but all the time? Surely there are other things to try? So, for some reason Mr Andreyev has practically moved into Le Restaurant by deciding to patronize our place at least a couple of times a week, either for business lunches or a dinner in the evening. He likes the same table and he always orders the same food – beef carpaccio and the steak. He is undoubtedly on something like the Dukan, or DoCan't, diet, but, sadly for his waistline and probably his nutritionist, he always finds Giovanna's puddings irresistible.

I look across at Gina who seems to be settling into the bar well. She is only really mixing the aperitifs – the odd Russian Standard vodka here, a Sipsmith's gin and tonic there. What can I say? We are a Russian Standard bar here at Le Restaurant. They have the best reps, the best wholesalers and more money than God. The company is owned by a Tatarstani businessman, Roustam Tariko, who also owns the Russian Standard Bank and is worth about £1.1 billion. Their ambition is to make Russian Standard as big as Smirnoff and I am only too happy to help them on their way. Anyway, Gina is looking happy and rather decorative. I smile across at her. This could work.

I am just about to go over and have a chat with her when out of the corner of my eye I see the weirdest thing happen. Luca is walking towards the Voucher Vultures with two plates in his hand. One is belly pork and the other is the spatchcock chicken. He's got some momentum going. Then, for some reason he has to swerve around Mikus and suddenly the chicken slips off the plate, along with the couscous and a harissa sauce, and straight into the open handbag belonging to one of the pretty girls. Luca doesn't miss a beat. He serves the belly pork and heads straight back to the kitchen to order another chicken. Meanwhile I am left standing there, with Jorge next to me, both of us slack jawed.

'Jesus!' whispers Jorge, finally. 'Did you see that?'

'Yup.'

'And it's Marc Jacobs.' Trust him to be able to spot a label in a dimmed room at fifteen paces.

'How did that happen?'

'Why didn't he stop? Now one of us has to sort it out,' sighs Jorge.

'She hasn't even noticed,' I say, looking at her leaning in, running her hands though her long, clean, blonde, blow-dried hair. She is going to hit the roof. 'We could always not say anything?'

'What, and let her go home with a warm chicken in her bag?'

'Why not?'

'I think she just might guess where it came from.' Jorge shrugs and pops his best smile on. 'You did the dead man today, let me do the woman with a chicken in her bag.'

I watch him go over and very discreetly whisper something in her ear. She turns, looks down, looks up, and looks horrified. But before she can really react properly Jorge has picked up the bag, covered it in a napkin and disappeared out the back. I follow up the rear.

'I am so sorry, madam,' I say, arriving at the table. 'I can't think how it happened. We shall obviously pay for it to be dry-cleaned. Do let me offer the whole table some champagne. On the house.' Fortunately her friends appear to find the whole thing slightly more amusing than she does.

'It's a very expensive bag,' she begins, looking towards the kitchen to see where it's gone. 'And it's got my life in there. My mobile. Literally everything.'

'I can tell,' I agree. 'And we shall have it as good as new in no time.'

'It *is* new,' she says. 'And the lining is silk.'

'Silk,' repeats one of her friends, being a little more supportive, cocking her head to one side with concern.

'I am sure,' I concur. 'And we will absolutely sort it out. It's entirely our fault.'

'Well, it was hardly mine, was it? I was just sitting here,' she says.

'I know, I know, and we will sort the whole thing out. Here! Here it is.' I see Jorge come smiling out of the kitchen. 'Here's your bag.'

Jorge walks towards the table carrying the black and gold Marc Jacobs bag, devoid of chicken, couscous and harissa.

He has its more traditional contents in a white paper bag.

'So, madam,' he smiles. 'Here is your phone, all fine. Your purse, all fine. Your other things, all fine and your bag . . .'

That is looking distinctly less fine, I have to admit. The cherry-red silk lining is greasy and smeared and there is a distinct stench of chicken. Fortunately Gina arrives at that precise moment with a chilled bottle of Ruinart Blanc de Blanc. Not quite the bottle of house that I was after – this goes for £90 a bottle.

'Some bubbles, ladies.' I am now smiling so hard my cheeks are actually hurting. But there is so much oohing and aahing from her other girlfriends at the free fizz that Little Miss Chicken Bag is forced to join in the champagne appreciation society.

'I am sure it will be fine,' she says eventually as she knocks back a large swig of fizz. Funny how everything always looks a little better after some bubbles. No doubt we will get a massive dry-cleaning bill, but for the moment, any scene has been avoided. Which is all one can really hope for. I must remember to give Luca a bollocking at the end of the evening. How the hell he managed to pull that juggling trick off, I shall never know.

Just then the Russian, Mr Sergeev, shoots his hand in the air and clicks his fingers. He is looking directly at Gina. She stares back at him. He clicks his fingers again. She remains rooted to the spot.

'Girl!' he demands, adding another click. 'Girl!'

'Oh, I am sorry,' she says in her heavy Danish accent as

she ambles over to the table, 'were you referring to me?'

'Girl,' he says, nodding.

'You see, it takes more than two fingers to make me come.'

I just manage to contain my loud snort of laughter. I like her style, although I'm not sure it's conducive to working in a Michelin-starred restaurant where the customer is always right and you have to stand and smile and suck it all up. But she has a certain something about her. Maybe Adam could use her in Le Bar?

'I am sorry?' replies Mr Sergeev, his English still clearly in need of some practice.

'Good, just so long as you are,' she says. 'Now, how can I help you?'

I leave the Russian ordering a bottle of Ruinart, the sight of which has whetted his appetite, and I wander past the Voucher Vulture table. They are still nursing their one glass of house champagne, despite Jorge's best efforts, and have now moved on to pudding. They've all gone for the blood orange jelly and vanilla ice cream.

'Excuse me?' asks one of the men. 'What is this?' He points to what looks like droplets of blood scattered across the plate and another small puddle on top of the ice cream.

'Oh, it is nothing, sir,' I hear Mikus say. 'A little extra jelly.'

'Oh, right,' he nods. 'Because it looks like blood.'

'Blood? Oh no,' says Mikus, his ears pinking slightly. 'It is just a little extra bit of blood orange.'

As he walks away from the table, I grab him by his elbow and match him stride for stride back into the kitchen.

'What the hell *is* that?' I hiss in his ear.

'Blood,' he whispers.

'Blood!'

'Yes. There's been a little bit of an accident in the kitchen.'

8–9 p.m.

Mikus is clearly the master of understatement. There is not a bit of an accident in the kitchen, there's a fucking great car crash. It's like something out of a Tarantino movie. First of all, Barney, the commis chef, is sitting slumped on the floor, his arm in the air, his face as white as a sheet and there are pools of blood on the floor and all over the pass. And secondly, Andrew and Oscar are rolling around on the floor, in amongst the blood, the slops of water, and the curls of vegetable peel, smacking ten tonnes of shit out of each other.

'What's going on?' I just manage to refrain from shouting as I don't want the customers to hear.

'I've cut myself,' says Barney, his head lolling slightly. 'My finger.' He waves a blood-soaked tea towel at me. 'It's not as bad as it looks.'

'Well, it looks pretty shit to me,' I say.

'Get your hands off me!' yells Oscar, flat on his back, pinned to the floor under Andrew's substantial thighs. His fists are flailing, somewhat ineffectively, at Andrew's chest. Andrew throws a big punch which lands on Oscar's left cheek. Jesus, that must have hurt! A spray of snot and blood flies across the room. Oscar screams and pounds Andrew's chest even harder.

'You're a cunt! You know you are!' Andrew shouts, showering Oscar's face in gob.

'Get off me, you lunatic! You're fucking MAAAAD!' With one almighty push, Andrew goes flying across the room and lands, skidding into a pool of filthy water, under the sink.

'Can someone get me a bandage?' comes a plaintive cry from the other side of the kitchen.

'Service! Table Six!' says someone. I turn to see Matt, stepping over Oscar's dishevelled, blood-spattered body to man the pass. He looks completely calm, as if he's on a different planet. 'Service!' he repeats. Both Luca and Mikus stare at him, unable to comprehend exactly what he is saying. 'Go!' He shoves two pork, one steak, one rabbit towards them over the pass. 'Go and serve people.'

Finally the words sink in and the two waiters pick up the trays and take them through the swing doors.

'What the hell is happening here?' I ask, looking from one filthy head chef to another.

'The man's a cunt!' declares Andrew, getting up from under the sink. 'I can't work with him.'

'You don't have to,' I state, trying to calm the whole thing down. 'You're leaving.'

'I am leaving now.'

'You can't, you can't leave now, not in the middle of service, you really can't.' I realize I sound like I'm begging. But the restaurant is full, all the orders are piling up, there is no way Andrew can walk. I am pretty sure Oscar would be able to get some food out but he doesn't know all Andrew's recipes and it's a complication we really don't need. 'Honestly, mate, I'm sure we can sort it out.'

'You don't do that!' sneers Andrew and points a sharp, threatening finger. 'Cunt!'

'Man!' Oscar puts his hands up like he's surrendering in a gunfight in some cheap Western. 'All I did was borrow a knife.'

'Not *a* knife, you arsehole. MY knife!'

Oscar should have known that would not go down well. Most chefs hate it when someone else uses their knives. They love their knives, often more than their children, and they'll carry them, very sweetly and gently, from job to job, tucked up in their knife roll. They are very expensive, which is why chefs don't like lending them out, but they are also personal, part of the craft. They are the tools of greatness and that can't be shared. Well, that's what a great big egomaniac like Andrew thinks. Oscar, on the other hand, just needed to chop some parsley.

Or at least that's what I manage to glean from the brigade over the next five minutes. Oscar borrowed the knife. Andrew lost his rag and, unfortunately for Barney, he was caught in the middle and Andrew somehow managed to slice Barney's hand during the altercation. Barney then fainted because he hates the sight of blood, which is apparently why he prefers working veg in the first place.

Chefs have fallen out over less. And some feuds have gone on for years. Gordon vs. Marco is one of those most entertaining: the language used and the methods of subterfuge have kept the rest of us riveted from the wings for nearly twenty years. It is like some game of cat and mouse or, more aptly, Tom and Jerry, with one taking a camp swipe at the other and the other flouncing a swipe back. It's a load of old handbags really.

It all stems from the Harvey days when Gordon worked for Marco (1988–91) and Marco laid into Gordon so hard that Gordon started to cry. He was planning on leaving, and no one likes it when their sidekick decides to up knives, particularly if he's a talented sidekick. So Marco shouted and Gordon cried. Although, Marco did subsequently remark: 'I didn't *make* Gordon cry. He *chose* to cry.' Whatever, the animosity between the pair is continuously fuelled by little outbursts and flurries designed to wind each other up. Marco famously used to travel around with a Gordon Ramsay business card. The Ramsay was spelt 'Ramsey', just to irritate Gordon. And Ramsay admitted recently that he was the one who'd stolen the reservation book from Aubergine, only to blame it on Marco, apparently to prevent Marco from taking over as head chef. Marco then accused Gordon of not being able to cook because he's always on the telly; Gordon subsequently arrived with TV cameras to Marco's third wedding, although quite why he'd been invited in the first place is anyone's guess. It's ludicrous, and they are obsessed with each other; it's a perfect case of familiarity breeding contempt. Marco is notoriously difficult to get on the phone – he never picks up – however, leave a message saying something like: 'I hear Gordon's . . .' and you'll never be called back quicker.

But that's not to say that things can't get quite tetchy. Gordon's split with Marcus Wareing, when Marcus decided to leave the fold to set up on his own, is not quite so entertaining.

'If I never speak to that guy for the rest of my life it wouldn't bother me one bit. Wouldn't give a fuck,' said Wareing on leaving Gordon, despite the fact that Gordon was best man at his wedding. 'My advice to him is: put a gun to my head, shoot me, put me in a box and bury me because if you don't, I'll come back and come back. I'll never give up until I get where I want to go.'

The problem is that they have all graduated from the same charm school, which was started by Marco, curated by Gordon and whose head boy now is Marcus. Marco used to shout and scream and throw things and, much like children learn from their parents, so do the others. So Marco's famous story of hurling the Oak Room cheeseboard at the wall because some poor sod had put too small a piece of cheese on it, and others of him shoving chefs in the bins for 'time outs' or cutting holes in someone's uniform, like a colander, because they complained of being too hot, are legendary and a simple precursor to Gordon's hurling oysters, chucking bottles of truffle oil, calling everyone who annoys him a cunt or covering a commis in hot risotto.

Marcus is not that dissimilar. 'I bollocked people like Gordon,' he said. 'I acted like Gordon.' But when you work off and on for someone for nineteen years, and 'side by side, six days a week, for two solid years', things are bound to get hot, intense and to rub off.

'Never, ever did I get to bed before two,' Wareing once said. 'Never ever.'

Even the lovely, talented Clare Smyth, another Ramsay protégé, is not immune. 'I don't think twice about grabbing hold of a guy and screaming in his face if he gets it wrong,' she once opined.

However, all this appears insipid child's play when you hear that US chef and author Anthony Bourdain once had a young cook stripped, covered in blood and wrapped in cling film before popping him in the freezer. But then again, Bourdain would threaten a junior to hurry up or he would 'tear out his eyes and skull fuck' him.

Fortunately, Andrew is not yet at the skull-fucking stage with Oscar, but left to their own devices for a couple of hours, who knows? We all have our war wounds. Raymond Blanc had his nose, cheek and jaw broken when another chef threw a saucepan in his face. Tom Aikens allegedly branded another chef on the back with a hot palate knife and was fired from Pied à Terre. The chef ended up in A&E. The worst case I heard was of a head chef bottling a waiter. They'd been up drinking after their shift and the head chef lost it and hit the waiter over the head with a bottle. The waiter had twenty-three stiches. The police were called but no charges were ever pressed; there is a warped honour amongst culinary thieves.

I always think you are allowed to scream and shout if it's your own house on the line. If you've got your own money in the place, it seems reasonable to be able to lose your temper. Which is what I am on the verge of doing if these two idiots don't get back to work.

'Listen,' I say. 'We're full. We've just under three hours of service left. We've got some pop star coming in later— '

'Who's that?' asks Barney, obviously feeling a little better.

'How the hell do I know? Do I look like a bloke who follows the pop charts? Get this blood cleaned up, bandage up that hand, and let's get on with it.'

Oscar's pulled himself up off the floor. He looks even worse than when he came in this morning, if that were possible. His curls are flat, his face is smeared with mucus and blood, and he's going to have a massive black eye in the morning.

'Sorry about the knife,' he mumbles, pulling down his filthy whites. 'I had no idea it meant that much to you.'

Andrew doesn't say a word. He merely reaches across to take another tasting spoon out a large silver tin full of water next to the pass and pulls out a new order slip.

'One pork belly, two turbot, one steak,' he says.

'Yes, chef!'

I walk out of the kitchen slowly. I'm shattered and I am not sure how much longer I can keep doing this. I don't want to be in the micro-managing business, sorting out domestics. I want to be one of those restaurateurs who gets texted at one in the morning, just to be kept in the loop as to how many covers each of my highly profitable restaurants has done. I want to be able to have nights off, go on holiday, see my mates, not break up fights between hot-headed idiots who can barely write their own names. It's depressing. And not something I have been working this long in this business for.

'All OK backstage?' asks Jorge, looking more than a little tense. He's got a full room to manage and barely any food coming through the doors. The kitchen is in the shit and so is he.

'It is fine now,' I say. 'I'm sure we can claw it back. Just make sure the team keeps filling up everyone's glass.'

Talking of which, I am desperate for a drink. The restorative effects of my pint of lager are beginning to wear off. I decide I might sit quietly at the bar for a moment, not something I normally do, and down a quick vodka and tonic.

'Everything OK?' asks Gina, seeing the look on my face.

'Not great.'

'We could hear a lot of it in here,' she says. What is it with Scandis and the truth?

'Really?'

'It was quite loud,' she continues. 'I could hear a few "fucks".'

'Very Michelin star. Can I have a vodka? And tonic?'

'English measure?'

'No, something substantially stronger.'

While I sit and she pours me a drink, I feel my shoulders

come away from around my ears. There is always something so cathartic about sitting at a barstool having a drink. Maybe that's my problem – I have always found it easier to share with the person on the other side of the bar than I have with the women who followed me down the aisle. That was always Sketchley's gripe anyway, that I was never home, and when I was, I never told her anything. Gina arrives with a short, fat drink with a squeeze of lime and plenty of ice. It is almost as if she knows what I like.

'Here,' she says. 'I remember this is how you ordered it last night.'

So she does know how I like it. 'Was that before or after the jägerbombs?'

'Before. And anyway you only had two.'

'Two? How come you have total recall?'

'I don't drink that much,' she shrugs.

I take a long, cool glug. It hits the spot almost immediately. I feel it slip gently into my bloodstream and start to relax. Just then a flashbulb goes off outside. Then another. And another. Then there's a strobe effect, as another fifteen to twenty go off in quick-fire succession. There's some shouting and jostling and eventually a skinny little blond boy in a baseball cap squeezes through the revolving doors, with an entourage of eight. It appears our WKF plus extras have arrived.

They are a motley group. I am not sure what Claridge's are doing sending them to us because I'm sure they'd be a lot happier in a brasserie, my brasserie for example, where they can get chips with everything and lots of things 'on the side'.

We don't do anything 'on the side', we are not that sort of place, and we don't do chips, either. Although I am sure the kitchen could or would, given the right price. I remember Marco once charging an arrogant yuppie (they were called that in those days) £25 for a plate of chips. He said he'd hand cut them, blanched them and deep-fried them and it had taken him an hour (not actually him, surely?) so the cost was £25. The man had ordered a plate of chips, off menu, and had not been bothered to ask how much they might be, so obviously he could charge what he fancied.

Anyway, this lot – three women in their thirties and forties who appear to be in charge and five blokes all dressed in baseball caps with their trousers hanging off their thighs – all cluster around the desk looking a little uncomfortable.

'Hi, so sorry about all the paps,' says one of the women with a cantilevered cleavage and lots of fluffy blonde hair. 'Prinz Zee.' She leans over, resting her breasts on the front desk. 'We're nine.'

'Excellent,' I lie, feeling my takings for the evening slipping through my fingers. None of these boys look old enough to drink. 'I'll have Jorge show you to your table.'

'Can we go here?' She points a pink fingernail towards two tables in the window. 'Shove them together?'

'Actually, those tables are booked.'

'But we'd like to be in the window.'

I look through the glass, there are four or five photographers loitering on the pavement outside, fiddling with their equipment. The pop star obviously wants to be snapped.

I never quite understand famous people. They complain about press intrusion, then tip the press off themselves. How else would these guys be standing outside on the pavement tonight? It happens all the time. I remember a mate of mine had Catherine Zeta Jones and Michael Douglas's security people crawling all over his restaurant for weeks before the couple came to dine. They checked the entrance, the exits, he was told on no account was he to alert the media, which of course he did not. He was also told not to put them on the tables in the window, otherwise known as the 'glamour tables'. So he chose a quiet corner spot, only to have them breeze in and take a table at the window, where they were met by a blanket of flashbulbs. He looked out of the window and across the street, to see a bank of paps ready and waiting for their intimate close-up. He said Tom Cruise and Nicole Kidman, when they were together, were the same. The security was even more thorough, but this time they came in the back, arriving and leaving in separate cars. He left out the back and she did the photo call out the front.

But it is quite simple to go out to dinner and not be bothered, even if you are a Hollywood movie star. You go to your local, round the corner, or somewhere quiet that doesn't attract that sort of crowd. I never really understand the 'don't-snap-me' pics of celebrities leaving The Ivy or Nobu; if you don't want your photo taken, don't go near the place. However, if you want to publicize your dramatic weight loss, your new haircut or husband, have dinner at The Ivy. It's not exactly rocket science.

I have a quick conversation with Jorge about where to place

Prinz Zee or whatever he's called, and we decide that in order to keep Claridge's happy we'll bend over backwards and accommodate them. We put the two fours together and split the eight towards the back of the restaurant. Which seems to make everyone happy. Especially the two ladies and their chicken-bag chum who seem to recognize the diminutive Zee. The giggle factor goes up as the pop star's entourage approaches. I'm sure it won't be long before they start getting their i-Phones out, sneaking photographs.

Food is beginning to come out of the kitchen again, which is rather a relief. The Russians are on the second bottle of Ruinart and it looks like the Voucher Vultures might be ready to leave. As predicted, they have turned down any extras, and it looks like Jorge is going to lose his bet. We still have a couple of tables about to arrive and we'll turn the voucher table as soon as we can kick them out into the street, to join the paps. Prinz Zee laughs. A few more flashbulbs go off. I think I might go outside and have a word. After all, how many photos of what looks like a giggling twelve-year-old drinking Coke Zero does the Fourth Estate actually need? Suddenly Michelangelo walks past me with a small smile on his face. He is carrying a bottle of Louis Roederer Cristal at £350 a bottle towards Prinz Zee's table. All of a sudden I find myself warming to the man.

My phone goes. It's Adam. I walk towards the door.

'Mate, we need you down here. I've got the police here and they need to speak to the licence holder.'

'Right,' I reply, my heart sinking. 'Trouble?'

'You could say that.'

'On my way.'

I am just about to walk down the street when a party of eight people come through the door. I look at Anna, she looks at me. They are young and well dressed.

'Hi,' says a particularly charming-looking chap. 'Table of eight.'

'Yes?' Anna sounds hesitant.

'Jack, Jack Russell?'

I'm afraid I walk straight out the door.

9–10 p.m.

Walking down the street I can see the blue lights flashing outside the Le Bar. It's always a good look to have the cops outside your place, I think; it's inviting, beguiling, good for custom. Not that I dislike the police in the slightest – we look after our local boys in blue. We have a very good relationship with them and it is essential that it remains so. We never call them out unnecessarily and we always remember them at Christmas. We are very generous with our festive bottles of whisky and cases of champagne, as the last thing we need in a knife fight is the police taking the long route round. Not that we have any knife fights; we're not that sort of place. But if you're a dodgy pub, with a dodgy licence holder, you'd be amazed how bad the traffic can be when you need a squad car.

'All right, chaps?' I say as I approach the two coppers who

are standing outside the bar. 'Evening.' They nod. 'I'm the licence holder here, what's going on?'

'A fight,' replies the shorter of the two.

'A couple of drunks,' sniffs the other.

'Any damage?'

'A couple of black eyes.'

'Really?' I'm surprised. It sounds little more than the punch-up I just refereed in the kitchen.

I walk in Le Bar just as the fighting drunks are frog-marched out of the place with their hands bound in white plastic hand-cuffs. Dressed in suits, with striped shirts and crooked silk ties, they look like a couple of beaten-up Billy Bunters. One of them has clearly come off much worse than the other. He's got a swollen right eye, a cut lip and a decidedly squashed-looking nose. This will certainly be a Christmas party he won't forget in a hurry.

Not that it seems to have put much of a damper on proceedings. The party appears to be continuing with little concern for their exiting colleagues. The music is loud, the lights are low and it's three-deep at the bar. Most of the women are sporting new festive party dresses. Red, sequins, velvet, and plunging necklines predominate. The blokes have barely re-accessorized since leaving work. They are, almost to the postboy, kitted out in shirts, ties and grey suits. A couple of standout wags have party hats on and a few are sporting streamers.

'What happened?' I quiz Adam when I find him in amongst the crowd. It's unlike him to call the police just for a fight. He's a great negotiator and normally manages to calm the most troubled waters. Except when he's pissed and high himself and then, of course, he's like a steroid-fuelled terrier with a virulent case of rabies.

'They wouldn't stop,' he says. 'I told them to pack it in about six times. I separated them twice and they just wouldn't cool off. I think they're both on some pretty crap cocaine because they were not giving up, no matter how many times I told them off. I had a word with the MD and he said get rid of them so they're going to get a P45 along their shit hangover tomorrow.'

'Which one's the MD?'

'He's the guy in the pink tie talking to that girl—'

'In the red sequin dress?'

'Yup.'

'How are we doing?'

'Not bad – shifting shit. I am pretty sure we'll be through all the pre-paid drink by about ten thirty and we'll be on to a cash bar.'

'I like the sound of that,' I smile. 'Oh, by the way, we've got Prinz Zee chugging back the Cristal down the road.'

'I didn't know he was old enough to drink?'

'So you know who he is then?'

'He's playing the O2 next week.'

'He's got that many fans?'

'Excuse me?' I turn around to see another police officer in front of me wearing a high-viz jacket. 'Are you the licence holder?' I nod as he gets out a notepad. 'Do you mind if I take a few details?'

While I stand and talk the constable through my name, age and address, etc., I can't help but think I am going to get Adam to take the wretched licence exam. If I bung him an extra five grand then he can deal with all this without me having to come down and have a chat every time some drunk eurobond dealer gets his fists out. The only reason my name is on the licence is because the last barman I had was so stupid he failed the test. Quite how he managed to do that I don't know. I studied for it the night before while drinking my way through a bottle of rather nice claret and came away with a 100 per cent pass. It has to be the easiest test I have ever done. The questions are multiple choice so it's like pinning the tail on the sodding donkey. They ask basic things such as: Is it illegal to sell alcohol to a prostitute? Er, yes? Extraordinarily, my ex-barman is not in a club of one; there are plenty of publicans, landlords and restaurateurs who fail the exam, which says rather a lot about the people in my industry.

It doesn't take long before the constable snaps his notepad shut and leaves. Over the other side of the bar I catch a look on Damon's face. He seems very intent on watching the policeman go.

'Adam?' He turns around. 'Could you keep an eye on Damon.'

'OK.' He looks up the bar and spots Damon; they both smile at each other.

'I think he might be up to something.'

'OK, mate,' he nods. 'Like what?'

'Dealing drugs.'

It has happened to me before. I had another Aussie barman, Rick, who came from Perth, the most isolated city on earth, which was one of the excuses he gave to me when I caught him. He said the bright lights of London had turned his head, that he was a small-time guy, that it wasn't a big deal. And I believed him because I liked the man. But the situation was untenable. We'd have streams of people coming into the bar but none of them would order a drink, as they wanted to be in and out as quickly as possible. They'd order a Coke along with their coke and that was it – much like Steve had witnessed earlier this evening. I remember going back to Rick's flat with him, while he continued to impress upon me quite how small-time he was. I searched the place and eventually found a suitcase under the bed, which exploded with money. There were thousands and thousands of pounds all scattered around the room and floating through the air. I kicked him out there and then and told him to never darken my door again. It transpired he was one of the main men operating around West London. I was furious. It nearly killed my bar because when you have a stinking egg like that, it pollutes the rest of the mix. The more Rick's reputation grew, the fewer real drinkers turned up at the place and the more transient the traffic. In the end, the takings were something like thirty-five cokes an afternoon. I should have been across it, but I was battling to get Le Restaurant set up and I had my mind on other things.

Back at Le Restaurant things are feeling significantly calmer. The mood in the kitchen appears to be a little better. Oscar and

Andrew are not exactly on joking terms, but they seem to be communicating, working together a little better and, most importantly of all, getting the food out. Barney has stuck his hand back together using a collection of blue catering plasters and is back in position, dipping beautifully cut savoy cabbage leaves into boiling water.

'Careful with the edges of your sea bass, Alfonso,' says Oscar as I walk past. Alfonso approaches the pass. 'What, chef?'

'They're too sharp,' Oscar points out. 'See here, they look better rounder, not with a sharp edge, you know softer. Like this.' He trims the edges off the sea bass. I stop to look. He's right. It's a better-looking plate. 'OK?'

'Yes, chef.' Alfonso nods, rolls his eyes slightly and heads back to his station.

I am not sure how many of my staff are going to remain once Andrew walks.

Back out the front and the Russians have moved on to the Cristal. Not to be upstaged by a teenager in a baseball cap they've started to competitive purchase. I suppose there must be nothing more galling for your average oligarch than to have your buying power brought into question by someone who cut his milk teeth on the Disney Channel. The Voucher Vultures have finally gone, only to be replaced by a middle-aged, balding bloke in specs who's eating on his own.

'I don't like the look of him,' says Anna as she follows my gaze.

'What do you mean?'

'He looks like an inspector.'

'Do you think?' She raises her finely plucked eyebrows. 'Michelin?' She turns on her black patent stilettos and walks slowly back to the front desk.

Shit! My blood runs cold. That's all we need, a fucking Michelin inspector. I watch him for a minute, my heart fluttering in my chest as a surge of nervous adrenalin courses through my veins. He looks the type, part-accountant, part-nit-picker. I have a terrible sinking feeling she is right.

'What's his name?' I ask her, following her to the computer.

'Mr Adams,' she replies with a click of the mouse. 'He booked two weeks ago.'

'For one?'

She nods. 'Who else but an inspector books for one, two weeks in advance?'

I go and grab Jorge. 'What do you think?' I ask, nodding as discreetly as I can at the bloke over my shoulder. 'Inspector?'

'Michelin?' he says, his eyes narrowing slightly. 'He looks like it. But you know they keep changing the type. They have women, too.'

'Fuck!' I whisper.

'Double fuck,' he agrees.

'Why tonight of all nights?'

They are entitled to come, of course. They are supposed to come in and check your standards aren't slipping, that you're still consistent, but it is the frequency that makes you paranoid. The more visits you get, the more likely it is you're going up or, more probably, down.

Getting a star puts you on the map. Just ask Ollie Dabbous and his packed reservations book. Or indeed look at Hedone in Chiswick, which was catapulted into the limelight when it picked up one star only fourteen months after it was opened by a former food blogger, Mikael Jonsson.

It's our equivalent of the Oscars, which is a little tragic when you think about how the whole thing was thought up by the Michelin tyre company as way to sell more tyres. The brainchild of Andre and Edouard Michelin, the guide, first published in 1900, was intended to encourage people to climb into their cars (with their Michelin tyres on, of course) and drive into the countryside in search of a charming, fine dining experience. By 1933 the brothers introduced the first country-wide restaurant listings and unveiled the star system for ranking food, with one star denoting 'a very good restaurant in its class', two stars being 'excellent cooking, worthy of a detour', and three stars 'exceptional cuisine, worth a special journey'.

And that's it. That's what all the fuss is about. Marco bust his balls to be the youngest chef in the UK to ever serve food that was 'worth a special journey'. It seems ridiculous that it matters so much. But it does. As far as we're concerned nothing else matters more. There are other guides such as Zagat and Harden's but none of them are Michelin. As Paul Bocuse, the chef who helped create the nouvelle cuisine movement, and whose restaurant near Lyons has had three stars for a record-breaking forty-five years, said, 'Michelin is the only guide that counts.'

And any chef who tells you he is not interested in the guide and stars is either lying, evidently not good enough, or has completely given up. Ask any chef who has won one, two or three and they will tell you exactly where they were when they heard. Andrew cried. He actually flopped down in one of the chairs at the back of the restaurant and cried like a toddler whose ice cream had been pinched. I have to admit I joined him, and then we both proceeded to get completely rat-arsed and called in the coke. We must have drunk for over fourteen hours so it wasn't pretty. But as Andrew said at the time, 'It makes eleven days off in seven months feel actually worth it.'

And it does. Financially it makes a massive difference. One star puts you on the map, two stars means your phone never stops ringing and three stars means you can charge what the hell you like. Here in the UK you can get away with £45–£50 for a main course and in France you can jack it up higher – £60 a main. So you can easily charge £150 a head without alcohol.

Even with one star your clientele changes. You can go from the funky coke and cabs brigade to gin and jag overnight. So you have to be careful. The last thing you want is for everyone to think that your restaurant has become a stuffy, boring place where you have to put a carrot up your backside before you sit down.

The guide has mixed things up a bit recently; they're trying to get a bit groovier. There is less of an emphasis on pale pink napery and dickie-bow service. They sent inspectors to New York quite recently in an attempt to capture a little bit more of the zeitgeist and they handed over three stars to the Chef's

Table at Brooklyn Fare, which is a tiny place consisting of one very talented man, César Ramirez, and eighteen chairs. And the food is delicious. When I went there they hadn't even got a liquor licence, so we had to bring our own booze which added to the fun as we shared glasses with other diners around the bar, including one couple who'd brought a particularly delicious port.

However, there is still plenty of chintz associated with Michelin and it is often accused of being too Franco-centric, preferring poncy food with heavy sauces and staff who interrupt to explain food you have just ordered. Which I suppose is true in parts. But I don't really care. All I'm interested in is keeping the sodding star, because once you've had a taste of Michelin madness you can't, don't, want to go back.

And it *is* madness; it is obsessive and addictive. Once you've got one star under your belt you want another, but you're also shit scared of losing the one you've got. Just as with most addictions, the first star is always the best; the second is known as the chef's star, so it is for the most brilliant/experimental cooking, and the third (and most elusive) is for the whole package – the service, the plates, the place.

There are only a hundred and four three-star restaurants in the world at the moment and the pressure to stay on the top of your game is immense. No one wants a demotion. Michelin was blamed for the suicide of Bernard Loiseau who shot himself in the head with a hunting rifle after hearing suggestions that he might be in the verge of losing a star. The man was a genius and a French icon with the Légion d'honneur (he was supposedly the inspiration behind the film *Ratatouille*). Chef and owner of La Côte d'Or in Burgundy, he had made it his life's ambition to be a three-star chef. Something he had managed to achieve and maintain since 1991. However, by 2002 Loiseau's classic cooking was losing ground to trendier fusion styles, his business was slowing and he was swimming in debt. *Le Figaro* published a story saying that he was skating on thin ice with Michelin. He needed the three stars to keep the finicky gastrobores coming. The loss of one star could mean as much as a 40 per cent drop in takings. In 2003 he managed to maintain his three-star status but still the rumours continued, again in *Le Figaro*, that his stars were on borrowed time. Two and a half weeks after the article was printed, and after a long day's work in the kitchen, he killed himself with a shotgun blast to the head. He was fifty-two.

'I'm going over,' I say. 'If he starts asking questions about the menu, then we know we're in trouble.'

Michelin inspectors always ask questions. They love trying to catch waiters out, to see if they're lying, making things up on the spot. Which, of course, we do all the time. Just so long as you warble on with a bit of confidence and a smattering of French or Italian, usually no one is any the wiser. They used to make up the names of the dishes at the River Caff. No one really spoke Italian so they'd cobble something together, hoped it sounded good and no one really cared.

'Good evening, sir.' I smile, checking him over for any inspector signs.

'Good evening,' he smiles back. He's perhaps a little too

jolly? 'I have a few questions . . .' That's it. He's an inspector. He's got questions. He's going to ask what is in every sodding dish. 'Can you tell me about the crab?'

What I can't tell him is that Andrew has the plates made up hours in advance and sitting in the fridge, or he did this morning. Let's hope Oscar's words then mean that we haven't slipped back into that old trick, because if anyone needs a plate of crab salad à la fucking minute it's this bastard. I explain to him the fresh provenance of every dish he quizzes me about. I tell him about the friends, relatives, parents and beauty regime of the steak and the marvellous life of the lamb. Husbandry, husbandry, husbandry. And I am practically grinding my teeth I am smiling so hard.

Finally I make an escape into the kitchen. Word has already reached them that the inspector is in and Oscar and Andrew are heads down, trying to concentrate. He's ordered the crab salad, the turbot and the rice pudding soufflé and all hands are very firmly on deck.

'No one fuck this up or I will fuck them and that is a fucking promise,' barks Andrew.

'Yes, chef!'

'Barney?' I say. 'What are you doing?'

He's got a whole load of salad leaves floating in a bowl of iced water. 'Crisping the lettuce,' he replies.

'How old is that?'

'Two, three, maybe— '

'Days?'

He nods. 'I'm working some life back into it.'

'Don't tell me it's for the crab salad?'

'There's nothing else left,' he says. 'There's been a run.'

'A run?'

'Fraid so.'

'So we are serving the Michelin inspector old leaves?'

'He won't notice when I've finished with them.'

There are plenty of tricks for reviving old food: shoving the lettuce in iced water, sprinkling the bread with a few drops of water and popping it in the oven to crisp up, even, if you're a really crap place, dipping the four-day-old fish into a bit of bleach and water. The only problem with that is it stinks; so you've got to cover it in a sauce, with plenty of tomato and garlic. Safe to say never order a fish stew in an armpit outlet on a Monday. Not that *we'd* ever do that. It's more than our star is worth, but I wouldn't put it past L'Italiano. I'd be amazed if anything made it out of their fridge without contracting herpes simplex at the very least.

Oscar has put himself in change of getting the crab out, while Andrew is on the main and I imagine Giovanna will make at least three rice pudding soufflés in order to send the best one out.

'Everything OK?' I ask as I stand at the pass sweating like a sixteen year old about to lose his virginity. 'This one counts, yeah? Consistency? Right? Everyone? Right.'

'Right,' nods Andrew, glaring at me from the heated lamps. His dark eyes are looking madder than ever, and as he slowly licks his spoon, his long, white-coated tongue runs all the way up the side. 'Salt!' he shouts.

'Yes, chef!'

Alfonso scurries over with a small bowl. Andrew shoves his fingers in the bowl, showers the sea bass in crystals and pops his spoon back into the sauce and licks it again. He then picks up a pan, takes a spoonful of roasted cauliflower purée and smears it across a plate; he lays the fish on top, fans out some savoy cabbage leaves and, using the same spoon, dribbles on a langoustine sauce. 'Service,' he says, still staring at me. You can almost hear the steam coming out of his ears. I suppose it is my fault for trying to teach such a cantankerous cunt to suck eggs.

Back in the restaurant, I am off to check if the inspector has wine or an aperitif when Michelangelo corners me by the bar.

'The Russians,' he says, his eyes larger than our petit fours saucers.

'Has the inspector got a drink yet?'

'Have you seen the Russians?'

'What?' I turn and look across. The two men are sitting there, as is one of the girls. 'And?'

'And look at the tablecloth, the tablecloth!'

I turn and have another look. I can see a pair of red-soled Louboutin shoes poking out from underneath the table.

'What is she doing?'

'What do you think?' he replies, his expression somewhat incredulous. 'Look at his face. The fat one.'

'Mr Sergeev?'

'I think he's about to come.'

10–11 p.m.

I have to say that's the first blow job we've had in the dining room during service in a while. Or indeed, ever. I do remember hearing from a friend about a well-nourished restaurant critic who once turned up very drunk at his place, with a rather venal and vituperative writer, plus two more plastered hackettes, only for one of the girls to disappear under the table to perform fellatio on the fat critic. My mate, who was maître d' at the time, couldn't believe it. Firstly, that the girl could find the fat critic's penis, when surely he himself hadn't seen it for years, and secondly, that she couldn't wait until the main course.

'It was during the starter!' he said.

'How big was the restaurant?' I asked.

'Not big enough,' he replied.

He had no idea what to do. The critic was important and he

couldn't boot him out into the street, scrabbling at his fly. Anyway, it ended in tears. The girl's. Apparently she came up for air, drank another shot of vodka and was so appalled by her own behaviour that she promptly ran out of the place in tears.

A blow job in the room is quite rare. We've had a few hand jobs and some pretty full-on footsie before, where the ladies – and I use that term loosely – have removed their underwear and the gentleman has taken off his shoes. They think they are being discreet, but you can usually tell by the silence at the table, or the concentrated look on the bloke's face. Plus we've had quite a few pairs of pants that have been cleared away along with the napkins, having been left behind on the floor. But normally if someone can't control their tumescence, they'll retire to the lavatories. We have endless liaisons in our toilets and, fortunately, they are little larger than anything you'll find on an airline, so you don't need a trick pelvis to enjoy them. Although sometimes you'd be amazed quite how athletic seemingly ungymnastic middle-aged customers are. A few weeks ago one of the cleaners called me over to show me the men's loo. We'd a couple who'd disappeared for about twenty minutes during dinner the night before, and here was the reason why. Halfway up the wall, to the right of the loo seat, were two perfect stiletto prints on the new cream paint. It was so weird. Everyone came in to investigate. She must have had extremely flexible hips to get her legs that high in the air. It was impressive. But you know, if you can manage it in a broom cupboard in Nobu, you can manage it anywhere. Talk to anyone at Nobu and they'll say it was the staff room, although Boris Becker himself said it was the stairs – as if that's any better!

'What shall we do?' I ask Michelangelo, still staring at the pair of red soles poking out from under the table. I glance around the room. I am desperately hoping no one else has noticed. But the WKF and his gang are too confident that everyone else is looking at them to see any of the other customers and the three girls on the next-door table are providing the perfect audience. It's the inspector I worry about. Although, you never know, he could throw in a couple of red knife and fork symbols, or couvert, our way denoting the restaurant is a 'pleasant place to be', with good décor and, indeed, service. But somehow I doubt it. 'How much longer do you think she's going to be?'

'Judging by the look on his face, not long,' replies Michelangelo.

'Do you think?'

We both stand and stare. It is hard not to. Mr Sergeev's face is puffed and pink with drink, his eyes are bulging slightly and there is a smirk of pleasure playing on his chapped lips. His forehead is covered in a dank film, his thin mouse hair that was combed carefully over the top of his smooth domed head when he arrived, now hangs in a few sweaty strings. His small mouth suddenly opens like a goldfish gasping for air. He raises his thin eyebrows with surprise, coughs once and then reaches for his glass of champagne.

'There,' nods Michelangelo.

'Really?' I'm pretty sure I'd make rather a lot more noise than that.

But he's right. The red-soled shoes move and a skinny black-clad backside emerges from under the cloth and the dark-haired woman appears, dabbing her mouth with a napkin. I look across at the inspector; he is fortunately busy picking his way through the last of his crab salad. I can't help but breathe a small sigh of relief.

'Oh, by the way,' says Michelangelo, 'have you heard that Jorge is planning to leave? Apparently he's been in negotiations for a while.'

'Yes.' I nod. I feel a smart of irritation – why am I always the last to know anything? 'It has been brought to my attention.'

There's movement from Prinz Zee's table as they all get up at once. There are five empty bottles of Cristal on the table and a pile of cash. He can come again any time he wants. He saunters over to the table with the three girls and, pushing his cap at a 45-degree angle, proceeds to give them all a high-five. This seems to go down well as the level of giggling and hair flicking reaches fever pitch. One of the girls gets out her phone and Zee poses next to the other two, sideways on, with his index finger pointing towards the ceiling like a gun. There is more laughing and the chicken-bag girl manages to snatch a kiss. I am hoping she is now so thrilled with her evening she'll forget the dry-cleaning bill. Zee and his entourage are about to leave when he turns and walks towards me. His fist is extended.

'Man,' he says, giving me a punch on the arm. 'Great evening.'

'Thank you.' I am not really sure if I am meant to punch him back. The man's barely capable of growing facial hair. I could be had up for child abuse. So I resist and fiddle with my cufflinks instead, like Prince Charles. 'I am glad you had a nice time.'

'Man, you've got a good place,' he nods, looking around the room nodding some more. 'Cool.'

I am not sure how many Michelin-star places he's ever eaten in but I'll take any compliment. 'I am glad you liked it.'

'Yeah,' he says. 'I met your PR, Caz, the other night. Great lady.'

'Caz?'

'Yeah, we had fun.' There is a vague snigger from a couple of the younger men in the entourage. 'We had, like, a very good time.'

'Excellent.' I smile. So this is Caz's handiwork. I must remember to thank her.

He ambles towards the door, his baggy trousers belted to the bottom half of his buttocks, his cap on sideways; even with a distinct heel to his trainers he can't be more than five foot six. Outside the paps who'd remained encamped despite the chilly conditions have their dedication rewarded, with single shots of Zee doing peace signs in the street and a couple of up-close-and-personal shots with the entourage. I expect I'll see those as Biz-Bits in all the tabloids tomorrow. The fluffy blonde with the Grand Canyon cleavage calls a halt to proceedings and pops them all into a nearby blacked-out people mover.

Could Caz have really shagged *that*?

'Excuse me, sir?' Mikus is by my side whispering in my ear. 'You are needed urgently out the back.'

I look at him. 'Urgently?' He nods.

I walk into the kitchen, just as Luca glides past with a perfectly plated turbot destined for the inspector. Inside the kitchen is looking remarkably chastened and taciturn. They are looking towards the back door. I open it.

'Jesus Christ!' I recoil. Standing in front of me are four men in stab jackets crowding into the door.

'You the manager?' barks one, his freezing breath bellowing out of his mouth like a charging bull.

'Who wants to know?' My mind is racing. My heart is pounding. Who the hell are these guys? There are no markings. The first thing that comes to mind is that Big Pete has sent some heavies round.

'Immigration,' says one of them. He unzips his jacket and flashes me his UK Border Agency badge.

'But I've got customers,' I say.

'And we've got a job to do.' He sniffs. There's a crackle on his radio and I hear the muffled words. 'Go! Go! Go!'

Four guys storm in the back door, flattening me against the wall as they pass. Another eight pile in the front. They are swift, vocal, armed and they mean business. It takes less than four minutes to corral everyone together in the kitchen and they don't use the softly-softly approach. It's physical and there's plenty of pushing and shoving. The agency KP makes the mistake of continuing to polish the silver. He is yelled at and told in no uncertain terms to 'PUT THE KNIFE DOWN!'

Out front it's chaos. Anna is trying to assure the customers that everything is fine. But everyone is standing up, milling round, asking what is going on, wanting to pay their bill, trying to get their coats. The Russians look particularly perturbed. There's nothing like a vanload of armed officials with heavy boots and small weapons to get an oligarch to pay up and piss off at speed. Within seconds of the boys bursting through the door, two other burley blokes in suits appear at the restaurant window with fat necks, cropped hair and earpieces. A blacked-out Merc screams on to the pavement, Mr Sergeev drops £1,500 in cash on the table, and within two minutes the party of four are gone. His bill was just over a grand so he left a £500 tip, which is generous in anyone's book.

The other customers are a little less organized. It takes another ten to fifteen minutes to empty the place. The table of three girls giggles out into the street, pronouncing it the most exciting night they'd had in years – what with sitting next to a pop star and witnessing a police raid, I can pretty much now guarantee we won't have to pay for the bag. Everyone else leaves in a polite and charming fashion, quietly collecting their belongings and walking single file as they would during a school fire practice.

The last out is the inspector who, I note, did manage to finish his turbot despite the interruptions.

'I am terribly sorry,' I say, holding out my hand to shake his.

'These things happen,' he replies, giving me a weak tug on the arm.

'They could have waited another half-hour,' I said. 'But I hope you enjoyed your food.'

'It was good, very good. I shall have to come back and sample the rice pudding soufflé, I was looking forward to that.'

'It's amazing.' I smile. 'Delicious. Do you have a card on you? Mr . . . ?'

'Adams. No, I am afraid I don't at the moment.' He moves towards the door. 'But I shall be back for the pudding.'

'Yes, do!' I call after him. 'And maybe bring a friend.'

'Maybe.'

The man is definitely an inspector, definitely. I feel it in my bones. At least if he comes back we'll know this time what he looks like. Although I am pretty sure he probably won't because they'll surely send someone else. However, you never know. Sometimes they do make themselves known to you; they can even leave a card, just to inform you that you've been inspected, just to make you a little more paranoid, if that were possible. Anyway, at least we won't be judged on tonight. Or I bloody hope not.

Back in the kitchen and all my staff are lined up as if they are about to face a firing squad. Some of them look terrified and the others look bored, jaded and just keen to get home.

'Right,' says the tallest, broadest bloke. 'I need IDs and I need them now.'

'I'd just like to say that I am the owner and I know there is no one illegal here, so all we need to do is go through things politely and calmly and everything will be OK.'

'With all due respect, sir,' he says, his nose is a little too close to mine for comfort, 'we have information that tells us otherwise.'

'Oh, that's ridiculous!' I laugh. 'I wouldn't employ anyone illegal, I just don't. It's not worth it. It used to be, I grant you, I mean we all did!' I laugh again, attempting to lighten the atmosphere. 'But now you guys can pop in whenever you fancy, we don't. I don't, none of us do.'

'We'd like to see your paperwork.' He exhales in my face and his breath smells of cheese and onion crisps.

'What, now?'

'Yes, now!'

'But I've seen all their IDs! I have photocopies of their passports in the safe and I've checked them all and they are all fine.'

I am now beginning to sweat a little. I quickly thank my lucky stars that Gina is Danish, because I haven't even got her sodding telephone number, let alone her passport details.

'We need to see the paperwork,' he repeats.

'Fine,' I reply. 'It's in the office in my other place up the road.'

'Get it. We'll send a couple of our officers with you. In the meantime, you lot can stay here.'

'Well, actually, can I just point out that I am a UK citizen,' says Andrew, running his hands through his long greasy hair. 'You may have heard of me? Andrew James? I've been a judge on *MasterChef*?'

'Yeah, well,' replies the officer. 'Cooking is not really my thing.'

On the way up the street to Le Bar, I start talking to the

officers who are escorting me. Called John and Conner, they are quite nice blokes and apologize for the heavy-handed approach, saying they are always quite tense before they go in, because, despite the intel, they never quite know what they're going to come across. They go on to tell me some story about how two of their colleagues were attacked with machetes when they raided the bowels of a Chinese restaurant in Soho.

'They play dirty, those bastards,' says John as we arrive outside Le Bar. 'Raiding Soho is not a job we're queuing up for. They both ended up in hospital with serious wounds.'

'Hello, sailor!' purrs a plastered brunette as she spies John in his uniform. She and a couple of girlfriends are curled around an outdoor gas-burning heater, puffing away on cigarettes.

'I'm not a sailor, I'm an immigration officer,' he replies, ignoring her advances.

We enter the bar and the place is mobbed, everyone the worse for cocktails. Like molecules treated with heat they are moving around, dancing, zigzagging and constantly bumping into each other. I catch Adam's eyes and he gives me a puzzled look as he takes in my two escorts.

'Immigration,' I mouth. His eyes widen and he comes over immediately, pushing his way through the crowd.

'Everything OK?' he shouts above the loud music.

'Fine, I've just got to get the paperwork.'

'All right, gentlemen.' He attempts an ingratiating grin. The officers remain stony-faced.

The back office is a complete mess. The large black desk is covered in piles and sheets and random bits of paper. There are at least three half-drunk Starbucks cups that have separated into a layer of cold coffee with a thick milky head. There are two jam jars crammed with a collection of barely working pens, pinched from hotels all over the world. There's a saucer of spare change, endless Juicy Fruit wrappers and a sprinkle of fag ash all over the place. The walls are painted dark claret red, three cork noticeboards line one side of the room, covered in staff rotas, photos and invitations to trendy Shoreditch pop-ups. In one corner, there's an old wooden hatstand overloaded coats, scarfs and plastic bags. Opposite sits a black filing cabinet with a large, slowly dehydrating spider plant on top and next to its shrivelled leaves is a small, suspiciously smeared-looking mirror and a curled £20 note. I pick up the note and put it straight in my pocket, hopefully quick enough for Immigration not to notice.

'I am sorry about the state of the place,' I laugh, slowly pushing the mirror under the plant. 'The records are in the safe.'

Inside the safe there are plastic files with photocopies of everyone's passports along with wads of cash, bags of change and my divorce papers. There is also a padded brown envelope that I am pretty sure contains at least four grams of cocaine.

'Here we are!' I say, swiftly shutting the door.

Back at Le Restaurant and only a small gang of the staff remain standing to attention in the kitchen. Andrew, Oscar, Barney, Matt, Davide, Anna, Luca, Gina and a few of the others who have managed to prove their human right to be here are sitting around at one of the back tables drinking wine. I am not sure where the bottle has come from, but given the day we've had, nor do I care. There's still a group of sweaty nervous individuals who need my help proving exactly who they are.

'OK,' I say, licking my finger and leafing through the photocopies. 'So this is Alfonso, he's Italian, from . . . Capri. Capri?' I say, turning to look at him. 'I never knew that?'

'You never asked,' he replies.

'Yes, well.' I nod. 'And he's thirty-eight years old.'

'Right.' One of the officers leaning on the pass ticks the names off his list. 'Next.'

'Next is Mikus . . . something unpronounceable. Polish. Gdansk. He is twenty-four years old.' I hand over the photocopy and they check it over carefully. 'And here is Jorge de los Rios – Cadiz, Spain.' I smile at Jorge, handing over the photocopy of his passport. He is standing with his hands behind his back, chin up, like he's on parade. 'He's forty-three. Forty-three?' I exclaim. 'You've worn well.'

'It's the genes,' he replies, raising his eyebrows.

'Where are you from, mate?' asks the officer, leaning on the pass, scrutinizing the papers.

'Cadiz, Spain,' says Jorge.

'What's your date of birth?'

'Um, sixteenth of May nineteen sixty-six, no, sixty-nine.' There's silence. I look at Jorge. The officer looks at Jorge.

'These papers are forged,' says the officer on the pass. Another two go to verify it.

'Forged! Don't be so ridiculous!' I can't believe it. 'Forged? But Jorge has been here for years, he's my right-hand man, he's one of the best maître d's in town. He's brilliant. He's fantastic with people.' He is also a disloyal tosser, but let's gloss over that. 'They can't be forged. The man is—'

'From Brazil,' says the officer on the pass.

'Brazil?' I stop in my tracks. 'But he's Spanish.'

'Brazilian,' the officer corrects. 'Usually it's a Portuguese passport. But it happens all the time. Your industry is packed with Brazilian chefs who come over here on a student visa where they can work sixteen hours a week and they end up doing nine shifts a week of seven hours a day; they work for two years, max out on their credit cards, pay sod all off and leave having built a new home in São Paulo.' He sniffs and looks a Jorge.

'Well, firstly, Jorge is not a chef, secondly, he's been here for years and thirdly, he doesn't have a house in São Paulo.'

'And fourthly, here is his student visa.' The officer holds it up. It is so old Jorge's photo is almost unrecognizable.

'Christ!' I turn and look at him. 'You're *illegal*?' He shrugs. 'How long have you been in the country?'

'Over ten years,' says the officer.

'You've been illegal for all the time?' He smiles and nods. 'And you're from Brazil?'

'São Paulo,' he confirms.

'So you have built yourself a house in São Paulo?' I am so shocked, I have to hold on to the pass. I have been out and about with Jorge, we've got drunk, we've shared secrets, he's been my right-hand man for the past five years, and now it transpires that everything I know about him has been a lie.

'I am sorry,' he says. 'What can I say?'

'A little bit more than sorry,' I replied. I feel bitter and hurt, as if I'm being dumped by another one of my many girlfriends.

'Come with me, then,' says the officer closest to the door, reaching into his back pocket for a pair of handcuffs.

'What will you do with him?' I ask, suddenly feeling very nervous for my duplicitous friend.

'We'll take him to the station for processing and then he'll be straight on the plane.'

'What, deported?'

'Deported.'

They cuff him and lead him away out of the back of the restaurant.

He stops and turns. 'I am sorry,' he says, cutting a forlorn-looking figure in his Armani suit and his shiny shoes. His dark eyes are red with tears. 'Can you get someone to clear out my flat? Send my things back?'

'Won't you be allowed to go home?' I ask, somewhat stunned. Everyone shakes their head. That's it. He's gone. A six-year friendship goes up in a puff of smoke.

By the time I come back out of the kitchen, everyone looks miserable. I plonk myself next door to Gina on a banquette and stare vacantly into space as I try to take in what's happened. My phone goes. It is not a number I recognize.

'Hello?'

'Good evening,' says a very Russian voice. 'My name is Alexander Petrovsky, I am the owner of—'

'I know what you own.'

'I just wanted to say that I have asked your maître d', Jorge de los Rios, to come and work for me and he has gladly accepted my offer and he will be starting with me as of Monday.'

'Right.'

'I gather you are supposed to tell the person,' he says and pauses. 'So consider yourself told.'

'You're welcome to him. Although I suggest you get yourself down to Soho nick.'

'I am sorry. I do not understand. Who is Soho Nick?'

I hang up, while Gina pours me a very large drink.

11 p.m.–12 a.m.

There is nothing like the loss of a major player, or indeed a part of the family, to bring the rest of the team together. We all sit round a few tables at the back while Barney and Alfonso bring out some food. It's an odd selection. There are a couple of orders that were waiting to go out before the raid, a few rabbit, a steak, two sea bass and a pork belly, plus the most fantastic selection of puddings that had all been prepped and ready to go. There's a temptation to see if any of them can fight and live to see another day, or tomorrow lunch at the very least – however, I can see no one is in the mood for me to be a tight-wad.

Anyway, I can't help but think this is a more civilized way of behaving. Rowley Leigh, the cleverest, most charming and one of the few men in whites ever to have gone to Cambridge University, is famous for always sitting down in his own place for a spot of supper after service. During the Kensington Place days, when it was the hottest place in town, he would often be joined by various select customers and then other chefs and maître d's from restaurants round the corner would tip up for a tipple. Sometimes it could turn into quite an evening. Obviously, Rowley's smart and knows what he's doing, but you have to be so careful when it comes to the old hospitality. Before you know it you're on the brandies, offering around the port, drinking the profits, and you're the arsehole who wakes up with a headache, having spent over £500 of your own money at your own bar. Also, if you're always the 'hail-fellow-well-met' type, then the customers begin to expect it, so if you don't fancy a drink or you've got something better to do, they take offence. They'll see it as a personal snub: you've turned them down for a drink, you never turn people down for a drink, you didn't want to join their table, you're now clearly an arrogant git with no depth or profundity. It is a lose-lose situation.

'I can't believe it,' says Luca, shaking his head. 'He was always so fun.'

'He was certainly gay,' interjects Andrew who always found Jorge's exuberance, particularly the kissing, hard to handle first thing in the morning. 'Although I will never forget him kicking a rowdy bunch of very drunk men out into the street and one of the blokes shouted at him: "I'm bisexual and I wouldn't fuck you!" At which point he replied: "It's my night off, darling!" '

Anna laughs. 'My favourite was him telling you which men

gave him the eye during service. They were always with women, but were always in reality gay. He says he could turn anyone.'

'He was very good at his job,' I conclude, taking a large slug of my wine. It's a very nice red Sancerre. There is rather a large collection of half-full bottles on the table, gleaned from the fleeing guests. There is nothing we like more than finishing off that half you left behind, anyway. Often we'll serve it back to you by the glass the next day. Double bubble, if ever I've heard it. But I don't remember anyone ordering the Sancerre Rouge. It is one of my favourites and it's so good I take another look. This is a brand-new bottle. 'I didn't know we had any of this left?' I say to Michelangelo, who is sitting opposite me.

He smiles. 'We have a few. For special occasions.' Honestly, bloody barmen and sommeliers, they could hide a corpse if they had to. And I'm not joking; ask them to squirrel away something – anything – and even if it were a dead body, you could have PricewaterhouseCoopers crawling all over them like maggots looking for a flesh wound and they'd come away with nothing.

'Well, it's very good,' I say lamely. 'How many do we have left?'

'I'm not sure.' He does that puzzled look very well. 'A few?'

'Why don't you go and get them?' I suggest. 'I think every-one could do with a drink. Especially Oscar.' He is talking to Matt and hears his name. 'You'd like a drink, wouldn't you, mate?'

'A small one,' he nods. 'Then I should really get home. We've got a new baby.'

'You have?'

'I didn't know you were married,' says Anna.

'I'm not,' he replies.

Before I have the chance to hear the details of Oscar's domestic arrangements I get a call from Pippa who's filling me in on the covers she's done tonight. She's had 63, which I suppose isn't too bad for a forty-seater restaurant. They've managed to turn a few tables, but we're not far off the Christmas season and we should be turning everything at least twice. If you think Russell Norman can get fourteen hundred covers out of seventy-seater Polpo in the first week he opened, we should be able to do a little more than one and a half tables in the run-up to Christmas.

I am seriously worried about La Table. It is not a bad site. It's No-Ho – not quite Soho – but close enough that it should be picking up the media mafia, film and TV bods wanting an alternative to endless sticks of chicken teriyaki at Roka or flicking a salad around at the Charlotte Street Hotel. There was quite a good place on the site before we moved in. Which is helpful, as I often think it is hard to turn around the bad energy and bad karma of a place if it's always been crap.

The top end of the Brompton Road, I think, has always been a disaster. There are always road works, there's not much passing footfall, and nobody lives around there except the French. Nearby Racine is doing well, but apart from that, the French are so fussy and annoying when they go out, like the world owes them a fine dining experience. Honestly, I'd rather some coked-up traders than a table of French – at least I might flog some wine.

There are dead spots all over town, where no amount of banker's bonus money thrown at the hand-tiled wall will make any difference. A shite site is a shite site, haunted by the ghost of miserable evenings out. There was a place at the bottom of Portobello Road and Golborne Road, however, which had always been a disaster, playing host to a succession of failing businesses. It is now working, but it took the might of Nick Jones and Pizza East to turn that energy around.

So it's not the site that is plaguing La Table, and I'm beginning to think that perhaps it is the menu and the lack of glittering staff. Pippa sounds miserable on the phone. There is nothing worse than a place that isn't working. It's depressing, debilitating and enough to drive you to drink. So I ask her over for one.

'We've got a very nice Sancerre on the go,' I suggest and she says she'll be over as soon as she's cashed up. Which reminds me, I haven't been through tonight's takings and I haven't sorted out the tips.

Like most places we have a tronc system, where the tips are pooled and paid out at the end of the week. The amount of cash is supposed to be written down by the troncmaster, usually the manager or the maître d', and you're eventually supposed to pay tax on the tips. In the past, restaurants like Conran used to use the tronc to top up staff wages. So instead of paying minimum wage, there was a term called 'housepay', which could be anything as low as £1.88 an hour and the remainder came from the tronc. Often the service charge used to go directly to the restaurant and the waiters would only ever see cash tips, as credit card tips would also miraculously disappear.

I am quite careful with the cash, as I remember a few years ago, one maître d' I worked for famously used to skim the tronc. He was always the most generous bloke when it came to buying rounds in the pub – perhaps it was the guilt. It was only when he went on holiday we found out what was going on. Another waiter checked the tronc only to find out it was three hundred quid short. Poor chap wasn't as bright as all that and he'd written down the amount of money that was taken during the week *before* he pinched it. Eventually he was fired.

Industry standard, however, these days is for the restaurant to take the credit card tips, pop them into a PAYE account and dish them out after tax has been paid. The Revenue are so pathetically keen to get any cash at the moment that they watch you like a hawk. But it's tempting with that much cash swilling around. You need to pay a supplier, or you're a couple of hundred short of an evening, raiding the tronc is the easy answer. The problem is when you need to pay it back.

I suppose any port in a storm in these austere times. Recently I have noticed a couple of restaurants playing fast and loose with the service charge. Usually it's 12.5 per cent, but at a few dinners out in the last month I've found myself shelling out 14.5 per cent, which is a massive £25 added to a bill of £175. I am not sure what the extra 2 per cent is for. Some very fine napkins? Or topping up the wages of the bar staff?

Tonight, due in part to our generous pop star and the swiftly exiting Russians, who were so desperate to get out of the place they chucked money at the problem, we have just over £1,000 in tips, which might be enough to bring a smile back to the faces of the brigade.

'Can anyone smell anything?' asks Oscar, putting down his second glass of wine. His black eye is beginning to puff up nicely.

'Don't start being rude about my cooking now,' says Andrew, belching out of the side of his mouth. He must at least be three-quarters of a bottle down, not including any swigs he's helped himself to in the kitchen.

'No, mate,' replies Oscar, looking rather jaded by the constant battering he's getting from his older, much-less-wise, pissed, previous mentor. 'There really is a bad smell coming from somewhere.'

'You're correct,' nods Michelangelo. 'It is not nice.'

'It smells of waste,' says Oscar.

'Shit,' agrees Andrew, curling his top lip. 'It smells very strongly of shit. And it's coming from my kitchen.'

He is right, there is an eye-watering stench and it appears to be coming through the swing doors. Andrew looks at me, Oscar raises his sandy eyebrows and Michelangelo waves his hand in front of his nose. It is my restaurant, my baby and, anyway, I am closest to the doors.

It's only when I swing them open that the full hideous, gagging, retching, weeping, sinking hell becomes apparent.

'Oh my God,' I say, covering my mouth at the horror. I have never seen anything quite so disgusting in my life. The whole of the kitchen is about an inch deep in sewage. There is shit and loo paper and condoms and tampons and all sorts of effluent floating in a pool of revulsion all over the floor. The grill on the main drain, which sits just to the right of the stove, has been lifted off and is floating, rocking from side to side, in a tide of turd.

It is all I can do to stop myself from vomiting down myself and onto my shoes. The smell is intense and there is not enough mind bleach to rid myself of the vision. I close the door and, coming coughing and spluttering over to the table, the smell comes with me. It's in my hair, in my suit. Don't tell me it's on my shoes?

'Anna!' I yell so loudly she jumps and spills her wine. 'Get Rentokil. Now! And tell them it's a fucking emergency.'

'Rentokil?'

'Yes, Rentokil!'

'Christ? Really?' says Andrew, flopping back on to the banquette. 'Don't tell me it's the drains? Again?'

'Tell them we need the drains jetted, we need the whole VIP fluffing fucking service.'

I run into the toilets and retch so hard I think I am about throw up my colon. There goes my beetroot salad. Despite its virulent pink, I don't dare flush the loo. There's no telling what chaos that might cause. I shiver. I really can't stand the smell of shit, let alone half the capital's excrement floating around in my one-star kitchen.

Rentokil are supposed to come and sort our drains out every two months. They come with cameras and jet blasters and it is absolutely revolting. You see all sorts down there, but mainly that the sewers are crawling with rats. When they say you are never more than six feet from a rat in London, what they mean is that your butt cheeks are literally a U-bend away from their yellow, gnashing teeth because there are swarms of the bastards, scurrying around right underneath your feet.

Truth be told, our Victorian drains just can't cope with the stuff we put down them. And it's mainly the fault of restaurants and it's mainly fat. The whole system is packed with fatbergs: lumps of coagulated fat that collect in the drains under the kitchens of the West End. The situation got so bad recently that Westminster Council had to remove over 1,000 tonnes of fat from underneath Leicester Square. Like the clogged arteries of a heavy smoker, the gobs from endless irresponsible kitchens, usually from fast-frying cooking oil, had stuck to the sides of the pipes. Some of it was four feet thick in places. They eventually removed enough putrid fat to fill nine double decker buses. I am only extremely glad I was not around to see that. Nothing turns my stomach more than a lump of fat full of loo paper, old syringes and human hair; it makes me want to barf more than the smell of shit in the first place.

The other thing that is really putting pressure on the system at the moment is a weird problem particular to Soho, namely protein shakes. My mate has a place on Old Compton Street and he's been plagued by the problem. The new buff gay clientele that his place attracts means they've had to call the plumbers in three times in the last six months and they have all said the same thing: there is so much protein in his customers' urine after drinking one of these shakes that it coagulates in the drains and makes a type of jelly, which eventually blocks the drains. He now has his drains done once a month as a precaution. We don't have the buff, back and sac brigade, so we don't have a protein piss problem, but what we do have is a preponderance of other restaurants nearby who regularly pour any old rubbish down the drain, so we are much more likely to succumb to a fatberg.

And it makes such a mess, as well as the stink. I remember when I was working with Maitre d' Spencer we had an explosion during the lunchtime service. We were full, we had a hundred and fifty covers and I was on Table Ten, the VIP table, taking orders, when he tapped me on the shoulder and told me to cancel the order and help him get everyone out. The downstairs kitchen was flooded with so much effluent that it was beginning to come up the stairs. Amazingly Rentokil came and sorted the place out and we were back serving lunch the very next day. Restaurants can be amazing like that. They can fall down and get up extremely quickly: they just throw manpower at the problem.

Which is what I am about to do. No one is going to thank me for it, but there's not much I can do. We need to be open for lunch – tomorrow.

Anna puts down the phone. 'They're on their way. With everything,' she says.

'How long?'

'Half an hour maximum.'

'Half an hour? OK,' I reach in my pocket and pull out the wad of cash that was destined for the tronc. 'Who wants to make some extra money?' Barney's hand goes straight up as does Mikus's and the agency KP's, who's so spavin and pale and clearly straight off the ferry, he's not looked anyone in the eyes since he's been here.

It's at times like this I miss Sean; despite being a drug-taking tosspot, he was always very hands on and practical in a crisis. Unless he'd been to a club, of course, then he was bloody useless.

'Anyone else?' I lick my finger like a car dealer and start peeling off notes. I am up to £100 when Luca finally puts up his hand.

'Done! Great. You lot, I have to say I love you for this – and I don't often say that – you need to get any old linen that we have and stuff what is stained or ripped or anything and stop the shit coming into the restaurant, because once it hits the carpets we're fucked. The rest of you, hold your noses, and tiptoe into the kitchen and grab your stuff, if you can, and I'll meet you all up the road at Le Bar for a drink. You lot – Mikus, Barney and you –' I point to the luminously white KP, 'you all come up there when you're done and Rentokil are here and I'll buy you a drink. Make sure you come,' I nod. 'And Barney?'

'Yes?'

'You're in charge.'

I just have to get out of there. The smell is making me feel so awful. I also think because I have seen the hideous hell that is behind the door my imagination is working overtime.

257

Free, out in the street, I shake my hair in the breeze. I am desperate to get the cloying sweet smell of sewage out of my clothes. I light up a cigarette – surely it's better to smell of Marlboro Light than crap? Can this day actually get any worse?

12–1 a.m.

The office party at Le Bar is reaching its closing stages. Those who are going to cop-off for the night are already hooking up, talking to each other, moving in a little too closely, laughing just that bit too loud. The MD, whose pink tie is hanging as loosely as he is, appears to have got the blonde in the red sequin dress hemmed into a corner in a pincer movement worthy of an SAS execution squad. The remainder of the party, the great unclaimed, are left to wander around, dribbling, flopping, staggering, teetering, working a liquid face, that moment when their make-up and cheek muscles give up the ghost and gently collapse south.

Adam has turned the music down a little so it is no longer obligatory to scream loudly into someone's ear and it is now possible to have a conversation. He finds us two adjacent booths at the back of the room and I sit down with Andrew and Oscar while the others shuffle in next door. Adam piles in the drinks. There are a couple of bottles of red, five or six vodkas and he tries to flog us the gag-inducing coffee tequila. Andrew, of course, is the first to try. I honestly think there's nothing that hasn't passed that man's parched lips in the past twenty years. No liqueur is too monstrous-looking, no cocktail too lurid, no stickie too sweet. He went through a terrible absinthe stage about eight years ago, which I seem to remember we all had a go on, but he was the only one to drink a whole bottle and decide he was going to walk to Clapham, taking the direct route, through people's gardens and over their walls. He was in quite a state, apparently, when he walked in the door. Looking at him, knocking back his second coffee tequila shot, I can't help but think, having heard all the stories about him, that perhaps I should never have hired him in the first place.

But sitting there, chugging back a filthy drink, Andrew, I am pretty sure, would argue he's not a big boozer searching for oblivion in something that is 45 per cent proof. He'd say he was just 'decompressing'. There is a huge mythology surrounding chefs and the need to 'decompress' after a service. It's the adrenalin, they say, it's like running a marathon with your eye on the clock, in the heat, with all that talent, all that pressure of expectation, all those turbot to plate. We can't just go home, have a shower and go to bed! So you hear endless stories of chefs' 'decompressing' routines. Some of them are very *Knight Rider* and involve flogging a motorbike around town for an hour. Others are a little less dramatic and involve watching the telly for the next three hours. Or indeed, the very popular jogging home via a decompress-fuck with a handy waitress at a nearby restaurant. Some go to the Groucho Club, and others go home and drink a pint of red wine and smoke ten fags in total silence in the dark. Although my favourite is the jolly fellow who just went home to sleep, no drama, no histrionics, no need to decompress; no wonder he is no longer behind the pass. In fact, he now owns a few rather successful restaurants of his very own; cooking was apparently not for him.

'So how actually was France?' Andrew asks Oscar, as he slithers down on his elbow. 'All that fine dining shit is dead, you know.'

'Not in France,' says Oscar, reaching for a vodka and tonic. Clearly the baby is going to have to wait. 'In France they'll go out to dinner and spend something like 800–900 euros on dinner for two in a two- or three-star restaurant.'

'They'll pay that?' I ask.

'Yeah,' he nods. 'They've got loyal customers who come out once a month and shell out that sort of cash. But they don't do that here.'

'No, it's not our thing. No one is going to pay that for a bit of supper, no matter how many fucking stars it's got,' agrees Andrew, nodding away.

'It's all about Spain,' says Oscar. 'The Spanish are on the rise. The elBulli may be closed but I had the eight-course tasting menu at El Celler de Can Roca in Girona last summer and it was amazing, right down to the olives on the bonsai trees.

There's some wit in Spanish cooking and so much skill. It was voted the best restaurant in the world and you can see why.'

'That's not my thing.' Andrew looks like he's swallowed a wasp.

Oscar takes another swig of his vodka. 'But London is rocking. Honestly, I can't tell you the difference since I have been away. The atmosphere is different and there are so many restaurants.'

'It's all gone Polpo as far as I am concerned,' says Andrew. 'Small plates, all convenient, no booking. Some hard drinking, some delicious food, some good chat. In. Out. Fuck off. Polpo, da Polpo. They are all fucking packed.'

'Yeah, packed with facial hair.' I roll my eyes. 'I went to the Social Eating House the other day, Jason Atherton's new place, and I literally couldn't move for tweeds and three pieces. There's hip, there's hipster and there's food hipster.'

'You should have waited a few weeks,' says Oscar. 'When that crowd have moved on to the next pop-up.'

'If you want hipster,' grins Andrew, 'have you tried The Clove Club in Shoreditch Town Hall?'

'Instagram cooking,' says Oscar. 'Literally, food porn for bloggers. They don't eat it; they just rub themselves up next to it, photograph it and pop it on the Net. Doesn't taste of anything.'

'I thought it was quite good,' Andrew chips in.

'Really? I'm quite bored with photo-food, I have to say,' replies Oscar.

'What, already bored?' I chip in. 'But this little wave has only just started.'

'I suppose it's better than smears,' laughs Oscar.

I look at Andrew; fortunately he is chuckling in agreement, unaware that most customers would put him in the smear category. There is nothing he likes more than creating some sort of vegetable purée skid mark on a plate before placing some meat/fish/fowl on top.

'I had a mate who worked for Simon Hopkinson at Bibendum – you know, who did *The Good Cook* TV show and book? He's an awesome chef.'

'Yeah,' agrees Andrew. 'He's pretty good—'

'And he said he taught him all the stuff that was correct and what was not bloody correct. Like foam? Isn't that the stuff you get rid of when you skim something? Why would you use that? Smears? Why would you drag a sauce across a plate and off the side when the plate is supposed to be clean? Sprinkling? There are times when a nice sea salt works well, but you should season with the right amount of salt in the first place.'

'No, you're right,' nods Andrew, laughing and knocking back the tequila. 'Don't forget the powders and the granitas.'

'Although I did have the most amazing oysters with grape-fruit granita and caramelized seaweed in a pub in Kent.'

'The Sportsman?' asks Andrew.

Oscar nods. 'It's a grotty pub near the sea but the chef Steve Harris makes his own butter, harvests his own sea salt and grows his own veg. The lamb we had came from a field next door but one from the pub and he does a twelve-course tasting menu for £65.'

'Sixty-five quid? How can you make money on that?' I ask.

'Small portions,' they both reply.

This sudden outbreak of harmony is a little disconcerting. If only I had got them drunk this morning, we might have all had a much easier time of it.

'Everyone OK?' asks Adam, slipping on to the end of the banquette. There is nothing he likes more than the suggestion of a lock-in, and he'll do his damnedest to keep it all going. 'Can I get anyone any cocktails? Drinks? Vodka?' He glances at me to see if it's OK. Quite frankly, I'm tired, I have one failing restaurant and one that is currently full of shit; I don't care how much drink he serves, just so long as my glass is not allowed to run dry.

'I'll have a martini,' I say.

'Really?' He looks at me a little surprised. He knows I mean business.

'You see – talent copies and genius steals,' says Oscar, draining his glass. 'Oscar Wilde said that.' He waves his finger at Andrew. 'It's OK if someone takes your idea and moves it on. But if they take your idea and do nothing with it, they just copy it, then not only is it extremely irritating, but it is unlikely to work, because you need energy to make things work and if it is not your idea you are much less likely to put the effort in.' Andrew looks a little lost at this point. He's a great chef but he's not that brilliant when it comes to ideas. 'OK, take Polpo.' We both nod. 'The mini clipboard for the wine list? The exposed brick? From the Fatty Crab in the US, and the bar? You'd never guess it was from Williamsberg. But you know he's taken it and he's moved it on. You are allowed to do that. What you are not allowed to do is copy.'

They both nod sagely.

'Do you know what I hate?' I pipe up.

'What?' ask Oscar.

'A twelve-course tasting menu. There is nothing more depressing than being the last sod in the restaurant with your Addison Lee car waiting outside while you have to work your way through the last of the three desserts. It is it not my idea of fun. It's crap.'

'So you're a Polpo bloke then,' grins Andrew, about to welcome me on to his team.

'No,' I shake my head. 'I'm too old to queue. I like a good table, some nice lighting and good, charming staff.'

'Corbin and King,' says Oscar. 'Or a bit of Nick Jones.'

'I always see those two as the Paul Newman and Robert Redford of the London scene. Zuma's Arjun Waney is Omar Sharif. Nick Jones is Steve McQueen.' Andrew pauses.

'And you are?' I ask.

'Javier Bardem,' comes back his very obviously well-considered reply.

'And I'm Brad Pitt,' smiles Oscar.

'And I'm Angelina Jolie.' I smile. 'The thing is, the age of the super-chef is actually dead. It's all about the owners now.' They look at me as if I'm joking. I'm not. 'Does anyone really know, or indeed care, who is cooking in any of Chris and Jeremy's places? Who's the chef at Cecconi's? Who's cooking tonight at Zuma? No one really knows. There are still a few big names rattling around but mostly the chefs have gone back into the kitchen.'

The whole thing has come full circle. Cuisine in this country really took off with the arrival of the French chefs who'd fled France after the Revolution. Having removed the heads of the mouths they fed, they moved into the vast baronial halls of this green and pleasant land and got cooking. At that time they were below-stairs staff who rarely, if ever, saw the light of day. But as the finances of the posh were slowly depleted due to death duties and the First World War, so the chefs to the gentry had to find alternative means of employment and started to work in restaurants. Mrs Patmore in *Downton Abbey* will surely be working in some London restaurant come series seven, eight or fourteen set in 1955. Then, slowly but surely, what had been downstairs' staff started to stare out through the glass porthole window. Occasionally, they were invited through, to be applauded for their fine work. It was at that moment they saw the pretty girls and the rich men and decided they wanted a piece of the action.

The Roux brothers were among the first to cross the Rubicon and they opened the door for everyone else to follow. But now the door is closing. I don't think people are that interested in who's cooking, just so long as it's good, the restaurant is fun and the service is quick, slick and not intrusive. Surely there are only so many times you can watch a man dressed in whites scream at another over the soup?

'You're just bigging yourself up,' says Andrew.

'OK, then,' I agree. 'But tell me who are the hot chefs at the moment?'

'Ollie Dabbous,' says Oscar. 'His coddled egg was one of the best things I have eaten in my life.'

'He *is* great, but you can't get into his place for months, which is a disaster. The longest waiting list you should have is six weeks. Otherwise you just have the Happy Birthday crowd in, or people who are prepared to wait six months for a bit of grub. It's the quickest way to lose the buzz. It'll fly like anything for a year, maybe more, and then die slowly.'

'He is great, though, and Heston. Dinner is my favourite place to eat in London,' says Oscar.

'I'll give you that, it's bloody delicious.'

'I like St John Bread and Wine,' says Andrew. 'Fergus Henderson.'

'Yup,' I nod.

'The Ledbury? Brett Graham? Two stars. Voted thirteenth best restaurant in the world?' Oscar looks at me.

'I've been there once,' I reply. 'The food was great, but it wasn't fun. Did I have a laugh? No. I wanted to relax, chat to my friends, be entertained. I'd rather have a conversation with my guests than have to spend every tenth minute acknowledging the waiter, while he waits for our conversation to expire and explains to us the intricacies of a dish that we have already ordered.'

'I'm with you,' sniffs Andrew, pouring himself another shot. 'The places I like are anything Mark Hix does, the Pitt Cue, Meat Liquor, Meat Market, and I love the specials board at

Koya – you meet half of London's chefs there and I love that other Jap, Sushi Tetsu – it's only got seven seats.'

'Christ!' I say, holding my head. 'Where's the money in that?'

'The scene is split three ways at the moment,' Oscar pipes up. 'The first is clean, cooking big flavours, no sauces. Simple, proper stuff like Polpo, Polpetto, etc. Then you've got the crazy stuff, Heston, Noma, Dabbous, James Knappett's Kitchen Table, the blow-your-head-off stuff that you'd have never thought of, and then there's your classic cooking.'

'But you can have too much crazy humour with your food. I went to elBulli a while ago and I have to say I got more than a little pissed off,' says Andrew.

'Really?' replies Oscar. 'I loved that place.'

'There were elements that were funny and clever and there was craft and good use of ingredients and all that, but the chef had gone mad with the yuzu sauce, so I asked the waiter if the chef had been to Japan recently and he said "Yes". I felt like saying, "You're supposed to be a Catalan cook, back off with yuzu. I'm glad you had a nice time in Japan but we don't want to see your holiday snaps as well." '

'I'm over Asian confusion,' says Oscar. 'It's all full of salt, sugar and bloody MSG, you can taste the stuff as soon as you dig in.'

'Anyway, I'm out of here,' announces Andrew.

'Are you sure you won't have another drink?' I look up at the other table, at the others who are all knocking back the wine and cocktails and about to get on a par with the remainder of the office party crowd.

'Not here, *here*,' says Andrew, refilling his glass. 'I'm going private.' I look puzzled. 'I've got a position in a private house, big posh family just outside Henley on Thames. Stacks of money – well, a nice £90,000 anyway – great hours, holidays and, best of all, *no bloody pressure*.'

'When did you decide that?'

'A while back.'

'You're going back below stairs?' I ask. 'Like *Downton*?'

'It's not bloody *Downton*, and anyway, I can always come back into the game in a couple of years. And who knows? I might save up some cash and get my own place.'

Good luck to him, I think, as I have another stiff swig of my martini. I'd like to see how Andrew fares when he has his own place, so he is not in the shit, but cleaning it up.

1–2 a.m.

Rentokil turned up at Le Restaurant and immediately set to work jet-cleaning the drains and sweeping up the effluent. Barney and the gang all lent a hand in the initial clean-up but were eventually told to leave it to the professionals. So by the time they make it to Le Bar, they are parched and a little unfragrant. They join the other table and Adam makes sure they have enough beer.

'How's it all looking?' I ask Barney, trying not to sit too close to him.

It is amazing how a stench that strong clings to your clothes. When I first started working in kitchens I had a girlfriend who complained I smelt of onions whenever I turned up at her place. It was a nightmare. I used to spend hours in the shower after service trying to get rid of the smell of food, scrubbing under my fingernails, washing my hair. But I could never get rid of it. Even as I lay there, cleaner than a disinfected whistle, I could whiff the aroma of frying emanating from my skin. It was as if I had been irradiated and the stench of the kitchen had somehow inveigled itself in my bone marrow or my DNA at the very least.

'It's not that bad,' says Barney. 'They're on top of it already and they've managed to unblock the drain.'

'Was it fat?'

'Yup,' he nods. 'Not a massive fatberg, but just enough to screw us over. Anyway, most of the stuff has gone back down the drain and now they are cleaning and disinfecting.'

'How long do you think?'

'At least another three hours, maybe the whole night,' he says, licking his lips as he eyes his bevy.

'Tuck in!' I say, patting him on the back. 'And thank you all for such a great job. Very kind of you.' I look at the rest of the table. 'Thanks, guys, for all your hard work.' They all stare at me; their eyes are haunted and glazed with tiredness. There is nothing like a double shift followed by some shit shovelling to really finish you off! 'Here,' I say, digging into my pocket. I hand round £50 each, which I think is probably enough; it's never good to be too generous in this business, as it doesn't take long for everyone to think you're a soft touch, to see you coming, and for them to take the piss.

In the meantime, Andrew and Oscar have moved on from the perils of Asian fusion and the joys of going private, and are now discussing the merits of a consultancy and, indeed, a supermarket range.

'You can make quite a bit on these deals,' says Andrew, whose elbow has now slid to a 45-degree angle. He must be on at least his fourth or fifth tequila shot, but, despite the relaxed arm, the rest of it doesn't appear to have touched the sides. 'I mean, I'm happy to take Tesco's dollar.'

'You would?' Oscar's head wobbles with alcohol and incredulity. '*Tesco?* The devil incarnate? The great big gobbling vampire squid on the face of farming?'

'We can't all live next to farmers' markets and eat steak that had fucking parents and membership to the Groucho Club,' says Andrew. 'Some people have less than twenty quid a week to spend on food.'

'But Tesco's?'

'I wouldn't mind hopping to bed with Sainsbury's.'

'You wouldn't mind hopping into bed with anyone,' comes a languid voice laced with Marlborough (College). I'd recognize those posh tones in the morgue.

'Caz!'

'Hey, darling!' She flops a skinny buttock down on the banquette, and, entirely encased in black, she looks like a stick of liquorice. 'You've met Jason, Jason Stone?' she says, flicking a hand in the general direction of the tubby little critic who'd been chomping on our best-cooked steak less than twelve hours ago.

'Hi, Jason.' I smile, pulling my service industry face out of my back pocket and popping it firmly back on. I wish Caz wouldn't do things like this. Just when everyone is beginning to let their hair down, relax, she brings along someone whose arse you are supposed to lick. 'How are you?'

'Fine,' he says, belching through the back of his teeth and wobbling slightly on his soft-soled shoes. The man is slaughtered. He can barely speak. Andrew budges up the banquette and pats a seat next to him.

'Hey, dude, sit down.' Andrew has an irritating ability to think he is Californian when pissed. He imagines himself in shorts, with a deep tan and a surfboard under his armpit; instead he's in whites, with a matching skin tone and an Oyster card in his back pocket. 'How's it goin'?' he persists.

It transpires that it is 'goin' fine and dandy' in the world of Jason Stone. In fact, I'd go so far as to say 'terrific'. After a very fine one-star lunch at my establishment, he then went on to a champagne reception at the Landmark Hotel, where he knocked back some very delicious Laurent Perrier bubbles and followed a dim-sum-carrying waitress around a party, where he got to speak to the charming Russell Norman, the very witty Fernando from The Ivy and a nice bloke from the Ritz. He also bumped into Caz, who was propping up a pillar in her black dress, trying to ponce fags off anyone who was going outside, and who eventually persuaded him that he should 'go on'. So they'd had dinner at Little Social and then they'd had a cocktail at Dean St Townhouse and, just in case either of them had a little space leftover for anything extra, they'd popped in here.

'It was one of those awards when the usual suspects all won,' proclaims Caz, fossicking around in her handbag for what I am not yet certain. 'I mean, Colbert won restaurant of the year, I ask you.' She hiccups slightly and pulls out a red lipstick, which she then proceeds to apply with remarkable

273

precision bearing in mind quite how plastered she is. 'I mean, it is a lovely place – last time I went in there Nigella was in one corner, Joan Collins was next to her with full shades action, and hunkered down to the right were Pippa AND Carole Middleton!'

'Did you see her arse?' asks Andrew.

'No.' Caz gives him one of those pitying looks posh girls reserve for Jeremy Clarkson. 'But it is so terribly predictable,' she continues. 'The food is nice. That toasted sandwich is lovely.'

'It's fried in butter,' says Jason. 'Anything fried in butter is good. You'd be amazed how much butter you lot put in the food.' He points a wavering finger down the table. 'Grilled fish? Shove on some butter. Bit of steak? Shove on some butter. Butter. Salt. Sugar. All your food is slathered in the stuff. No wonder all us critics get fat. Most of us can only eat one meal a day because all your food is so packed full of calories.'

'You don't seem to be holding back today,' I suggest.

'No,' he grins, patting his rather mobile stomach. 'And I'm off to Plymouth tomorrow.'

'What's in Plymouth?' I ask.

'Don't know,' he says. 'Just call me the restaurant critic's Shabbos goy.'

'Their what?' Caz's face crumples up like the back end of a pug. She's cut back on the botox in these austere times. 'What is it with you critics and your Yiddish?'

'What do you expect? Eating and moaning – what better job is there in the world for a nice Jewish boy like me, than to moan about food?' says Jason.

'Yeah, but what's a bloody Shabbos goy when it's at home?' asks Caz, checking her lips in the back of a spoon.

'A Shabbos goy is a person who helps us out on the Sabbath, turning on a light or whatever, a sort of dogsbody, which is what I'm going to be. I'll be the bloke to test drive all the places, travelling to Plymouth to eat a Chinese, so those other illustrious souls don't have to.'

'Really?' asks Caz. 'I thought that was Jay Rayner?'

'I am sure if I did ever manage to winkle out a gem, they'd all come running.'

'You lot always go to the same places anyway,' I say.

'Never to return!' adds Caz. 'The critics descend like a plague of locusts, along with the foodsters and bloggers and it is literally like nailing a supermodel. They're in, they're out, they notch it up on the bedhead and they're on to the next thing. What we in the trade like is a nice loyal clientele who keep on coming back.'

'Here, here,' says Oscar, raising his glass of vodka and tonic. 'AND you nearly always agree with each other.'

'We don't,' says Jason.

'You do,' says Caz.

'That's rubbish.'

'Well,' starts Caz, 'you always give anything that Chris and Jeremy open a good review; those two are untouchable and it's only because you all want to get tables at The Wolseley and Scott's. Breakfast at The Wolseley is always soooo full of fashion PRs and journalists, it's a joke.'

'You'd know, Caz,' I say, taking another large glug of my martini. 'You've practically got your own table.'

275

'Don't be rude to me,' she says, putting her hand in front of her face. 'I've had a bad day. Quite apart from your launch, which you barely managed to turn up to, I had to fill a restaurant for bloody Adrian bloody Gill, which no doubt he'll slag off anyway. And then I had a phone call from another place I look after who told me that some cheeky sod of a hack was taking the piss and ordering £200 bottles of wine and shoving it all on the bill. Honestly, you give them a three-course dinner with a bottle of house red or white AND a bloody aperitif, and they start getting all grand and ordering expensive bottles of wine and expecting the restaurant to foot the bill. So I've had a blazing row with him and I am fucking never working with that tosspot ever again. *And* I haven't been paid.'

'Who hasn't paid you?' I ask.

'Oh, some restaurant,' she says, shaking her head.

'Who?'

'This really sleazy man who has some crap place around the corner from here. I've done more than three months' work for him and he's not going to pay me.'

'But that's not allowed.' I am feeling a little protective of Caz. She's a one-man band and she hasn't got backers or investors to help her out. If she doesn't get paid, she'll have to cover her expenses and wages out of her own pocket. 'How much does he owe?'

'Seventeen K. I'm pretty sure he's some drug-dealing fuckwit and he told me to back off today and that he was never going to pay me. He was quite threatening and there's absolutely bugger all I can do about it.'

'But that's terrible and illegal. All that work.'

She sighs. 'Shall I have a cocktail?'

Caz and Jason spend the next few minutes perusing the cocktail menu. I am not sure if either of them is really capable of vision, because they both laboriously go down the pages with their index fingers and then, incapable of deciphering the print or indeed making a decision, they both plump for a vodka martini. Not that either of them needs any more.

'Shall we go clubbing?' Caz suddenly suggests, wrinkling up her nose and cracking a smile. 'Club? Club? Club?' she asks each of the boys around the table, pointing at them with her sharp index finger. They are all far too terrified to demur. 'We could go to the Arts Club?'

'I am not sure they'd let half of us in in our whites,' I say. 'And the rest of us smell of sewage.'

She looks puzzled. 'Yes, I was wondering . . . didn't really want to say, but what is that weird smell?'

'We've got a few drain problems.'

'Ew!' She pauses. 'We could go to that club around the corner, your local, where they let you in the back door? That one? They wouldn't mind you and your stinking chefs, you'd blend in nicely.'

'Ah. There's a slight problem with that.'

Being part of a community works quite a few ways. So we lend L'Italiano milk and butter and whatever stuff they've run out of, on the condition that they pay it back eventually and that their waiter doesn't come ambling through our restaurant during the middle of service, bottle of milk in hand, ogling the pretty girls at the same time. We'll also give various other owners of various other bars and restaurants in the surrounding streets a few free drinks here and there in Le Bar, just to keep everyone happy. In return we get a few free drinks around and about, as well as access to a few clubs.

In the olden days when I was a bit younger and firmer and could pull a WAG, we'd finish our shift and call up our mates at China White and they'd let us in through the kitchens. In the capital, as in any city, there's a whole subsection of urban night owls who only begin to get going at around two in the morning and who all know each other. We know the bars that stay open late, the places where you can still get a drink at five and how to get into most places for free. It is a mutual back-scratching exercise and in theory it works. If we all keep scratching, that is.

However, a few months ago I tried out a couple of bouncers at Le Bar. I don't know what I was thinking, really, because it's not that sort of place, and we've never had that many problems there, nothing like tonight even. But anyway, I thought it might look good. I was hoping for a doorman vibe, a little bit Scott's, a little bit Wolseley, a little bit kidding myself, because what I got was a couple of monosyllabic cage-fighters looking for a fight and an outlet for their steroid abuse. So I terminated their services, only to find they had friends in lots of places who didn't like me 'dissing' their mates. As a result, I can no longer take my lame arse dancing at the local club and I am not welcome at the pole and lap the other side of Regent Street. And there is even a small coffee bar just down the road that won't take my custom. None of it is any bad thing – there are only so many times you can go to places like The Box and watch a man anally ingest a wine bottle and still keep your dignity. But I am quite pissed off about the coffee, though, as they have some very nice buns and one of the best baristas in town.

'I'm afraid I can't get anyone in there these days,' I explain to Caz.

'Oh.' She looks a little whiplashed. It is not often she doesn't get her own way.

'Umm, sorry to interrupt,' says Adam, tapping me on the shoulder. 'We've got a problem at the front.'

Caz shifts her skinny backside enough for me to move. I am feeling distinctly the worse for wear now. I am also shattered. I am thinking I might help Adam sort out the dregs of the party and then I might crawl back home to bed. The White Company bed is beckoning.

At the front there are two bare-legged, short-skirted girls leaning on the coat-check desk. Adam rolls his eyes slightly before he approaches. We have both been here, so many times before.

'Evening, ladies,' I say. 'I gather there is a little bit of a problem.'

'Well, not that little,' says the one with short dark hair. 'You lot have nicked my coat.'

'I don't think we have,' I say, very calmly.

Poor Larissa standing behind the desk looks absolutely exhausted. The coat check is possibly one of the least palatable places to be in a bar, or restaurant, as these days people are so abusive. I don't know what has happened to all those British manners and reserve, but now people arrive doused with entitlement and dripping superiority. They want it, they want it now, and don't you know who they are? The coat check is one of those irritating inconveniences that often brings out the worst in people. For us, there's a possibility of earning tips, which is what makes it bearable, but judging by the four pound coins in Larissa's pathetic saucer, none of this lot are very generous.

'Yeah, well it's not there, is it?' she says.

'Did you check it in?' I ask.

'What do you think this is?' She waves a small pink raffle ticket in my face.

If there is one thing worse than a pissed person at the coat check, it's a pissed person with a lost coat. I hate it when we lose a coat; the customer always gets so arsy and, you know, they are right to be. But it's difficult. If someone actively sets out to pinch someone else's coat there is very little we can do. They are often very calculating about it. They'll pretend they've lost their ticket, they say it's black and ask the girl to go through the coats ('No, not that one – that one') until they find something expensive and they'll claim it as their own. Most coat checks are closed off these days, to stop thieves from being able to pick the ones they want in advance, but still it is hard to gauge what is a genuine mistake and what's a deliberate fraud. This is where a door policy comes in. You want customers, but you also want people whose faces fit. It's very subtle. But the good manager can stop trouble before it's even got out of the taxi and crossed the road. Obviously the office party is less exclusive and not so easy to manage.

'Let me have a look,' I say, taking the ticket and opening the cupboard.

'It's black,' she says. Aren't they always? 'MaxMara.'

'I have looked, I really have,' insists Larissa as she watches me climb into the cupboard. I'm sure she has but this woman is so cross and tricky she is definitely an insurance claim waiting to happen.

'Anything like this?' I ask, digging out something made of black wool.

'Nah!' she sniffs. 'You see, I told you, you lot have lost it or nicked it. Honestly, I thought this was a posh place. I would never have trusted you lot with nothing, had I known.'

'How about this?' I pull out another black coat, thinner, that was so far at the back it was halfway to Narnia.

'Yeah, that's it,' she says, snatching it out of my hand. And without a thank-you or a tip or anything, she and her red velvet rump sway out of the bar.

'Excuse me?' says a rather squiffy-looking blonde, leaning backwards on her heels. 'Have you seen Leonard?'

'Who?'

'Leonard? Our boss? His car is outside, waiting to take him back to Wimbledon.'

2–3 a.m.

Much like a captain of a ship is supposed to be the last man standing, you always hope that the person who is throwing the party stays soberish, maintains a certain amount of decorum and remains perpendicular enough to sign off on the bill. However, this is often not the case.

The office party is beginning to draw to a close now. Adam has very much called the last, last, last drinks at the bar and we are trying to clear the place of the swaying, staggering dregs. There are half-drunk glasses everywhere, a couple of stray scarfs on seats, a bag, a jacket and one fluorescent pink shoe. You'd be amazed what people leave behind once they've had a few. We quite often get shopping bags full of expensive clothes and shoes abandoned by the tables at Le Restaurant after lunch. The owners usually come back to collect them a few hours later when they realize what they've done but sometimes not. Sometimes we have Burberry coats and McQueen shoes sitting behind the reception desk for months before they get claimed. We always have a couple of jackets, the odd glove and hat left behind, but fortunately no children or dogs. I remember a very old mate of mine who worked in a nightclub once telling me that when the lights came on the stash of stuff left behind on the floor was incredible. Wallets, belts, hand-bags, shoes, money, credits cards and an endless supply of drugs: pills, baggies of weed, and wrap after wrap of cocaine. It was one of the perks of the job to pilfer what you fancied as no one ever really expected it back. We, on the other hand, are very nice. We log everything in the cloakroom and we keep it for at least a year before either using it ourselves or sending it off to Oxfam.

The booths are all empty now, except for the Le Restaurant gang, and there are a few stragglers heading for the door. There are two persistent groups, hunkered down on the sofas, still nursing their cocktails, who are not that keen to go. I indicate to Damon to start helping them to move on.

Leonard's PA, whose name is Melanie, is following me around like a lost dog, looking rather anxious.

'I haven't seen him for about twenty minutes,' she says, mincing her hands and glancing in the direction of the waiting cab. 'The taxi was booked for one thirty and the driver's saying he'll only wait another ten minutes.'

'He's wearing a pink tie, isn't he?' checks Adam. She nods. 'I last saw him talking to a girl at the bar. I'll go and have a look out the back, he might be in the Mews having a cigarette.'

'He doesn't smoke,' she replies.

'You'll be surprised who does, particularly after a few drinks,' he counters. You'll be amazed what *anyone* does after a few drinks.

'I'll go and check the lavs,' I say, not sure why I'm volunteering. It must be the martini making me strangely helpful.

Checking the toilets at the end of the evening is one of the most unpleasant jobs, and something I always try and avoid. Quite apart from the terrible mess, the paper everywhere and the water all over the floor, there are the endless accidents when punters haven't quite managed to get whatever they are doing into the bowl. And it's never just urine.

Oddly the women's loos are often worse than the blokes'. You're generally guaranteed that some sanitary products haven't made the steel bins and, more often than not, there's some sort of obscure U-bend blockage. Everyone always thinks that women are tidier and cleaner than men; one thing that nearly twenty years in this business has taught me is what a fallacy that idea is.

However, if women specialize in making a mess, men are much more likely to fall asleep. Either they lock themselves in a cubicle with a view to actually using the lavatory or they simply go there for a timeout and fall soundly asleep. I remember one extremely drunk man who disappeared off to the gents during dinner at Le Restaurant. They were a party of four, so when he didn't return after twenty minutes, his absence was glaring. His wife pulled me to one side and hissed in my ear for me to find her husband. As I walked into the loo it was patently obvious what had happened. His snores were so loud they were rattling the cubicle door. It took another five minutes to wake him and another five to get him straight enough to return to the table. I have never seen a wife more livid in my life. Her knuckles were white with fury by the time the old boy finally sat down. Their taxi ride back to Chelsea must have been fun.

But it's the blokes asleep with their pants down who I find the most unpleasant. Mostly you find them slumped in the corner, a turd still floating in the pan, and so not only do you have to flush the lav for them but you usually have to help them pull their pants up. I draw the line at wiping their actual arses. There are parameters and that is one of them.

I walk into the ladies, which is surprisingly tidy. Just one bin overflowing with paper towels and what looks like a pair of pants in the corner. There are two eyeliners left behind in front of the mirrors and a few suspiciously smeared lines on the windowsill and a couple on the back of the black cisterns. I have a mate who covers all the flat surfaces in his place with WD40, which basically melts any cocaine. But as someone who was/is occasionally partial myself, I do think that's a little mean. I am in the hospitality industry, after all. Although I do remember seeing one rather canny way of putting off the drug-taking punter. There was a drinking establishment in Soho which had a hand-dryer above what looked like a very handy silver shelf. Customers would chop out their lines on the shelf only for the blasting hand-dryer to be triggered as they leant down to take the stuff. The funniest thing was to watch the people's faces as they came out of the toilet. Their expressions of fury at the injustice of it all really were something to behold.

'Leonard!' I shout. 'Leonard! Are you in here?' There is one cubicle that appears to be in use. I don't want to hang around as I am not really supposed to be in here. 'Leonard! Is that you?'

'No,' comes a distinctly female reply.

I close the door and move next door to the gents. The smell of alcohol and urine or alcoholic urine is overpowering. There are a couple of blokes standing with their backs to me at the urinals.

'Sorry, chaps,' I say. They both look over their shoulder at me. 'But I'm looking for Leonard?'

'What, the MD?' asks one. 'He was at the bar, talking to Denise, who works on reception. But that was about half an hour ago.'

'Have you not seen him since?'

'Fraid not.' He shrugs.

I come back to my table to find that most of the Le Restaurant brigade has disappeared, gone to take the night buses home to their various far-flung bedsits in undesirable and unfashionable parts of town. I am now left with the decidedly hard core. Caz, Jason, Andrew and Oscar. Caz, Jason and Andrew are all remarkably perkier than when I left them. One of them clearly has a wrap of class A that they have shared with the group because they are all significantly less burpy and bleary and are now having a very intense conversation about PR. Or rather, Caz is having an intense conversation, while the others try to get a word in edgeways. Only Oscar is very obviously the worse for wine or vodka or whatever headache-inducing combination he has moved on to. He's not a boy who does drugs – he's far too ambitious – and, as a result, he's no longer capable of banter, but merely sits, his mouth slightly ajar, as he stares, with one boxed eye slowly closing, at Caz.

'What you want, though, what you want, what you really want, though,' says Caz, her finger in the air, forbidding any form of interruption, 'is a scandal. No PR will ever tell you this, but something like a celebrity sex thing or a fight is brilliant for a restaurant.'

'Really but—' Jason leans in, his leg is jigging up and down under the table. You can see that, as a journalist, he is desperate to get in on this.

'Can I just finish?' snaps Caz. 'You see, d'you remember when Russell Crowe had that fight at Zuma? D'you remember? When he hurled plates and everything?'

'It was broken up by Ross Kemp,' chips in Jason.

'Whatever,' says Caz. The details are tiresome. 'Anyway, that – that went global. Gobal, totally global, round the world,' she nods, taking a sip of her martini. 'You can't buy that.'

'Yes but—' starts Jason again.

'And the Boris Becker in the wardrobe, or wherever it was. Also global. Completely global. You can't buy it. You can't buy global, you just can't. Global is gold dust, celebrity gold dust.'

'But it's really good for the restaurant?' queries Andrew.

'Of course it is!' replies Caz, leaning right in and ticking points off on her fingers. 'It says this is a cool place to be. It says this is where famous people go and it also says that if you're lucky enough, and you manage to get yourself a table, you might, just might, get to see them misbehave.'

'So is all publicity good publicity?' ask Jason.

'Yes,' she says emphatically.

'Except a bad review. That's actually bad,' ventures Oscar.

'Yes, that's obviously bad,' she acknowledges, turning to eye him like a velociraptor. There really is nothing more annoying than a very drunk person puncturing the premise of your argument.

I am about to ask if any of them have seen a drunk, middle-aged bloke wondering around in a pink tie, when Adam arrives and whispers in my ear.

'We've found him. And it's not pretty.'

'Where?'

Adam can only shake his head, which is bad news, as Adam is almost entirely unshockable. Firstly, he's been a barman and manager for over ten years and secondly, he's Australian. I follow him past the lavatories and down into the tiny basement kitchen where we heat up sausages and pitta bread, churning out the few small plates. The skeleton staff has long since gone home. These guys don't work beyond nine thirty to ten as the hot bar snacks are only really an early evening thing to get the punters in straight after work. He walks past the fridge towards the door to the bins.

'You're kidding,' I say, not that keen to approach. These bins are fetid. They are full of old sausage, half-eaten Scotch eggs,

French fries, slops, bread, tartar sauce, ketchup. These are not Michelin-starred bins, they're bar bins. They are rank; they are truly awful. They are disinfected twice a day but the last thing you want to do is ever, actually, go inside the bin-room. We are a few feet away from the door and already I can almost taste the stink.

'You open the door,' I say to Adam. He pauses, his nose wrinkled, his eyes half closed like he is scared.

'Must I?'

'Yes.'

He pulls open the double doors and there, at it like hammer and tongs, is Leonard and his receptionist Denise. It is quite shocking. She is on her back, her red sequin dress up around her armpits, with her legs in the air, shoes still on, covered in rubbish. He is half on top of her, his trousers round his ankles, his striped boxer shorts round his calves, pumping away like his life depended on it. They both seem completely oblivious to the fact that they have been interrupted. I can only hope they have taken some sort of drug, because this is not normal behaviour.

'Excuse me!' I say, clearing my throat. They carry on. 'Excuse me!'

She has potato peeling in her hair; he has some chips and ketchup stuck to his thigh. Neither of them seems to care. They are oblivious to me, Adam, the smell, everything. Short of going into the room and slapping him about the face I am not sure what to do.

'Fuck it,' says Adam with his sanguine Aussie charm. 'Let's leave them to it.'

'Really?'

'Well, d'you want to go in?'

'No.'

'Neither do I. He can't last much longer – he's over fifty, for Chrissake.'

'OK, then,' I nod. 'Another ten minutes and then we come back.'

'You're kidding me, right?' he says. 'I'm going off to get the rest of the gang. This is one of the most disgusting things I have ever seen! They've all got to come and have a look.' I look at him, a little bit shocked. 'Oh, come on, mate,' he says, giving me a smack on the back. 'Live a little. It's got to be one of filthiest shags I have ever seen – and I mean that literally. You've gotta share that with the group!'

Adam's generosity knows no bounds and within a few minutes most of the bar staff have nipped down to have a gawp. Poor old Leonard, he has no idea what a complete fool he's making of himself. His taxi back to Wimbledon has long since departed, his secretary is weeping on the banquette, and half of the Le Bar staff have seen his fat, pink backside. He is going to have a little bit more than a hangover to contend with when he comes to, tomorrow morning.

Eventually, Adam manages to decouple the couple and, after another ten minutes, they appear in the bar. It is difficult to determine if they know or realize quite what a scene they have caused. But Adam is remarkably professional and it doesn't take long for the stinking, fetid shaggers to be dispatched off in their minicabs.

I go back to the banquette with Andrew, Oscar, Caz and Jason, who have clearly been to the lavatory for a re-up. Andrew is beginning to speed drink as the alcohol is no longer touching the sides; Jason's right leg is bouncing so vigorously it is drilling a hole in the floor, and Caz is having an argument with herself. Poor old Oscar is now so tired and drained and completely exhausted, his chin is resting in his hands, and he is unable to speak; all he can do is move his head from side to side playing conversational ping-pong. I sit down and take a sip of my rather warm martini.

'Oh my God!' says Adam, crashing in next to Caz. 'Was that the most filthy sex evah! I don't think I've seen worse. Never. Never. Honestly. Don't you think, mate?'

I shake my head. 'No, I've seen worse.'

'You can't have!'

'I have!'

3–4 a.m.

In fact our staff parties are worse than that. Quite a lot worse.
I remember one particularly debauched affair a while ago now,
when I was younger and significantly more badly behaved. I
was working in a restaurant which had a very cool bar
attached, and it was one of those cold, dull nights in January
when those of us who actually work in hospitality have our
Christmas parties. Santa comes late for us. We're always too
busy providing the festivities for everyone else to have any fun
ourselves. Weirdly, a whole load of canny firms are now joining us. Companies who are tired of paying Christmas
mark-ups or who can't be bothered to elbow themselves into
their favourite spots are choosing to celebrate in January as
well. It's cheaper, easier, and they know they can bargain us
down for a better deal.

Anyway, it was something like the sixteenth and everyone

was tucking into the vodka cocktails when someone, I think it was Stew behind the bar, poured a whole load of cocaine into the punch. And everyone went mad. There is always quite a lot of sexual tension within our industry. You have young, usually quite attractive people all frotting around each other for long hours at a time with plenty of alcohol. Quite apart from the erotic rush for a session on the warm napery, I have seen staff having sex in the lavs, in the cupboard, and, most extraordinarily of all, in the middle of service. I was working next to two chefs who simply couldn't contain themselves any more and went for a quick one in the disabled toilets. They were done and dusted even before I'd managed to cook my duck.

I have a mate who used to work in both the restaurant and the music business, and he once said to me that in rock and roll they talk about sex all the time but don't do it; in restaurants we just get on with it. You can get fired for it, obviously. I had a female colleague who was really rather naughty and quite up for it. She was fired for having sex with a sous chef in the staff showers where we worked and she then moved on to a rather cool gastro pub, only to be fired from there for doing coke during service. I remember her calling me up and asking me to collect her, only to find her marching out of the front of the restaurant with a fish as large as a small child under her arm, which she'd pinched in a fit of high dudgeon.

But this night was something else. The sensible ones had managed to get home early enough to avoid the coke-punch (why am I never one of those?) but the rest of us stayed till five.

And what happened was a little Roman to say the least. Everyone got to it. Anyone who had ever flirted with anyone during the last six months decided that tonight was the night to follow it up. There were people having sex on the floor, there were waitresses doling out blow jobs under the table and the maître d' was running around totally naked. In fact, not many us kept our clothes on. However, there was one girl who kind of surpassed herself and knelt on all fours on a table in the middle of the room; I am not sure how she ever looked anyone in the eye ever again. But then, I don't suppose any of us particularly showered ourselves in glory that night.

'Oh my God, d'you remember that terrible night with that poor woman who became totally hysterical?' asks Adam, plonking down a selection of the alcoholic samples Martina had left him this afternoon. I can't help noticing they are all half bottles, instead of the usual 75cl. Austerity appears to have hit the drinks business at last. 'D'you remember her?' He looks at me.

How could I ever forget? One of the downsides of this business is that sometimes you see quite how destructive the influence of alcohol can be. Over the years I have seen some awful fights, arguments between friends, between best friends, best girl-friends, husband and wives – it can be incredibly depressing.

But this was terrible. It was very late, about two thirty in the morning, and Adam and I were trying to clear Le Bar. We'd had a bit of a bash and had a DJ in, something I try not to do very often. We'd done our usual trick of pumping up the aircon, making the place properly chilling, ruining the atmosphere, to try and get them out, when we heard a woman scream. There was something in the scream that made your heart stop and understand that it was serious. When we finally found her outside the loos, she was hysterical. I had noticed her earlier in the evening, as she was part of a foursome who looked well-heeled and well glam. Adam and I took her back into the main room and sat her down on a banquette; we couldn't understand what she was saying, she was jabbering away that mad and sad. What was obvious, though, despite the booze and the rambling, she was pretty and clever and quite a catch. After a few minutes I managed to calm her down enough to ascertain she'd gone into the lavs and found her husband having sex. Her world had fallen apart and she was so upset it was terrible to watch. After some more digging I found out the rest of the four were her ex-boyfriend and his girlfriend, and her husband of five years. So I attempted to calm the situation even more. I said something along the lines that her friend had probably drunk a bit too much wine, I was sure that she regretted it and that if she had a chat with her in the morning it would be OK. She then turned and looked at me, like I was completely half-witted.

'My husband was not fucking my girlfriend,' she said very slowly. 'He was fucking my ex-boyfriend. He turned round and told me he was gay and he had been gay ever since I married him and he no longer wants to be married to me. He wants a divorce.'

The things is, we had all been enjoying the story up until that point, it had been little bit amusing, a domestic in the lavs, but the tone changed and everyone suddenly felt very sorry for her. Adam even offered to pay for her taxi, which is unheard of for him.

'What drinks have you got here?' ask Andrew, turning the selection of bottles around to face him, his eyes narrowing slightly as he tries to read the labels.

'They are mainly rums,' replies Adam. 'It's all about rum at the moment.'

'Yeah,' nods Jason. 'There's that place, the Rum Kitchen in Notting Hill.'

'Have you reviewed that?' asks Andrew.

'Not yet,' says Jason. 'I haven't been in the job very long.'

'Jason's going to be very nice about Le Restaurant, aren't you, Jason?' states Caz, her large turquoise eyes staring at him from across the table. It's more than his bollocks are worth to disagree.

'Of course,' he nods.

'Because we all know it is so much easier to be nasty, that it's more fun to be a little bit wicked and make hilarious jokes at everyone's expense,' she says.

'Expense being the operative word,' I say.

'But it was a first-class lunch, wasn't it?' She smiles, like she's admonishing a small child.

'Yes,' he agrees.

'What do you actually know about food?' Andrew suddenly chips in. 'I mean, really?'

'What was it A. A. Gill said about Giles Coren?' Oscar suddenly speaks, like Lazarus risen from the dead.

'"A mouth like a fisherman's glove but great on a waitress"?'

'But none of them know anything,' continues Andrew. 'Could they actually cook anything?'

'That's not really the point though, is it?' says Caz. 'The critics have changed along with the food. The lifestyle hack who can sew a fine sentence has taken over from the bore who could wang on for hours about the ingredients. We want writers who can be funny about the décor and the waitresses and the experience, about the craic rather than the crackling.'

'Probably,' says Andrew.

'People's attitudes have changed; it's only the twats at San Pellegrino and their World's Best Fifty Restaurants who want to eat twenty-one courses at El Celler. I mean, I couldn't think of anything more dull – morels with milk skin and curried walnuts? I'd rather starve,' says Caz, spoken like a true drunkorexic, like her ability to survive on fresh air and atmosphere is news to anyone. Given the choice between any morsel of food and starvation, Caz would always choose the later. 'People are much less scared of going into restaurants; it used to be a terrible social faux pas not to know what something was, and now no one cares. They don't care about mispronouncing stuff. Mainly because no one knows what half the stuff is anyway.'

'I suppose so,' acknowledges Andrew. 'Fuck it all, what I want to do is open a bar. That way I can serve nice cocktails and be done with it.'

Adam starts to laugh. 'A bar! You! You can't open a bar, it would kill you.' Andrew looks at him, his expression that of 'mildly-insulted-with-booze'. 'You can't be the frontline man for very long, otherwise it kills you off. You're the last person out and you have to balance the books. I remember a bloke I used to work for before, who was a complete basket case. He'd always be pissed doing the bought ledger and he'd stand and stare at it and then decide to have another beer and a fag before trying to deal with it. It made even less sense to him the next morning.'

Over Adam's shoulder I can see Damon and the remainder of the bar staff doing the final wipe down behind the bar. The glasses have been cleared, the dishwasher stacked and all the used straws and sliced lemons and limes cleared from behind the bar. Damon is chatting away to another couple of staff, punching fists and slapping them on the shoulder. As I watch Adam go over to thank them for a job well done, I still think that Damon is up to something – although he is clearly rather good at it, otherwise I'd have been to able catch him red-handed by now. I make a mental note to have a proper conversation with Adam about it in the morning. In a situation like this, you have to be sure. As I am pretty certain Damon's gleaned a few bits of choice information on both Adam and me during the eights months he's been working here. An amicable split is always preferable to anything resembling a dismissal.

The place is now entirely empty but for Andrew, Caz, Jason, Oscar and Adam who keeps bringing out lots of different flavoured vodkas for everyone for try. I can't help wishing that Jason would disappear, sod off, in fact. I am quite fond of a few critics and happy to go out on the piss with them, but I don't know Jason and I'd really rather just unwind with a few familiar faces than have to add his ego into the already ego-heavy mix. I should also perhaps put Oscar in a cab. His wife/girlfriend is probably wandering where the hell he is, although I am pretty sure she's used to being a Hospitality Widow.

I think it must be quite tricky being married to a chef. They only really like hanging out with other people in the industry. They're like politicians, who only really enjoy each other's company. There's nothing they like more than obsessively talking shop. Where have you been? Who's good? Who's doing well? Where's the next hot place? What's the next hot thing? It's very hard for civilians to join in, as there really is a limit to a normal person's interest in the texture of the beef suet 'candle' at Story. Or whether the Gramercy Tavern's Danny Mayer is actually going to take over from Gordon Ramsay at Claridge's now that his services are no longer required.

But it is also a massive excuse for sublimely selfish behaviour, or at least that's what both of my ex-wives accused me of. There is that male ego thing about work. 'I have to work till one at night and I have to go back again at seven in the morning. Don't give me a hard time! This is what I do! My work, my business, I am doing it for us!' Which is obviously bollocks. It is just that they/we prefer the company of customers and other chefs to our wives or children.

In the end it's Adam who persuades Oscar to get into a cab. The poor bloke is not really capable of speech. In fact, it is quite hard for Adam to ascertain his address. Fortunately he is used to the slurred ramblings of drunks and so he pieces together some address near Mile End. As we both escort him out into the waiting minicab, my phone goes. It's the boys from Rentokil, saying they are almost finished cleaning up Le Restaurant. The fat has been removed, the drains are now clear and would I like to come down and inspect the place.

Obviously there is nothing I'd dislike more, but if I am to open up tomorrow, needs absolutely must.

4–5 a.m.

Rentokil are just finishing up when I arrive. The kitchen looks immaculate. The floor's been scrubbed and the steel worktops are cleaner than when the commis normally sluice down at the end of service. The ovens, the least popular job at the end of the night, look more than passable, as do all the white wall tiles; even the grouting doesn't appear too stained. The smell of bleach and cleaning products hangs heavy in the air, but it is in welcome contrast to the previous stench. Although, if you breathe in deep enough (and I try very hard not to), you can still detect a back note of sewage. But all in all they have done an impressive job. I don't know how many bodies they've thrown at the problem but it is hard to imagine that less than a few hours ago the whole place was swimming, ankle deep, in the finest contents of the capital's drainage system.

It takes another ten minutes for me to go through all the

paperwork, signing off on drain blasting and deep cleaning. A rotund grey-haired bloke in charge tells me, with the relish of a proper obsessive, the actual size of the fatberg they'd managed to retrieve from under the main drain.

'The size of two dinner plates,' he enthuses, demonstrating the actual size with his huge thick fingers. How he can type his report into the computer encased in a thick grey plastic suit-case is anyone's guess. 'It's enough to cause a major obstruction,' he sniffs. I feel like saying 'no shit' but that would be the martinis talking and perhaps not the sort of joke he'd enjoy. So instead I thank him and his team profusely for turning out at such an unearthly hour to deal with such an unpleasant problem. 'It's part of the service,' he shrugs, picking up his computer. 'Could you sign here, here and here and rate the service here.'

A few minutes later and I am entirely alone in Le Restaurant. I lock the back door and walk through the bleach-soaked kitchen, turning off the strip lights. Through the swing doors, it is dark. The tables have been cleared, only the linen cloths remain, and the orange street lamps cast the room in an eerie glow. The silver bar reflects the outside light; it also catches off the rows of spirit bottles lined up on the glass shelves behind. Empty restaurants are weird places; there is something rather haunting about somewhere that is normally so full of life and energy rendered so totally still. To be honest, I have always found them a little scary. And it is usually just as you are closing up that you come across the unexpected.

I remember when I worked in a small restaurant in

Kensington, walking around checking all the doors when I heard this terrible moaning sound coming from the courtyard out the back. It was enough to make your blood run cold. I remember my heart beating in my chest and my palms growing clammy. It was a pitiful noise, a low and painful mewing. I slowly opened the back door to find some poor bloke wandering around the enclosed courtyard. He'd gone to the loo only to have gone out through the wrong door and fallen asleep. He'd woken up several hours later, after service had long gone, and had not been able to find the exit. He was wandering around like a caged animal making this weeping noise that didn't sound human at all.

But then again, coming across one of my chefs passed out, stark naked in the office once, surrounded by the dregs of a cocaine binge, was worse. For a start, I thought he was dead. It looked like the ultimate rock 'n' roll suicide. His flesh was so white, luminous in the moonlight, the hair on his body was so dark, so saturnine, and he was motionless. He looked like some sort of giant pupating slug, a sheen of sweat all over him. It took me a while to get into the office as his comatose legs were blocking the door. By the time I had managed to force my way in I was ready to call 999 and it was only when I heard him belch that I realized he was simply out for the count on the floor.

I sit down at one of the bar stools and yawn. I catch a glimpse of my dishevelled reflection in the mirror behind; it is not a good look. My hair needs a cut, I have stubble that's just reaching the George Michael stage and I have bags big enough for the Kardashians to take on holiday. What a day! I am vaguely thinking about helping myself to a vodka and tonic. I have been up for nearly twenty-three hours and I could really do with going to bed. I am absolutely exhausted. Only I am loath to leave Adam and the others with a free rein at Le Bar. I have been in Caz's company enough times to know that come this time of day/morning she is impossible to stop. She's one of those girls who says: 'Oh, just one more. Just one more for the road. One more can't hurt. How about another tiny one?' For someone who looks like a cocktail stick she has the stamina of Oliver Reed. There's no telling how much stock they'll get through before six, Adam's cut-off point. He is always out before the cleaning staff. That's his rule. No matter how many battalions of Bolivia's finest he's had up his nose, he's out of there, for a shower, a shave and a laundered Paul Smith shirt before coming back in at eight, fresh as a proverbial daisy.

I lock up and head back towards Le Bar. The streets are deserted now but for a homeless person curled up in a doorway. Lying horizontal, covered in a cardboard box, I recognize his shoes. He is one of the local old boys who occasionally turns up to go through the bins around eleven at night. I know Barney is always leaving out a few choice things within easy reach, plus the occasional tot of whisky of a cold night. He's nice like that.

It is still pitch black outside. The sky is a deep, dark granite and a couple of confused birds are belting out some tunes. It really is time to go to bed. Sadly, as I arrive at Le Bar, the level of laughter and banter makes me realize that I'm the only one who thinks that.

'So I am standing there,' says Adam, out of his chair, acting. 'And this thirteen-year-old girl stood up and barfed all down my trousers. I was holding a tray of food, so I couldn't do anything. All I could think was "I have been here since six this morning and I really don't need this," so I walked up to another waiter and said: "You'd better take this," and I walked very slowly out of the room.'

'That's disgusting,' says Caz.

'Happens all the time,' says Adam. 'We've had people throwing up at the table. They eat and drink too much or too quickly. It's the excitement.'

'I imagine it's the drink,' says Caz, as she pours herself another. They've moved on to what looks like Amaretto on the rocks. It's one of Adam's favourites, especially when he's staying up all night. Personally, I think it already tastes of a hangover.

'There's nothing I like more than deep-frying someone's steak when they're pissed and have sent it back, asking for it to be well done. "That well done enough for you, sir!" It's like a fucking old boot.' Andrew sneers and helps himself to another drink.

'And before you fry it, you've wiped your arse with it and kicked it about the floor,' giggles Adam.

'No – afterwards,' grins Andrew. 'No point in doing it before, totally defeats the point.'

'Morning,' I say.

'Ah! There you are,' says Adam. He clicks his fingers at me like an oligarch ordering a hit. 'D'you remember the woman with the plastic leg you had at Le Restaurant?'

'What? Last year?'

'That's the one!' He starts to laugh. 'So she turns up a little bit pissed and asks to use the toilets.' He looks at me to confirm that this true. 'Anyway, she then passes out in the loo, as you do, only none of us could get in to get her out. Anyway, finally, we poked our heads over the top of the loo and realized that her leg had come off and was blocking the door. So you pulled the leg out, and we got the woman out afterwards. She was out cold and we, you, wanted to close up. What could we do? So we went through her bag and found £500 in cash. So she was minted, but there was no ID. Eventually she mumbled "The Cumberland Hotel". So we got a cab, popped the leg on the back seat, and we were really laughing because it was so crazy, and we turn up at the Cumberland. We carry her in, holding the leg on, and the doorman is standing by the door. He immediately recognizes her and starts telling us to "Fuck off! I am not having that woman in here! Fuck off now!" It is now, what—?'

'Two,' I say, sitting down next to Jason and Andrew and pouring a vodka shot.

'And we're stuck. We've got a nameless woman and her leg and nowhere to go.'

'So what did you do?' asks Jason, his leg still bouncing up and down.

'We dropped her off at a police station and scarpered!'

splutters Adam, now laughing so hard he has little tiny tears of mirth welling up in his eyes.

'You did what?' Jason is taken aback. 'You dumped her?'

'Yeah!' says Adam, nodding and laughing. 'What else were we supposed to do, mate? Take her home? Check her into a hotel?'

'It's tragic,' says Caz. 'Almost as tragic as when David Hasselhoff came in, d'you remember? And he left a cash tip and a signed photo of himself that no one had asked him to sign and no one picked it up.'

'I love the Hoff,' says Jason.

'We all love the Hoff, mate,' agrees Adam. 'I'm just not sure we need a picture of him on our wall.'

Just as we are about to mull over the pros and cons of the Hoff, my phone goes. It's Pippa.

'Hi, Pippa!'

'Tell her to get her arse down here!' shouts Adam, beckoning with his hand.

'What happened? You were supposed to come here for a drink,' I say, suddenly sounding a little bit worse for wine myself. 'We missed you. You never called. Nothing.'

'The alarm's gone off at La Table,' she says, ignoring all our overtures.

'Oh, right.'

'Now, I'm happy to go and check on my own if you want, but I would rather not.' I can hear her sounding terribly brave.

'Don't worry, I'll do it, stay at home.'

'No,' she says. 'I don't need to stay at home, I'd just rather not go in there on my own.'

'I'll come and I'll bring a baseball bat with me.'

'Good. You just don't know who's in there.'

'It could be anyone.'

'Anyone,' she confirms. 'See you there. Wait for me. You can go in first and, I promise, I'll be right behind you.'

5–6 a.m.

I could really do without this at the end of such a long and difficult day. Dawn is on the verge of breaking now and I am marching along the street clutching a baseball bat, like the Pied Piper of pissheads, being pursued by Adam, Caz, Andrew and, for some irritating reason, Jason, who clearly has no home to go to and who now thinks he's on to some story. It's like he's on the frontline of hospitality, competing with his pals in Mogadishu, waiting for me to go wading in with my bat in the name of my Gaggia coffee machine.

Actually, it is almost never the machines; it's always the money. And it is usually some inside job. A disgruntled employee, or someone who just can't resist the lure of cash. If you're going to get turned over it almost always happens on a bank holiday. You've got extra takings, you haven't managed to get them to the bank, obviously, and that's when they'll walk off with what might be up to £40,000–£60,000 that's sitting in the safe.

'Hang on!' begs Caz as we stride down the street. 'I've got heels on!'

'Listen, Caz!' I say, turning around. 'This is not a party, you will not be missing out on some fun if you don't come now. There are no famous people. There's no one to gawp at. The alarm has simply gone off at La Table. It could be nothing. It could be a cat. A tramp fancying a nice kip—'

'Or an armed gang,' says Jason, his wired eyes widening.

'Or some teenagers,' yawns Adam, whose two-day bender appears to be catching up with him.

'Or a problem you need to find a PR solution to,' replies Caz, indignant at my suggestion that she's only come along for the ride.

'Or—'

'FIRE!' yells Pippa, running towards me, dressed in an unforgiving pink T-shirt top and matching tracksuit bottoms. Her large bosom is flying to the left and then the right, with a momentum all of its own. 'La Table is on FIRE!'

'Fire!' I reply, suddenly becoming totally sober. 'Where? How big? How did it start?'

'I don't know,' she says, shaking her head and beginning to mince her hands. 'But there are *flames*.'

We all turn the corner together and there is a collective intake of breath. La Table is indeed on fire and there are flames licking at the front windows and smoke pouring out of the door.

'The glass could blow at any moment,' says Adam, casting an expert eye over it. He didn't live in the armpit of Australia without picking up a tip or two about bush fires.

'Yes,' agrees Jason. 'It looks dangerous.'

'Have you called the fire brigade?' I ask Pippa.

She nods. 'As soon as I got here. They won't be long, they said. But it's spreading fast.'

In a matter of minutes the curtains Sketchley and I had spent so long trying to hang correctly, or, more accurately, telling two designers called Camilla and Liz to hang, go up in flames. I thought they were supposed to be fireproof? The orange-yellow glow that we can see through the windows grows even more fierce. In the far distance, above the noise of the birds and the occasional early-morning car, I can hear sirens. The fire brigade, wailing a way off. And I'm compelling them, willing them, TO HURRY THE FUCK UP.

Suddenly there's a loud bang and smash and the tinkling of glass as one of the upstairs windows explodes. We're standing in a row, on the opposite side of the street and we all look up.

'Shit! Mate! Your flat!' exclaims Adam, turning to look at me, his wide eyes shining orange with the glow of the fire. 'Your flat,' he says again.

It takes me a while to react. I've been so busy reflecting on the damage to my business, on how much of it is about to go up in smoke, that I had completely forgotten that I live above the joint. It's my flat. With all my stuff. I can feel my heart pounding in my chest. Could things get any worse?

The fire engines screech around the corner and within

minutes the whole area is crawling with vehicles, hoses and blokes in yellow helmets. They cordon the place off and repeatedly question both Pippa and me to make sure that there's no one left in the building. I suddenly panic that Gina might be in there.

'Has anyone seen Gina?' I turn and ask the group.

'Gina?' ask Adam.

'Gina? The pretty girl who was working behind the bar today? Andrew?'

He shrugs. 'Not since staff supper.'

'Has she got keys?' asks Pippa.

'Keys?'

'To the flat?'

'No, I don't think so.' I am pacing about, overcome with anxiety. There's nothing like a bloody great fire to make you completely irrational and send you rapidly over the edge.

'Did you give her any?' asks Pippa, taking hold my shoulders and looking me in the eyes. 'Did you? *Think?*'

'No.' I pause. 'No, I didn't.'

'Well then, she is not inside then, is she?'

'No, no, good. You're right. What's the matter with me?'

The fire brigade have got their hoses out now, pouring thousands of gallons per second onto the flaming building.

'It's going to be all right, mate,' says Adam with a large sniff as he pats me on the back. 'You're insured, right? You've got all the right paperwork?'

I nod as I watch the smoke and flames still pouring out of the building.

'Look on the bright side,' says Caz as she rattles around in her handbag for lipstick. 'It's the perfect opportunity for a refit. One of my clients had a fire the other day and he was over the bloody moon. It was a bit touch and go to start off with because the insurance company were bastards and took bloody ages to pay up, and he had to bankroll the first hundred thou himself but, you know, it came through in the end. He was quite smart about it. He got half his staff to help out with the refit, and the other half he sent on compulsory holiday.'

'Clever,' agrees Adam. Staff have a compulsory four weeks off a year. Two weeks of their choosing and the other two when their boss says they are allowed. 'Although I don't see Pippa here sanding tables!'

Pippa laughs. 'I don't know, my DIY skills are second to none. I have been known to put up Ikea shelves.'

'Christ!' says Adam. 'I've never managed to put anything together from there.'

Caz is right. It's the perfect opportunity for a refit. Truth be told, most restaurateurs love a fire. There is an old restaurant joke.

'Where's the fire?'

'Shhh, don't tell anyone. Next week.'

There are also numerous little tricks and dodges that make it even more worth our while. Smoke damage is our friend. You'd be amazed how terrible and destructive it is when you go round the ashes of a place with the loss adjustor. Smoke gets into every nook and cranny and soft furnishing. It destroys tables! Lights! Sofas! Everything! However, once the insurance company has paid up, you'd be amazed how tables can come back to life after a quick scrub down. Send the soft furnishings to the dry cleaner's and suddenly you have two sets of cushions or curtains for the price of one. Smoke damage really is the restaurateur's very best pal indeed.

Equally, what better way to get rid of a failing place than having a 'terrible accident'. I had a mate who did torch his own place as it was losing him £4,000 a week. He couldn't carry on playing for it, so he dropped a fag, a bit of this, a bit of that and a bit more besides. A few months later he was back in business with a new groovy design and some young groovers packing the place out. Although I have to say he was lucky that no one found out.

'They look like they've got it much more under control now,' says Adam. 'It won't be long. I always think fire is like vomit or blood. It always looks much worse than it is.'

He's right; it feels a lot less hot. The intensity has dissipated and there are a couple of firemen going into the building, hauling in hoses to put out the last pockets of flames. The smell of the smoke and water is really rather unpleasant; it's acrid and catches at the back of your throat.

'Excuse me,' says Pippa, grabbing a passing fireman who is broad and butch and strip-joint handsome.

'Yes?' he says, turning to look at both of us with his pale blue eyes. I am just glad Jorge is not here, otherwise he'd be liable to squeal.

'Do you have any idea how it might have started?'

'Not sure,' he says. 'It could be petrol through the door.

There's a smell of fuel. Do you have anyone who, how shall I put this, doesn't like you?'

'Doesn't like us?' Pippa looks puzzled.

'Enemies?' he suggests.

'Enemies?' Pippa repeats.

'He's just gone through quite a sticky divorce!' says Andrew, rather unhelpfully out of the blue.

'Yeah!' agrees Adam. 'Sketchley doesn't do the woman scorned thing very well.'

The fireman looks at me. I am sure he's wondering what sort of name is Sketchley and why on earth would a woman ever bother getting her gusset in a twist over some half-baked, unshaven loser like me. Let alone resort to arson.

'It could also be a coincidence,' he says.

'So it's not a chip pan, then?' asks Pippa, obviously harbouring some sort of not-so-terribly-secret guilt.

'We can't rule that out,' he says.

'What can you rule out?' I ask.

'Nothing at this point,' he says.

It could be Big Pete, I think. This is not beyond his remit. No! What's wrong with me? Surely arson is a little big heavy at his juncture? Even for him? I mean, I only said I was interested in the terrible Greek place and it is not as if I've got a plan together, or got the money to do it.

I stare over the road at my smouldering restaurant and the thirty or so firemen stomping through the ashes with their great big boots and heavy hoses. It is a piteous and pathetic sight and yet I don't feel cowed. You never know, I think (I

315

have always been a glass-half-full person), given some clever accounting this could all turn out to my advantage. It could be OK. I could do up this place and properly throw my hat into the ring with the Covent Garden dive as well. I could have the beginnings of a proper empire. I could get myself a proper little brasserie. I should think snazzy, I should think of turning those tables and getting the slebs. I should get my skinny arse down to Balthazar and get my notepad out, check out the red leather seating and see what all the fuss is about. To be inspired, not steal. Obviously.

'Christ,' says Adam, checking his ridiculously expensive watch. 'Is that the time? It's nearly six. The cleaners will be in soon.'

'And the butcher,' sniffs Andrew. 'I should go home, have a disco nap. Haven't we got a hundred and fifty covers to do today?'

'Something like that,' I say.

'You could always come and stay at mine for a bit if you need to, darling,' says Caz, looking across the road at my smoking apartment. 'Gerry won't mind if you stay for a while.'

'Thanks,' I say, patting my back pocket for a packet of fags. 'Do you know what? I've got quite a lot to do today.'

'Really?' She tries to frown.

'Yes. What's another twenty-four hours at the coalface of the hospitality industry? It's five to six. What else is there to do but push on through? I need to talk to the butcher anyway, find out about the turkeys – after all, it's nearly Christmas.'

Imogen Edwards-Jones is the bestselling author of *Hotel Babylon*, *Air Babylon*, *Fashion Babylon*, *Beach Babylon*, *Pop Babylon*, *Wedding Babylon* and *Hospital Babylon*, as well as novels such as *My Canapé Hell* and *Shagpile*. She lives in west London with her husband and their two young children.